Suzy — love from Mr & D.
Xmas '86

GARDENERS' QUESTIONS ANSWERED

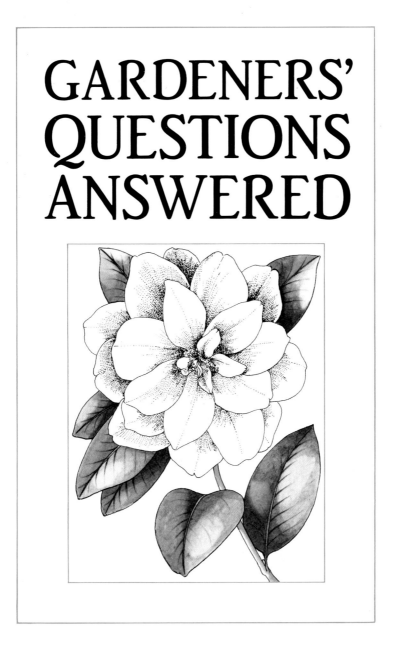

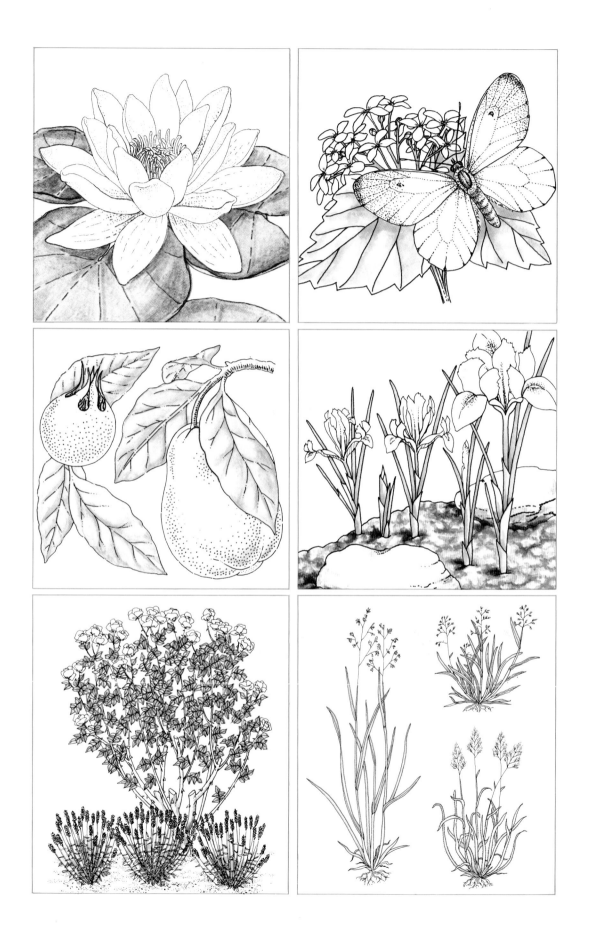

GARDENERS' QUESTIONS ANSWERED

Expert advice and practical solutions
for your gardening problems

Dr STEFAN BUCZACKI

of The BBC's Gardeners' Question Time

COLLINS

First published 1985 by
William Collins Sons & Co Ltd
London · Glasgow · Sydney
Auckland · Johannesburg

Conceived, edited and
designed by
Marshall Editions Limited
71 Eccleston Square
London SW1V 1PJ

Editor: Gwen Rigby

Designer: Simon Blacker / Elgin Press

Research: Jazz Wilson

Production: Janice Storr

Originated by
Reprocolor Llovet, S.A. Barcelona, Spain

Typeset by
Composing Operations, Tunbridge Wells, Kent, U.K.

Printed and bound by
Printer Industria Gráfica, S.A.
Barcelona, Spain

British Library Cataloguing in Publication Data

Buczacki, Stefan
Gardeners' questions answered : expert advice
and practical solutions for your gardening
problems
1. Gardening
I. Title
635   SB450.97

ISBN 0-00-410414-5

Contents

In memory of my father, who loved his garden

Introduction

Gardeners are a fascinating, inquisitive and extremely numerous fraternity. At the last count, it was estimated that there are about 18 million gardens in Britain, and, one must assume, not far short of that number of gardeners. For although, in my travels around the country, I see neglected gardens from time to time (some of them masquerading under the vogue term of 'wild garden'), they are unquestionably in the minority, and our designation as a nation of gardeners seems not altogether inappropriate. Nonetheless, to talk in generic terms can be misleading in the extreme, for among that 18 million gardens will be rolling acres of manicured turf, allotments of leeks, orchards of apples and almost every imaginable grade of garden size, shape, colour and content.

If gardens are diverse, gardening is more so, and few subjects of popular appeal can embrace so wide a spectrum. But the subject, the gardens and, above all, the gardeners themselves, have one thing in common. They thrive on problems. Put two gardeners together and you will have two ways of attempting to achieve any given objective. And yet, by and large, they are always willing to listen to the other person's point of view; although to take heed of it is quite another matter!

Reading recently through the correspondence columns of old gardening magazines and listening to old recordings of *Gardeners' Question Time*, I was struck by two things. The questions have not changed much over the years, but the answers most certainly have. Partly this is because advances in the science of horticulture have filtered through to its amateur gardening cousin, and partly because professional gardening experts, those who answer the questions, are but one species of gardener. They have opinions and viewpoints just as diverse as those of their amateur colleagues, with the difference that they air them publicly (and that many of them think they are always right). So, although the questions have remained the same, the answers have changed because the experts have changed; which may explain why some of the answers you will find in this book are different from those in other gardening books you may read or from what you expect.

I have selected the questions that experience has shown me to be those asked most frequently, and I have answered them on the basis of my own experiences, as a scientist, a gardener and an observer. I have adopted the maxim of trying, wherever possible, to give some of the 'why' in addition to the 'how' of each problem, for I firmly believe that if you understand the nature of the difficulty you are part of the way to overcoming it. I have made no attempt to disguise personal bias in certain areas and have even permitted myself a small helping of dogma.

One of the most contentious aspects of modern gardening is that relating to the use of chemical pesticides. I have always advocated the use of non-chemical solutions to a problem where I believe they will give satisfactory results. Where a chemical seems the only effective answer, I have suggested materials that I believe to be the safest available. Nonetheless, I certainly do not wish to imply that modern gardening is dependent on modern pesticides, and I discuss this issue in some detail in the book. If, however, you do employ garden pesticides (or, indeed, any other other synthetic chemical), I cannot stress too strongly the importance of reading the manufacturer's directions most carefully *before* you start to use them.

It seemed most convenient to divide the book into sections based on the questions that arise in relation to different types of plant, but I have tried, wherever possible, to give cross-reference to related questions and answers in other sections. In some instances, the illustrations are used to amplify points in the text; in others, they cover aspects not otherwise dealt with.

STEFAN BUCZACKI 1985

SOILS, FERTILIZERS AND CLIMATE

The basic ingredients

of gardening

How much do I need to know about the type of soil I have in my garden?

A good deal of what you need to know can and will be learned best by experience, for there is great variation in soil types and it is impossible to describe the precise horticultural characteristics of each. But you should understand the properties of certain broad categories of soil — clay, sand, chalk and peat especially — if only to prevent you from spending time and money on plants that will never succeed in your particular soil.

Soils are a blend of living, once-living but now dead, and never-living components. The living comprise plants and animals that range from the microscopic (eelworms, tiny arthropods and algae, for example) to the relatively enormous mammalian forms such as moles, together with multitudes of microscopic and submicroscopic organisms that perform most of the chemical processes taking place in soil.

The once-living component of the soil is humus — the remains, predominantly of plants, that are broken down into their chemical constituents by the living micro-organisms. The never-living bulk of the soil is the mineral matter, derived from the breakdown of a 'parent' rock. While the humus content of the soil is largely the remains of plant life that once grew on the site or has been deliberately added to it by gardeners, the mineral make-up of the soil may not bear any close relationship to the mineral content of the underlying rock.

As rocks are weathered and broken down, the surface layers that comprise the soil are subject to agencies, such

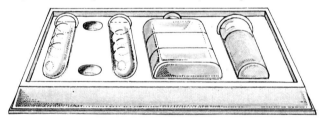

Soil-testing kits usually contain some chemicals, small graduated test tubes and a chart. To find the pH level, take a number of soil samples from various parts of the garden; mix the soil and chemicals and match the colour of the solutions with the chart.

LEVELS OF LIME REQUIRED BY SOIL TYPES

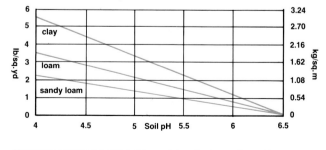

Most crops prefer soil with a pH of around 6.5; alkalinity can be raised by adding lime in the amounts shown above. Lime may also slightly improve the structure of clay soils.

See also:
Chalky and clay soil pp 12, 13
Soil preparation for planting
lawns pp 98–9
Soil preparation for planting
trees p 109

What exactly is 'topsoil'; should I buy some to improve my garden?

The topsoil is, in practical terms, the upper layer of the soil, in which your plants grow. Beneath is a region known as the subsoil, comprising the less well weathered parts of the underlying rock and, by and large, lacking any humus content. The relative depths of topsoil and subsoil vary greatly from site to site, depending on how easily the underlying rock breaks down; on the factors that have influenced this breakdown; the extent to which mineral matter has been transported from elsewhere and deposited on the surface and, conversely, the extent to which mineral matter has been removed.

From time to time, you will see topsoil advertised for sale, especially by builders, who have removed it from a development site (and have, thereby, probably created a problem for anyone hoping to garden there in the future). It is rarely cheap but, if you have an eroded site, it may represent the best, and certainly the quickest, way of producing a few small beds for growing plants satisfactorily. Bear in mind, however, that a cubic metre of soil weighs approximately 1 tonne and that, since you need at least 30 cm (12 in) depth to garden satisfactorily, this 1 tonne will cover an area of only 9 sq m (10 sq yds).

as wind and water, which can move them considerable distances. Thus, a garden sited in a river valley may well have a light, sandy soil as a result of the decomposition, over many thousands of years, of soil derived from rocks a long way upstream. A neighbouring garden, on slightly higher ground, may have a heavy clay soil much more similar, chemically, to the rocks that lie beneath them both. Because the organic content of the soil is a reflection of how the site has been cropped and treated in the past, so it can be amended by appropriate cropping and manuring. The mineral content of the soil, however, is not one that gardeners can influence to any great extent.

A physical analysis of soil is easy to perform by shaking up a sample with water in a tall glass container and allowing it to settle out, when the relative amounts of clay (at the top of the sediment), sand (at the bottom), and humus (which will largely be floating) will become apparent. Detailed chemical analysis of garden soil is not easy to do accurately and may give misleading results.

And what about pH? This is a measure of acidity or alkalinity on a scale of 1 to 14, especially important in gardens in relation to the soil. The mid-point is called neutrality, while values below 7 are acid and above 7 are alkaline. Garden soils rarely have pH values below 4.5 (very acid) or above 8 (very alkaline). Most types of garden plant, and certainly most fruit and vegetables, prefer a pH just on the acid side of neutral (about 6.5), although a few lime-tolerant species prefer it slightly higher, and a fairly large group of attractive ornamentals that includes rhododendrons, azaleas, camellias and many heathers prefers it more acid.

It is fairly easy to test the pH of garden soil with one of the small kits now available — usually, a test solution is added to a small sample of soil, the colour change noted, and the pH value read from a chart. In theory, the desired adjustment may then be made. This is not as easy as it sounds, however, for although it is possible to raise the pH of an acid soil by adding lime, it is difficult to lower the pH of an already alkaline soil. The addition of sulphur is sometimes suggested to increase acidity, but it is of limited value; if acid-loving plants are to be grown on alkaline soil, a peat bed is the best solution.

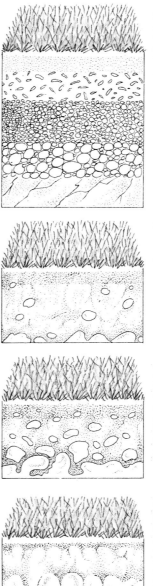

Several layers of increasingly degraded material lie between the topsoil and the bedrock. The best way to find out the composition of the soil in your garden is to dig a steep-sided hole about 1 m (3¼ ft) deep. This will reveal the various strata, show how deep the topsoil is and also how well the soil retains moisture.

The ideal soil for gardening is loam, which contains a mixture of sand, clay and humus. The darker the soil, the more humus it contains, the richer and warmer it is and the easier it is to work.

Chalky soil, particularly when it contains lumps of chalk, is one of the most difficult for gardening. The topsoil is often shallow and free draining, and nutrient deficiencies may be induced by the chalk. The soil can be improved and its alkalinity slightly reduced by adding peat.

The fine particles that make up a clay soil stick together when wet and cause it to become water-logged. Although rich in nutrients, clay must be lightened and aerated by the addition of compost or peat and by digging and turning.

What is the best way of making compost from garden waste?

Most gardeners will be familiar with the concept of the compost heap, although 'heap' is really a misnomer if compost is to be made properly, for it is important to confine the material in some type of container. For a medium-sized garden, the best plan is to build or buy a boxlike compost bin, approximately 1 to 1.25 m (3 to 4 ft) cubed, with slatted sides, no base and no lid. Use seasoned and treated wooden planks, approximately 10 × 2.5 cm (4 × 1 in), leave air gaps of approximately 2.5 cm (1 in) between each and use rustless nails or screws. Ideally, the planks comprising the front of the bin should not be fixed but should be capable of being slotted in, one by one, as the bin is filled.

For small gardens, it is possible to buy plastic, barrel-like compost bins, which work fairly satisfactorily provided they are well ventilated. But contrary to all the rules, some gardeners manage to make small amounts of compost surprisingly well in big plastic sacks.

Site the bin in partial shade with free air circulation all around. Place a layer of coarse rubble in the bottom so that air can circulate underneath. Then start to fill the bin with organic matter. Virtually all non-woody material can be included, although the toughest stems and roots (brassicas, for instance) are best chopped or crushed. Household waste may be added, including shredded paper, (but no plastic or animal remains, which will tend to attract vermin), together with garden weeds, lawn mowings, windfall fruit, straw and similar material.

It is important to keep a balance between the various types of waste; no more than one-third of the contents should be lawn mowings, for instance, since it is otherwise difficult to prevent the contents from becoming too slimy. Leaves tend to rot more slowly than most other forms of organic matter and can block up a compost bin by preventing air from circulating. They are used much more efficiently if stacked separately to make leaf-mould. The roots and rhizomes of some perennial weeds (preferably not couch) can be included, but they are best placed in the centre of the bin, where the temperature will be highest and decomposition most efficient.

Although all such organic matter should rot in a well-made bin, it is wise not to include brassica roots attacked by clubroot or onion roots attacked by white rot, for it is not worth taking the risk of spreading viable fungus over the garden in the compost. Some gardeners like to turn the compost from the outer part inward after a few months to ensure that all is rotted uniformly, but this should not really be necessary in a good bin. Although a tight-fitting lid is not recommended, some form of cover will help prevent the compost from becoming either too dry or too wet. The openweave plastic material sold as windbreak is ideal.

For every 20 cm (8 in) or so of depth, add a dusting of proprietary compost accelerator or a layer of fresh farmyard manure. This is essential to provide 'starter' nutrition for the bacteria and fungi that will bring about rotting of the organic matter. About 9 litres (2 gallons) of water should also be added periodically, while a dusting of lime may be included occasionally to prevent the compost from becoming too acid. During the summer, compost should be ready for use after about four months, but material added to a bin in the autumn will need at least six months to rot fully.

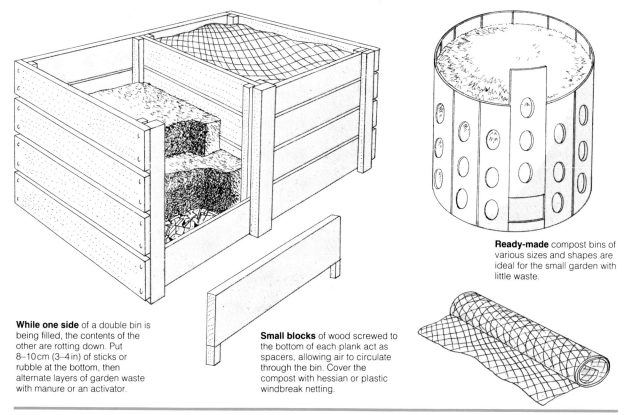

While one side of a double bin is being filled, the contents of the other are rotting down. Put 8–10 cm (3–4 in) of sticks or rubble at the bottom, then alternate layers of garden waste with manure or an activator.

Small blocks of wood screwed to the bottom of each plank act as spacers, allowing air to circulate through the bin. Cover the compost with hessian or plastic windbreak netting.

Ready-made compost bins of various sizes and shapes are ideal for the small garden with little waste.

See also:
Formulae for John Innes potting
   composts p 15
Ericaceous composts p 16
Garden uses for wood pp 17, 28–9

 ## Can I use garden-made compost for preparing seedling and potting composts?

If garden compost is well made, it should not contain any pests or diseases. It should, therefore, be perfectly safe to incorporate it in a potting medium, but I am always wary of using it for seeds and young seedlings. However good their compost-making ability, no one can be certain that every contaminating organism has been killed in the composting process and that it will not proliferate in the warm conditions needed to germinate seeds. The cost of purpose-mixed seedling composts is not so great that the risk is worth taking.

But there are many other valuable uses for compost in the garden. Larger plants grown in potting composts are much better able to survive, and since such mixes are needed in greater quantities, the economy of using home-made compost in them is particularly attractive. It is a good idea to pass the compost through a fairly fine sieve to remove fragments of wood and other coarse material before using it.

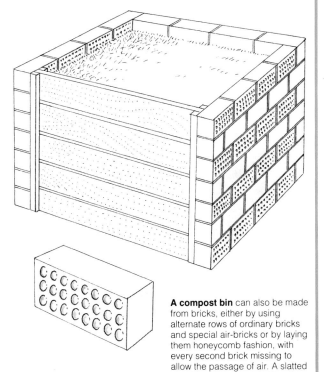

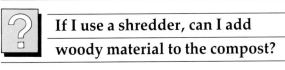

A compost bin can also be made from bricks, either by using alternate rows of ordinary bricks and special air-bricks or by laying them honeycomb fashion, with every second brick missing to allow the passage of air. A slatted wood front is still needed to allow easy access.

 ## Are the creepy-crawlies in my compost doing any harm?

Creepy-crawly is a generic term used to embrace a wide range of creatures, both beneficial and harmful. Red-coloured species of worm will commonly be found in compost and should be welcomed. They may not be present in the hottest part of a properly functioning bin, but elsewhere they will perform a valuable role in turning and aerating the compost.

Other forms of small animal life may be less desirable. Woodlice frequently invade compost, and their presence should be taken as an indication that the bin is not functioning as well as it should be, especially if they occur in the centre. Regular turning of the compost may help to ensure that it heats uniformly, and this will go some way toward discouraging woodlice. If they persist in spite of all your endeavours, incorporate a dusting of an insecticide powder containing HCH from time to time, as you fill the bin.

Is garden compost as good a source of organic fertilizer as farmyard manure?

There is little difference between well-made compost and well-rotted farmyard manure. Both contain approximately 0.5 per cent of the major plant nutrients: nitrogen, phosphorus and potash; relatively little, even by comparison with a general fertilizer such as Growmore. Think of them more as soil amendments, or conditioners, than fertilizers and use both. In most gardens, the amount of compost that can be made each season is inadequate for all purposes, and some supplement will be needed in the form of farmyard manure or even peat, which is more expensive and almost totally lacking in nutritional value.

If I use a shredder, can I add woody material to the compost?

Provided the shredder is a good, powerful one, the answer is generally yes. Some hand-operated shredders are little more than over-sized mincing machines and represent extremely hard work if you have more than a modest amount of fairly soft woody material with which to contend. The larger and more robust electrical appliances are much more satisfactory; and the big, petrol-engined shredders can cope with fairly thick branches. They are expensive but might be worth considering if you have a large quantity of woody material to deal with.

Are organic fertilizers better than artificial fertilizers?

Few subjects in gardening are more emotive than this, those who prefer organic fertilizers, in particular, arguing their case with passion and often invoking such terms as 'poison' to describe the effects of artificial fertilizers in the garden. Organic and artificial, and even fertilizer, however, do not mean the same things to all people. To me, a fertilizer, as opposed to a manure, is a substance applied to the soil primarily for its value as a plant nutrient. While an organic fertilizer is derived from some once-living organism, in contrast with an artificial one, which is derived from somewhere else (which may not necessarily be a chemical factory and could be a quarry or a mine).

Plants take up all nutrients in simple chemical form, and almost any fertilizer added to the soil will be broken down, usually by micro-organisms, into a state that plants can use. There is little scientific evidence to suggest that the original source of the simple chemicals makes any difference whatever to plant growth. Nitrogen to a plant is nitrogen, be it from dried blood or ammonium sulphate.

If plant growth is unaffected, what about the flavour of edible crops? Again, there is little evidence to suggest that additional substances present in organic fertilizers improve crop flavour (and it does seem strange that, if such substances exist, they should invariably change flavour for the better).

Finally, it should be said that certain organic fertilizers may be advantageous because of the form in which they occur. Bonemeal, for example, is a slow-release form of phosphate; it breaks down chemically in the soil over a long period of time and is thus beneficial when establishing new plants. There is no comparably convenient artificial form of phosphate. The wisest course, therefore, is to use organic fertilizers if they perform a particular task better than artificial fertilizers or are cheaper; but there is no reason to imagine they will automatically do everything better, solely because they *are* organic.

What special problems are there on a chalky soil?

Strictly speaking, a chalky soil is one derived from chalk rock, but the word is used colloquially to mean any highly alkaline soil — chalk is simply a rather purer form of calcium carbonate than limestone. Although perusal of nursery catalogues often seems to suggest that most choice trees and shrubs prefer or require acid conditions, there are, in fact, more garden plants tolerant of chalk than there are of high acidity. Our impression is simply biased by such gems as rhododendrons, azaleas and camellias.

The biggest problem with alkaline soil is that most mineral nutrients needed by plants are taken up less readily than they are in more acid conditions. So, although plants that are well adapted to such conditions (known as calcicoles) will grow satisfactorily, those more marginally tolerant of chalk will require certain special treatment if they are to thrive. In particular, an amendment, known as sequestered iron or sequestrene, will be necessary if the foliage is not to become yellowed and its function of providing the plant with nourishment thus impaired. This sequestrene should be applied annually at the start of the season; granular, liquid and powder forms are available.

The leaves of some plants turn yellow, with dark green veins, when they are grown on chalk, indicating that they are suffering from iron deficiency. This can be overcome by adding easily absorbed sequestered iron, or sequestrene, to the soil.

Climbing species of clematis, such as 'Nellie Moser', thrive on chalk, as does *Mahonia* 'Charity', an evergreen shrub bearing spikes of scented yellow flowers in winter.

Clematis 'Nellie Moser'

Mahonia 'Charity'

See also:
Compost and compost making
    pp10–11
Leaf-mould as a soil improver p 14

Peat as a soil improver p 15
Use of slow-release granular
    fertilizer p 18

Is there an easy way to improve a heavy clay soil?

The ease with which a clay soil can be improved depends on how you approach hard work, for there are no short cuts if the job is to be done properly. Most of the problems of a clay soil stem from its composition: fine particles of mineral matter that pack together extremely closely, preventing the free movement of water and air. As a result, water tends to accumulate in the soil and not drain away, and the inability of air to penetrate means that the soil tends to be cold — the warmth of the sun simply cannot reach more than a few centimetres below the surface. To improve both of these features, the clay requires 'opening up' — the solid, impenetrable mass must be changed into a finer, crumb-like structure.

At different times, various amendments have been suggested to bring about this improvement. Lime was recommended in the past, but while it does reduce the stickiness, its effects on clay are transient. Gypsum too has had its advocates but gives little long-term benefit. More recently, a number of proprietary 'soil-improving' substances have appeared on the market and much research has been conducted into the subject. At present, there is little evidence that the materials available to gardeners actually achieve anything approaching the magic answer they seem to promise; and many are expensive.

Almost all professional and experienced gardeners take the view that the thorough incorporation of large quantities of bulky organic matter is the only reliable way to improve the structure of heavy clay soils. It matters little what form the organic matter takes — peat, farmyard manure, garden compost — all are effective, and the choice really depends on local availability and cost. Whatever the material, it should be dug in as thoroughly and as deeply as is physically possible. The consolation is that, when the exercise is done, the resulting soil will be extremely fertile, for one other attribute of clay is that its tiny particles attract and hold many chemical substances needed for plant growth.

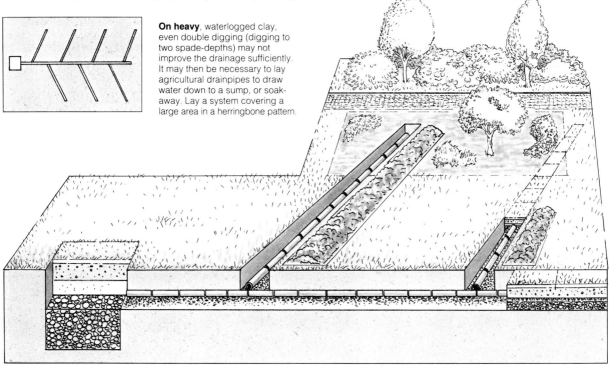

On heavy, waterlogged clay, even double digging (digging to two spade-depths) may not improve the drainage sufficiently. It may then be necessary to lay agricultural drainpipes to draw water down to a sump, or soakaway. Lay a system covering a large area in a herringbone pattern.

A soakaway should be sited at the lowest point of the area to be drained. Take off the topsoil to a depth of 30 cm (12 in) over an area at least 1–1.25 m (3–4 ft) square and keep it separate. Dig the hole as deep as it is square and half-fill it with large stones or broken bricks. Cover these with a layer of smaller stones, then earth, and replace the topsoil.

Trenches for the drainpipes must be at least 60 cm (24 in) deep and should slope gently down toward the soakaway. Lay the pipes on a bed of small stones with their ends just touching. Cover the pipes with more stones and gravel and replace the 30 cm (12 in) of topsoil.

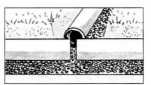

Where lines of pipes meet, cut one pipe at an angle of 45° and butt it up to the others where they join. Cover the junction with a flat stone or slate to prevent it becoming blocked by small stones.

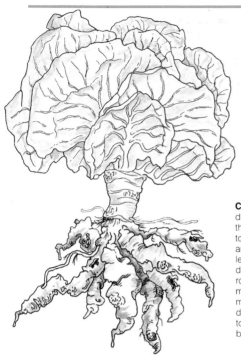

Clubroot is a fungal disease that causes the roots of brassicas to become distorted and swollen and the leaves to wilt and discolour. In time, the roots become a slimy mess, from which millions of spores disperse into the soil to infect other brassicas.

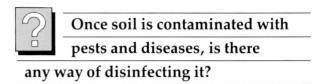

Once soil is contaminated with pests and diseases, is there any way of disinfecting it?

There is no reliable way of disinfecting soil in the garden, although small quantities can be treated quite easily for compost preparation. The easiest way to do this is to bake it in a domestic oven for about an hour at 150°C (300°F, Gas Regulo 2), or in 4-kg (8½-lb) batches in a microwave oven at maximum setting for eight minutes.

It is sometimes claimed that beds, borders and vegetable plots can be disinfected satisfactorily by watering on various proprietary solutions. These claims should not be taken too seriously, for such substances have only a localized and temporary effect on a limited range of organisms, and contaminated soil will soon be brought to the surface from below. With few exceptions, however, (clubroot and onion white rot in particular), most soil pest and disease organisms will die out if crops prone to the particular problem are not grown on the affected site for four or five years.

Does leaf-mould, collected from the woods, contain harmful pests and diseases?

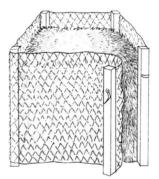

The best leaf-mould is made from small leaves, such as beech and oak, in a cage constructed from four strong posts sunk in the ground, with chicken wire firmly attached to three of them. Leave one corner loosely wired, so you can open up the cage to dig out the leaf-mould.

The only harm likely to arise will be that to you, if you have not obtained the woodland owner's permission before you carry away his leaf-mould. All woods, and their leaf-mould, belong to someone; but, provided you have permission to remove it, this is a valuable gardening material. You will see all manner of fungi and micro-organisms growing among, and crawling about in, the leaf-mould (as you will in garden compost); but these organisms all help to break down the material into a form that plants can utilize.

Provided you do not use 'raw' leaf-mould or compost in the greenhouse or for seedboxes (where the combination of weak young plants and extra warmth means that even a normally harmless soil organism could cause damage), nothing but good can come from their use. Leaf-mould is a valuable soil-conditioning and mulching material. Indeed, since leaves rot down more slowly in a compost heap than most other types of organic matter, it is worth making your own leaf-mould separately from the compost if you have a quantity of trees in your garden. A simple, wire-netting cage is all that is needed, with periodic watering of the layers of leaves and dusting with a compost accelerator.

Fork leaf-mould around roses, shrubs and fruit bushes as a mulch to protect the crowns in winter and to conserve moisture in the summer.

See also:
Propagators pp 43, 143
Disinfecting seedboxes p 43
Cold frames pp 44, 45
Mulching p 57
Disinfecting greenhouses p 143

Which is the best type of compost for seedlings and potting-on?

Not so many years ago, almost all potting composts, for sowing seeds and raising seedlings, for growing-on more mature plants or for striking cuttings, included at least some sterilized loam, with greater or lesser amounts of added sand, grit, peat and/or fertilizer. Largely because of the shortage, and consequent cost, of adequate quantities of sterilized loam, however, soil-less composts have become popular recently. Most are based on peat, although, ironically, that too has now become costly and alternatives are being sought, perlite and vermiculite being two that gardeners will see quite commonly.

Both soil-based and soil-less composts have their advantages and disadvantages, some of which are fairly self-evident, others more technical. Soil-based composts are more expensive to prepare properly and thus more expensive to buy; they are difficult to standardize and so liable to give inconsistent results. They are also heavier and much less convenient to handle. They do, however, contain a wider range of nutrients, and plants grown in them are much less dependent on supplementary liquid feeding.

Ultimately, for seedling composts especially, cost and ease of handling mean that most gardeners now use soil-less composts and find them satisfactory for most purposes. The main factor to watch closely is watering, for a peat-based compost in particular can easily become waterlogged but, conversely, is difficult to rewet once it has dried out.

For potting-on, the deciding factor will be that some plants simply grow better in one or other type of compost. When large pot plants in big pots are considered, the greater weight of soil-based composts is an important factor. Although a large pot filled with such a compost may be heavy and inconvenient to move, it will also be less liable to be knocked over accidentally.

FORMULAE FOR MAKING JOHN INNES SOIL-BASED COMPOSTS

Type of compost	Parts by volume		
	Sterilized loam	Peat	Coarse sand
Seedling	2	1	1
JI Potting No 1	7	3	2
JI Potting No 2	7	3	2
JI Potting No 3	7	3	2

To the above add: grams per cubic metre (ounces per cubic foot)				
	Superphosphate	Hoof and horn	Potassium sulphate	Chalk
Seedling	1186 (2)	—	—	593 (1)
JI Potting No 1	1186 (2)	1186 (2)	593 (1)	593 (1)
JI Potting No 2	2372 (4)	2372 (4)	1186 (2)	1186 (2)
JI Potting No 3	3558 (6)	3558 (6)	1779 (3)	1779 (3)
Homely measures:	1 cubic foot = ¾ bushel = 28.32 litres (6¼ gallons) = 3 slightly heaped 9-litre (2-gallon) buckets A box 55 × 25 × 25 cm (22 × 10 × 10 in) holds 36.4 litres (1 bushel) of compost loosely packed			

What exactly is peat and why is it used so much in the garden?

Peat is the partly decomposed remains of plants; only partly decomposed because the plants have died in poorly aerated, waterlogged conditions, where the bacteria and fungi that are responsible for decay processes do not thrive. The attributes of peat of greatest value in the garden are its water-holding capacity (several times its own weight) and its acidity. Added to soil, peat will improve the moisture retentiveness and, to a considerable extent, the acidity. For similar reasons, it is a valuable basis for seedling and potting composts. Its major drawback is that it has almost no nutritional value, and all plant food must be added in the form of fertilizer.

There are many different types of peat. The variation is due largely to the type of plant from which they are derived and, to a lesser extent, from the degree of decomposition they have undergone. For garden purposes, the two main types are moss and sedge. Moss peat, as its name suggests, is derived largely from mosses, especially species of *Sphagnum*. It is highly acidic, with a pH of around 3.5 to 4. Sedge peat contains the remains of sedges, with some wetland grasses and heathers. Sedge peats tend to be blacker than sphagnum peats and are more decomposed, but they have a lower moisture retentiveness and are generally less acid.

The most convenient way of buying peat, if more than a small amount is needed, is in the form of bales; they are lighter to transport from the garden centre than bags, for the peat is compressed and has had much of the water squeezed out. Bales are rewetted most easily by making a small hole in the plastic covering, inserting a hose-pipe and running it for several hours.

? Why is it difficult to grow rhododendrons, magnolias and heathers on some soils?

This is simply because these plants prefer acid conditions and will not thrive on alkaline, or chalky, soils. They are not alone in this preference, and the appeal of many of the most beautiful flowering shrubs is unfortunately limited by their preference for acid soils. Plants such as rhododendrons and azaleas and, to a slightly lesser extent, camellias and magnolias are unable to take up many of their required nutrients from alkaline soils, with the result that they lack vigour. In particular, they are unable to take up the element iron and develop yellowing of the foliage, which consequently cannot manufacture essential foodstuffs efficiently.

Unfortunately, too, it is difficult to increase the acidity of a naturally alkaline soil, especially if the soil contains lumps of chalk or limestone. The addition of large quantities of sulphur to the soil is sometimes suggested, but this is far from satisfactory and cannot really be recommended. There are, however, other possible courses of action. On a moderately alkaline soil, free from lumps of chalk, the thorough digging-in of large quantities of acid peat will make a considerable difference, although further top-dressing with peat will be needed annually.

Even so, a treatment with additional iron in a form that the plants can utilize will also almost certainly be needed — such iron is available to gardeners as sequestrene or chelate and should be applied at the beginning of each season. On such a soil, magnolias will thrive and camellias may also be successful. For rhododendrons and azaleas, it will be a matter of trying and seeing.

If this treatment fails or if the soil is highly alkaline, all is not lost, provided the gardener does not try to be too ambitious. Individual specimen camellias or rhododendrons may be grown in tubs containing a lime-free ericaceous compost or, alternatively, a small peat bed may be built. This is best constructed in a raised form, edged with rock, wooden logs or even peat blocks. In such a bed, filled either with ericaceous compost or with peat amended with a small amount of soil, many of the small and highly choice rhododendron species and hybrids may be grown successfully. The acid-loving types of heather (remember that the winter-flowering *Erica carnea* heathers are lime tolerant) and other dwarf shrub species will also do well.

Magnolia soulangiana reaches a height of 3–4.5m (10–15ft) and in April produces large white blooms flushed with rosy purple.

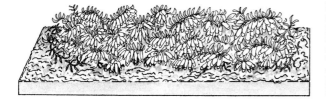

Heathers, camellias, rhododendrons and other plants that prefer acid soil will grow satisfactorily in a specially prepared raised bed containing a large percentage of peat or ericaceous compost.

Lime-tolerant *Erica carnea* grows about 30cm (12in) tall and provides good groundcover. Foliage colour ranges from yellow or bronze to light green with the variety, and bushes are full of white, red or pink flowers from November to April — some of the bleakest months of the year.

Compact, evergreen *Rhododendron yakushimanum* is ideal for growing in a tub or raised bed of acid soil in partial shade. It forms a rounded bush up to 1m (3¼ft) high, with a spread of 60–92cm (24–36in). Clusters of pink buds, paling to white as they open, appear in May and June.

See also:
Acid and chalky soils pp 8–9
Liquid and granular fertilizers p 18
Fertilizers for vegetables pp 118–19

Old railway sleepers or treated stout wooden poles can be laid in an interlocking fashion to form a sturdy raised bed — with the bonus of a built-in seat.

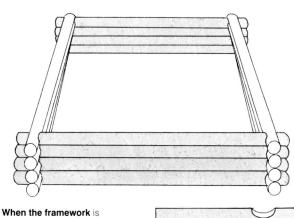

When the framework is complete, put stones in the bottom for drainage, then fill the bed with a mixture of sandy soil and acid peat. Plant it with heathers to flower year-round, dwarf conifers and other shrubs.

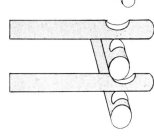

 ## Do I need special fertilizers for each type of plant, or will a general mix do?

This is one of those areas of gardening where the distinction between what you should do and what you can get away with is fairly clearly defined. Most gardening books and much of the gardening advice given in magazines, on the radio and on television, suggest that your garden shed should bulge at the seams with specific fertilizer mixtures for each and every garden task. This has to be countered by the fact that many, many gardeners have little fertilizer in their sheds beyond a bag of Growmore, which they use liberally and apparently successfully for a whole range of different purposes.

The answer is that, as with most things in life, there is a happy medium. The keen gardener, seeking the highest level of perfection, will want to have not only a wide range of fertilizers but also to mix his own blends from a stock of basic ingredients. The less keen gardener, the gardener with only a small garden or one with little time will 'manage' with commercially prepared mixtures and a fairly limited range.

Growmore is certainly the most useful, general-purpose solid fertilizer and contains 7 per cent of each of the three important elements, nitrogen, phosphorus and potassium. Nonetheless, there are some purposes for which one of these elements is required in greater or lesser amounts, and even Growmore should be applied at different rates for different crops. Because Growmore is an example of what is known as a balanced fertilizer, it will be found that for many tasks, if enough of it is applied to satisfy a particular plant's need for nitrogen, there will be adequate phosphate and potash present too. In some instances, however, the particular need plants have for phosphorus to aid root development, or for potassium to help flower and fruit formation, means that fertilizers containing proportionately more of these substances are required.

This short list of essential or desirable fertilizers should satisfy the demands of the average garden:

- [ ] A granular formulation of a balanced fertilizer such as Growmore.

- [ ] A balanced liquid fertilizer for general feeding during the growing season. One of the most popular contains nitrogen, phosphorus and potassium in the ratio 10:10:27, with the necessary additional trace nutrients in smaller quantities.

- [ ] A liquid tomato fertilizer, containing a high proportion of potassium for swift results on rapidly growing, flowering and fruiting plants.

- [ ] A lawn fertilizer for spring and summer use that contains a high proportion of nitrogen.

- [ ] Sterilized bonemeal as a source of phosphorus to aid root development; especially valuable when planting out perennials — trees, shrubs, herbaceous plants and bulbs.

 ## What is the meaning of the term trace element or trace nutrient?

The two terms mean the same thing: a chemical element required by plants in exceedingly small quantities and thus distinct from the major elements such as nitrogen, phosphorus, potassium, calcium, magnesium and iron. Normally plants receive all the trace elements they need from the soil or from fertilizers, although occasionally an element, such as boron or molybdenum, can be deficient in some soils.

Are liquid fertilizers better than powders or granules?

Ready-made liquid fertilizers are generally better for the people who sell them, since they tend to represent a more expensive way of buying a given quantity of nutrients. This is less true of the brands that gardeners make up themselves from powder and water, although it is important to realize that there is a place in gardening for both solids and liquids.

If you want the quickest cure for a headache, you should take a soluble medicament, dissolved in water, for it will be absorbed into your body more quickly. So it is with fertilizers. If you want the quickest way to place nutrient inside a plant, a liquid feed is the answer. This is especially true when plants are growing rapidly, as they do at the height of summer or at other times indoors or in heated greenhouses. Thus, tomatoes are almost always fed with liquid fertilizers for, as anyone who has grown them will know all too well, they put on foliage at a prodigious rate and, once the fruits begin to swell, they do so extremely quickly.

It is pointless, however, applying an expensive liquid feed to the soil in advance of planting or sowing, for it will be washed away by the rain long before the plants have had any chance to make use of it. At such times, a solid, even a special slow-release type of solid, is needed to give longer-lasting benefit.

Rake granular fertilizer into the earth between vegetables or around the roots of shrubs and herbaceous plants. Water will slowly dissolve it into the soil to provide long-term nutrient for the plants.

Feed fast-growing plants, such as tomatoes, regularly with liquid fertilizer as fruits set and swell.

Plant seedlings through diagonal slits in a growing bag; replace the flaps to retain moisture.

What about mixtures containing a fertilizer and a weedkiller?

These mixtures are sold for use on lawns and are essentially labour saving. Usually they comprise a high-nitrogen, spring and summer lawn fertilizer with one of the selective weedkillers from which almost every lawn will benefit. They have the great advantage of saving the time and effort involved in applying chemical to a lawn more than once. There is little to choose between the liquid formulations, for application with a watering can, and the powders, provided the latter are applied with a special spreader — they are difficult to spread uniformly by hand.

Dry fertilizer and weedkiller mixture is most easily applied with a wheeled spreader. The mixture is put into a hopper, which normally has adjustable calibrated rollers at the bottom that control the amount of powder released. Take care not to leave gaps nor to overlap the tracks of the spreader.

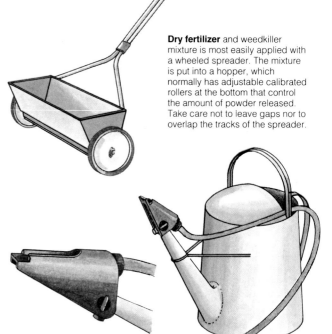

The easiest way to apply liquid feed and weedkiller is by means of a gadget that links a hose and a watering can. Screw the gadget to the spout of the can, containing a concentrated chemical solution, and push the short tube down the spout; the hose, too, is attached to the gadget. When the water is turned on, a metered mixture of water and chemicals is sprayed on the lawn.

See also:
Naturalizing bulbs pp 26, 68
Mulching p 57
Lifting bulbs annually p 69
Planting dahlia tubers p 77
Liquid feeding tomatoes p 147

Need I lift plants such as dahlias and gladioli every autumn?

The key to answering this question lies with the meaning of the term hardiness. A hardy plant is one that will survive all year round in the open in a particular area; a half-hardy plant will survive only during the summer; and a tender plant will probably survive outdoors only during the hottest part of the summer. The limiting factor is not rainfall or even the highest temperature that prevails — it is the level to which the winter temperature drops and, in general, half-hardy plants are limited by the occurence of frost.

Dahlias are a good example of half-hardy plants. The first autumn frost blackens and kills the foliage, and gardeners are usually advised to lift the tubers and store them in a frost-free place for the winter. The foliage of

gladioli does not blacken so dramatically but, by the end of October, in most parts of Britain, gardeners lift them, cut off the old leaves and store the corms indoors until the spring.

Generally the best advice is to follow the normal practice — check with the nursery or seed company that sold you the plants or consult any of the standard reference books regarding hardiness. But gardening is always most interesting and exciting if you are prepared to experiment a little. Try leaving a few of these non-hardy subjects (not your most valuable specimens) in the ground over winter. Cover the soil where they are growing with a protective mulch of peat or with bracken or straw held down with a spadeful of soil. Even in quite northerly areas, sheltered gardens or sheltered corners in more exposed gardens may permit you to leave at least some non-hardy plants outdoors.

Lift dahlia tubers carefully with a fork as soon as frost blackens and kills the foliage. Trim the stems back to a few inches and dry the

tubers upside-down. Wrap each plant in several sheets of newspaper.

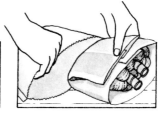

Then put each wrapped plant into a paper packet, leaving the top open. Stand the packets in a fairly deep box and store in a

cool, dry, frost-free place such as a loft or a cupboard inside the house or garage.

Is it possible to protect plants in a garden from frost?

This depends on the level of frost protection you have in mind, the part of the country in which you live and the overall frostiness of your site. A few guidelines are worth following, but it is important to distinguish between protection from normal winter frost and protection from late frosts in the spring.

Many slightly tender perennials will benefit from a small amount of frost protection over their crowns in winter. Bracken or straw packed in and among persisting leaves or branches is advantageous, and the simple expedient of delaying pruning or 'tidying up' until the spring will be of value to such plants as fuchsias and hydrangeas. Packing peat around the bases of small shrubs, such as tarragon, *Ceratostigma*, or the shrubby convolulus, *C. cneorum*, may make all the difference between a severe check to growth and satisfactory survival.

A screen of hessian or synthetic windbreak material will protect many evergreens and will help preserve the immature fruit of figs. Cloches are of inestimable value in ensuring the success of many winter vegetable crops, such as lettuce or Swiss chard. But remember that a plastic cloche can be counter-productive, since it quite commonly becomes colder inside than it is out.

Above all, the siting of plants in the garden may make all the difference between frost damage and the survival of a plant. Always remember two facts: first, cold air is denser than warm air and so the frosty areas of a garden will be the lowest-lying areas (sometimes actually given the name 'frost-hollows'); second, the damage to plants is caused not so much by the depth to which the temperature falls as the rapidity with which frozen tissues thaw — a quick thaw is much more damaging than a slow one. Tender plants should, therefore, never be planted where cold air collects and, paradoxically, they will often be much more successful against the north side of a building than against the south or east side, where the early morning sun will warm them up too quickly.

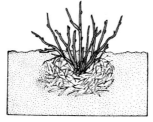

Straw, leaf-mould or dry bracken packed around the crowns and between the stems of half-hardy plants affords them some protection from frost. In exposed sites, young trees and evergreens benefit from being enclosed in a 'tent' of sacking or plastic windbreak material.

GARDEN PLANNING

The essentials of garden design

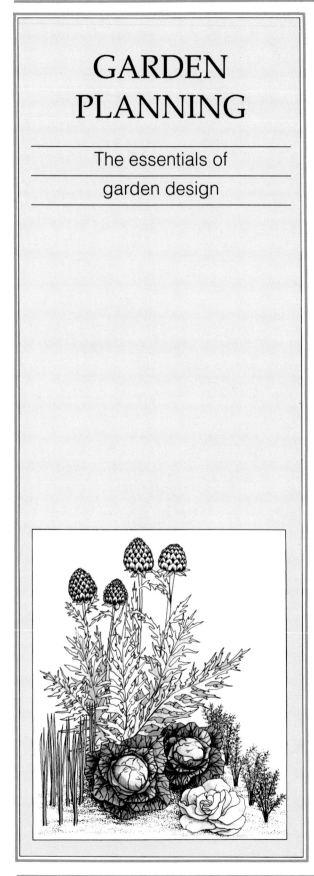

Are some sites impossible from a gardening standpoint?

Emphatically, no. It may seem so if you live on a northern hilltop, at the head of a beach lashed by the Atlantic, in a forest clearing, on an island in brackish water, or on a chalky hillside, where the topsoil extends all of 5 cm (2 in) below the surface. But there are gardens, and good gardens, in all of these places.

Some combinations of soil and climatic factors can try the most devoted horticulturist and, indeed, break the heart and back of some. It is always hardest to come to terms with gardening and planning a garden in extreme conditions when you have moved to such a site from

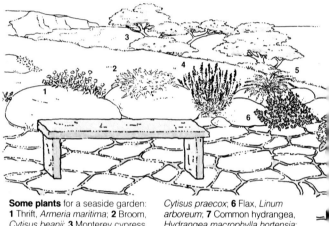

Some plants for a seaside garden: **1** Thrift, *Armeria maritima*; **2** Broom, *Cytisus beanii*; **3** Monterey cypress, *Cupressus macrocarpa*; **4** Old English lavender, *Lavandula angustifolia*; **5** Warminster broom, *Cytisus praecox*; **6** Flax, *Linum arboreum*; **7** Common hydrangea, *Hydrangea macrophylla hortensia*; **8** Spanish broom, *Spartium junceum*; **9** Rock rose, *Cistus purpureus*.

Is there anywhere I can learn about garden design?

Yes, an increasing number of professional garden designers now run summer schools or weekend courses on various aspects of the subject. The gardening press usually carries advertisements for these, and most of the better courses are announced in the columns of the Royal Horticultural Society's publication, *The Garden*. In some areas, local authority evening classes may include an aspect of garden design in general gardening courses. As with design itself, always check the credentials of those running the courses and satisfy yourself that they have extensive practical experience and are not merely recounting the advice from other people's text books.

See also:
Plants for boggy areas p 41
Herbaceous perennials for poor,
    shady sites p 56
Plants for north-facing walls pp 80–1
Hedges for seaside gardens p 114

some more mellow and hospitable clime. But look around, and you will see plants growing; wild plants, growing naturally in harmony with each other and with their environment. If nature can do it, then so can you. Indeed, 'difficult' sites are, above all, those where the gardener can learn from nature. Look carefully at the types of plant that are obviously thriving and start with their cultivated forms or with related but more desirable species.

Then look closely at the particular features that make your garden such a difficult one; is it the type of soil, the inadequacy of soil, the cold, the wet or the wind? Can you do anything to ameliorate the influence of at least some of these? Simplest of all, and often most important, is to erect a windbreak, for not only will this lessen the directly damaging effects of the wind but it may well

have the additional benefit of locally raising the temperature, conserving the topsoil and decreasing the impact of salt spray. Indeed, it may even impart benefits simply by allowing insects to remain in your garden long enough for flowers to be pollinated, and fruit to set.

Much of the pleasure of gardening comes from the companionship of others and from the exchange of views, ideas and plants. The newcomer to a problem site can benefit from this more than most, for there is no substitute for experience. Discussions with neighbours on the way they have met and overcome particular difficulties can be worth a hundred gardening books. Local nurserymen, too, are often happy to share their experience and offer their advice; but do repay this by buying their wares.

Some plants for a hilltop garden:
10 *Campanula carpatica*;
11 Cornish heath, *Erica vagans*;
12 Juniper, *Juniperus sabina* 'Tamariscifolia'; **13** Hinoki cypress, *Chamaecyparis obtusa*;
14 Cinquefoil, *Potentilla arbuscula*;
15 Bell heather, *Erica cinerea*;
16 Artemisia gnaphalodes*;
17 *Gypsophila repens*; **18** Heather, *Calluna vulgaris* 'Gold Haze'.

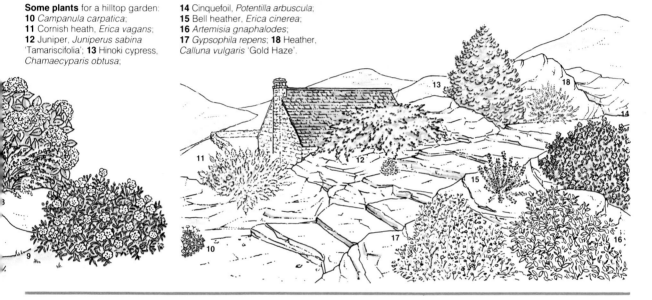

Is it better to design your own garden or to obtain professional guidance?

There is no simple answer to this, and even professional garden designers would hesitate before responding. As with many things in life, it is perfectly possible for an amateur to perform a task for which someone else is paid. The ultimate poser is to decide what your expectations are of your garden and how far you are prepared to stretch your resources to meet these expectations.

Most people with at least some gardening experience are capable of planning a garden of sorts. But few amateur gardeners have the combination of horticultural expertise, experience, plantsmanship and artistic vision to make the most of a given site, and it is this ability to achieve more than the obvious that sets the professional garden designer apart.

Certain points should be borne in mind. First, good professional advice is not cheap, although there are various levels at which assistance can be bought, ranging

from a 'walk-through/thinking aloud' service, which some designers may be prepared to offer, to a set of drawings and plant lists, or finally, to a complete design, planting and construction service, which naturally is the most costly. Second, always ask for references before you engage a designer; the gardening profession is peopled with as many 'cowboys' as any other, but a good designer will always be anxious for you to see examples of his or her work.

Lastly, do not imagine that to obtain a professional's services is in any way to discredit your own gardening ability; a good designer will always ask for your ideas and will be pleased to incorporate them wherever he can. In the long run he may, however, save you a great deal of time and money by pointing out at an early stage what is and is not feasible.

If, at the end of the exercise, you decide either that you cannot afford professional help or that you really want to do it all yourself, remember that there are now several excellent books on garden design; some of the best are listed in the Bibliography.

How should I go about planning and setting up a brand-new garden?

There are two types of virgin garden: the one that is, in effect, a building site, complete with half-bricks, lengths of broken drainpipe, subsoil and cigarette packets, and the one that consists of a fence (usually single-strand wire) around an area of field or woodland. They require different management, but the initial action should be the same in each instance.

Make a list of all the essential features you hope to have in your garden. Do you, for example, want a herb garden, a greenhouse, a garden shed? Do you want roses, rhododendrons or no shrubs at all? Are there particular types of tree you have always wanted if only you had the space; are the goldfish outgrowing the fishtank and in need of a pool to swim in? Do you like the idea of 'grow your own', rather than 'pick your own', vegetables and fruit?

Once you have drawn up this basic list, give a little thought to how much time you have to devote to the garden and more or less how much money you will be able to spend on it — initially and over the next five years. Remember, too, that the style of your garden should reflect the style of your house and the way you live: cottagey and informal, modern, clear and uncluttered, or somewhere in between.

The next step is to look at the garden from the highest vantage point you can find (usually this will be an upstairs window); take a pad of plain paper, sketch roughly the outline of the plot, then begin to doodle. No matter that you cannot draw; everyone can produce a sketch that they themselves can understand. Jot down where the basic features on your list might fit in. This is the point when you realize that there is not enough room for everything, so discard the less important, more expensive or more time-consuming items.

Now is the time, too, when a number of other questions begin to present themselves and when you will need to refer to other parts of this book for guidance. There may already be one, or two, or three fine trees or shrubs on the plot — how best can you incorporate them into your new garden? What is the best position for a greenhouse? Which way does the prevailing wind blow, and which of the planned features is most likely to be affected by this? Is the place you have chosen for the pool the most suitable? Is the soil really suited to roses, rhododendrons or other plants you hoped for?

Only when you have a fairly clear idea of what you want should you act. Depending to an extent on the time of year, the first move will generally be to lay some sort of paved area adjacent to the house. Begin your planting with the largest and most slow-growing items: the trees, followed by shrubs and hedging. Having established the framework of the garden, you can gradually move on to creating a lawn and, eventually, flowerbeds and a vegetable garden.

Transfer your design to squared paper when you are satisfied with your bird's-eye-view sketch, taking care to get the distances and dimensions of various features accurate. Bear in mind any slope of the land and don't crowd trees and shrubs; they may grow large quite quickly. Try to imagine how your design will look when you are standing in the garden; remember any curve drawn on paper will be exaggerated in reality by fore-shortening. Stick wooden pegs into the ground or lay a hose out to show the shape and position of beds, paths and so on.

See also:
Sizes of trees p 24
Water gardens pp 32–3
Shrubs for autumn colour p 78
Trees for small gardens pp 112–13

Vegetables to grow in a limited
  space p 121
Espalier and cordon fruit trees
  pp 132–3
Fruit cages pp 136–7

? What is the best course of action when one takes over an established garden?

In short, hasten slowly! Drastic alterations made within weeks, or even days, of moving to a garden, will almost certainly be regretted in years to come. This applies especially to the removal of large trees and shrubs for, once gone, they cannot be replaced, and new stock will take many years to reach significant proportions.

The first reaction, on seeing a huge tree close to the house or shading a large area of the garden, is that it must go, either because it will be damaging the foundations of the house or because nothing else will grow on a sizeable part of the garden. Neither of these things need be true. Many types of tree can grow quite happily and in close harmony with a building without posing any threat to the structure.

The effect of large plants on their neighbours depends greatly on the type of plant. Is it deep or surface rooting, evergreen or deciduous, and which side of the garden does it shade, for example? Above all else, therefore, wait for at least one season before removing anything large and woody. This apart, the plan of action depends to a large extent on how well established the garden is when you acquire it.

Gardeners, by and large, are a conservative and unadventurous fraternity. At a guess, probably 90 per cent of those moving to an already established garden hardly change the basic plan they have inherited, or do so exceedingly slowly and only slightly. There seems an innate acceptance of the status quo; the vegetable garden will stay where the vegetable garden has always been; even the shape of the lawn, inconvenient little twists and turns though it has, will stay the same. While bearing in mind my cautionary comments about instant upheaval, it is important to look carefully at the existing design to see if it works as well as it should.

Is the herb garden close to the kitchen; is the compost heap convenient for depositing household waste, yet screened from view? Are the winter-flowering shrubs at the far end of the garden, where no one goes in winter; are the scented plants in positions where someone will appreciate the scent — close to a seat, a door or a window? Have some of the shrubs, planted ten or twenty years ago, outgrown their original positions to the detriment of their neighbours? Some of these things will become apparent fairly soon; others, you will have to wait some months, if not a whole season, to appreciate. Moving to a garden in winter, for example, even the most experienced gardener may find it hard to identify all the leafless shrubs; and, until you have lived through a spring, there is no telling what bulbous treasures the apparently barren earth may yield.

In some instances, and for a few fortunate people, the management of an existing design may have more important implications. Your garden could be not just a subject of attraction or interest, but a significant piece of artistic creativity. If it is an old garden, it could be an important representation of a particular period of gardening activity or even the work of an important

A large tree close to the house can be an asset, even though, if they are shallow, the roots will deplete the soil for a considerable distance and the branches will cast their shadow widely. The area directly beneath the tree can be paved to provide a cool sitting-out place; or ferns, some varieties of geraniums and hellebores, and euphorbias, which tolerate deep shade, can be grown. Farther out, dwarf rhododendrons and camellias, perhaps in pots, will benefit from the partial shade, as long as the soil conditions are right.

garden designer, not all of whose creations are catalogued or even appreciated. Even such apparently unimportant features as moulded Victorian path and bed edgings or cast-metal plant labels should not be discarded simply because they do not meet your preconceptions of how your garden should appear.

? Is it possible for my garden to be 'listed' as an important old building is?

No, not in a strictly comparable way and you do not have to obtain permission before you change its design or appearance. However, if you wish to remove or lop trees, the consent of the local planning authority may well be necessary while the Society for the Preservation of Plants and Gardens (contacted through the Royal Horticultural Society) may be able to offer assistance if you believe that your garden represents an important or unrecorded example of a particular designer's work.

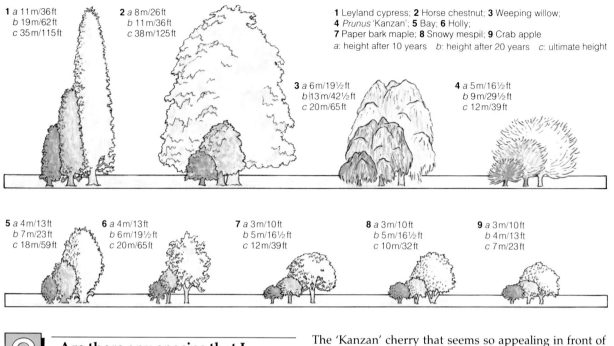

1 *a* 11m/36ft
b 19m/62ft
c 35m/115ft

2 *a* 8m/26ft
b 11m/36ft
c 38m/125ft

1 Leyland cypress; 2 Horse chestnut; 3 Weeping willow;
4 *Prunus* 'Kanzan'; 5 Bay; 6 Holly;
7 Paper bark maple; 8 Snowy mespil; 9 Crab apple
a: height after 10 years   *b*: height after 20 years   *c*: ultimate height

3 *a* 6m/19½ft
b 13m/42½ft
c 20m/65ft

4 *a* 5m/16½ft
b 9m/29½ft
c 12m/39ft

5 *a* 4m/13ft
b 7m/23ft
c 18m/59ft

6 *a* 4m/13ft
b 6m/19½ft
c 20m/65ft

7 *a* 3m/10ft
b 5m/16½ft
c 12m/39ft

8 *a* 3m/10ft
b 5m/16½ft
c 10m/32ft

9 *a* 3m/10ft
b 4m/13ft
c 7m/23ft

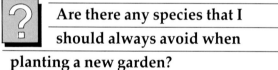

Are there any species that I should always avoid when planting a new garden?

All gardeners have their loves and hates among plants. Personally, and for various reasons, I would never plant weeping willows (which make a bee-line for drains and grow far too big for most gardens); sumachs (because their brief autumn colour does not compensate for their winter gauntness and dreadful suckering); limes and silver birches (because they, too, grow much bigger than you might expect and drip sticky honeydew on people, cars and garden furniture). I also avoid *Garrya elliptica* (because it makes dull winter days even duller); Leyland cypress, mimulus, calceolarias and picotee petunias (merely because I do not like them). Most of these are personal foibles, but there are certain factors that are sensibly borne in mind when choosing plants.

Size Every plant will grow larger than it is when you buy it. It is important that you should be aware of precisely how much larger, expecially if the plant is a tree or shrub that you plan to be an important and long-term feature of the garden. The ultimate size of herbaceous plants, too, should not be dismissed, especially when planning a properly structured border, although mistakes here are fairly soon rectified and can be put down to experience. It is not only ultimate size but rapidity of growth that needs to be taken into account, and many of the better nursery gardens now provide this information in their catalogues, giving an indication of height and spread after, say, ten and twenty years.

As an indication of how much variation there can be, the popular trees shown in the chart might all be bought at a height of around 60 cm (24 in) from a garden centre.

The 'Kanzan' cherry that seems so appealing in front of the house for a few years after planting will, quite possibly, be shading your bedroom windows within ten; and a weeping willow could be darkening the entire front garden after twenty. The lovely mespil, crab apples and small maples make much sounder investments.

Invasiveness Some plants, especially some herbaceous perennials, may not outgrow their welcome in terms of height nor in the spread of individual plants. Nonetheless, they may tend to reproduce rapidly, either through the production of seeds or by rhizomes, runners, far-reaching roots or tiny bulbs, called bulbils. Such invasiveness is a feature of many of the most successful weeds, such as couch and nettles, but several choice garden plants are quite capable of turning on their owners in this way too.

For this reason, my black list of plants, to which I would give only the most cautious garden room, includes *Helxine* (mind-your-own-business), lily-of-the-valley, some of the creeping campanulas, many ornamental grasses and bamboos, and St John's wort. On a smaller scale, be aware when planting alpine gardens and troughs of the invasiveness of such species as some of the alliums, helianthemums and dwarf phlox. Many of these plants are useful as groundcover, but once established among other plants, they are often difficult to remove.

Social undesirability The anti-social dripping of honeydew by some trees has already been mentioned, but other features to consider are the physically dangerous thorns or spines of some plants (almost needlelike with some of the yuccas and other succulents), and the poisonous nature of some or all parts of yew, laburnum, privet, and some spurges, especially in gardens where children will play. Many other plants, too, may be poisonous to animals or to humans, if eaten in large quantities, or will produce allergic reactions in some people when handled.

See also:
Frost protection for plants p 19
Rose hedges p 91
Clipping hedges p 94
Hedges for a seaside garden p 114
Suckering plants p 116

Is a windbreak necessary in the average garden?

Necessary, perhaps not. Desirable, very probably. The benefits will be seen in many, even most, gardens. On many coastal sites, some form of windbreak provides the only means of growing any other than the toughest species. For the drying effect of the wind and consequent stunting of bud and shoot growth is dramatically evident in the grotesquely leaning trees and shrubs of exposed cliff-tops. The benefits of shelter from the wind can also often be seen in meadows or cereal crops, where the plants growing close to a hedge are usually taller and more lush than those in the centre of the field. For practical purposes, the choice of a windbreak is essentially the same as the choice of a boundary, although an impenetrable barrier, such as a wall, may be counter-productive, causing wind eddies on the leeward side.

Is it better to have a fence, a wall or a hedge as the boundary to a garden?

There are three considerations when deciding on the form that a boundary should take: the financial, the aesthetic and the functional, usually in that order. The attributes of the three types of boundary in each of these ways are summarized below and although the financial will understandably usually take priority, the incongruity of fences in some gardens is almost painful to behold. At least one may hope that, when part of a wall falls down, it is not replaced by one or two panels of wooden lap fencing, and that the integrity of the whole is retained. On the other hand, the relative slowness of a hedge to develop could be balanced by erecting a screen fence initially, planting the hedge alongside (provided that side does not face north) and then removing the fence at a later date when the hedge is well grown.

	Cost	Appearance	Practicality
Fences	Relatively inexpensive	Can be monotonous; good support for climbing plants	Quick to erect; take little space; relatively unstable in high winds; wood tends to rot, so needs periodic retreating and replacement
Hedges	Moderately expensive	Attractive, especially flowering types; provide cover for wildlife; limited support for climbing plants	Slow to establish; take a lot of space; need clipping; provide shelter for pests; encourage weeds; deciduous types less effective in winter
Walls	Initially expensive	Attractive; excellent support for climbing plants	Fairly quick to establish; robust, need little maintenance; give rise to wind eddies.

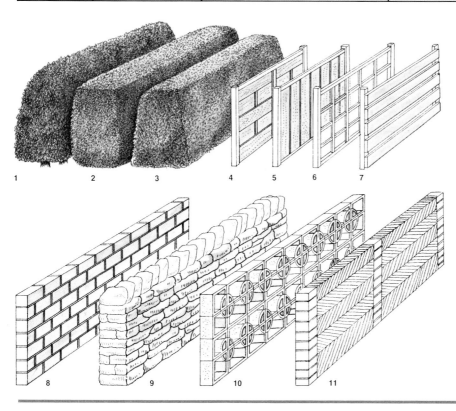

1 2 3 4 5 6 7

Although deciduous, beech, **1**, (all green or interplanted with copper varieties) retains its dead leaves so long that it remains an effective screen in winter. Formal hedges of yew, **2**, and privet, **3**, are evergreen but need clipping to keep their shape and prevent them from becoming leggy. Wooden fences, from woven to solid lap through trellis and spaced boards, **4–7**, take up far less room. They allow air to circulate and sunshine to reach shrubs and climbers.

8 9 10 11

Facebrick walls, 8, have good, clean lines, ideal in a modern setting; while mellow stockbricks give a softer, more rustic air. Building drystone walls, **9**, (closely packed stones with no mortar) calls for perserverence and skill, a job for the expert only. Concrete comes into its own with the use of patterned pierced blocks, **10**, that offer a good surface for plants to cling to and grow through. Use materials in combination too; one of the most attractive — and expensive — walls, **11**, has brick piers with rows of tiles set at an angle between them.

Is it possible to design a garden so that it requires only minimal attention?

Gardeners, as a group, may be conservative, but they cannot generally be called lazy for, almost by definition, gardening is not a pursuit for the indolent. There are those, however, who have a garden larger than they desire, which is an encumbrance; and there are those who, although enthusiastic about gardening, simply have insufficient time to do it full justice. Both of these groups need minimal maintenance or labour-saving, gardens.

Although a labour-saving garden need not necessarily be a small one, there is obviously a relationship between size and the work needed to keep the garden attractive and tidy — for that, after all, must be the objective. Anyone can, by minimal labour, produce a horticultural wilderness. Many of the principles of labour-saving gardening apply equally to large and small areas.

In a small garden, a quite appreciable area can be given over to an attractively paved or gravelled courtyard; there really is not much choice, however, given a big garden and little time and labour, but to grass a large proportion of it. Lawns may need mowing, but they do not require anything approaching the upkeep of beds and borders or of vegetable plots. The amount of mowing can be kept to a minimum by allowing the grass to grow long wherever possible.

Within unmown grass, daffodils and other bulbs can be planted in drifts to naturalize and provide attractive early season colour, while trees and shrubs not in need of careful annual pruning can be planted extensively. Those that grow fairly rapidly and supply good ground-cover are especially valuable, and the enormous range of low-growing conifers merits serious consideration. Consider also the value of heathers for groundcover, year-round colour in flower and foliage and the minimum of attention, apart from an annual clipping after flowering. If your soil is not sufficiently acid for the summer-flowering species, remember that the winter-flowering *Erica carnea* and *E. darleyensis* are lime tolerant.

Do not rule out roses for attractive colour either; but not the Large or Cluster-flowered modern varieties. Choose 'Old-fashioned' Shrub Roses, many of which will grow large. They need the bare mimimum of pruning and can, by careful choice of varieties, be selected to give bloom right through the season.

Clothe walls and fences with shrubs and climbers that do not need much attention to annual pruning — some of the vigorous clematis, such as *C. montana*, although, ideally, needing some pruning after flowering, can be allowed fairly free rein in unrestricted areas.

Above all, avoid trying to raise plants from seed unless you know that you have time to prick them out, harden them off and then plant them out into the garden. Indeed, if time is really limited, avoid annual bedding plants altogether. Many people also make the mistake of thinking that the only time taken up with hanging baskets and window boxes is that required for making them up at the beginning of the season and, in

Under fruit and ornamental trees, grass-cutting can be restricted to two or three times a year with a power scythe. But even on more conventionally lawned areas, limiting mowing to little more than pathways in the grass can have a most appealing effect.

Confine planting to the edges of the garden: lawns need less maintenance than borders. Plant good groundcover, such as low-growing heathers or vinca, and mulch around them with pulverized bark or even pea gravel.

consequence, buy them ready planted. They soon learn, however, that the real time-consumer is the daily watering throughout the summer. And, as with vegetable gardens, greenhouses, and tomatoes in growing bags, baskets and window boxes will inevitably suffer if you are away from the garden for days or weeks at a time.

Finally, give thought to what is one of the most labour-intensive of all gardening operations, weeding. Be prepared to use modern selective weedkillers but remember also the enormous advantages to be derived in weed suppression and moisture retention from surface mulching. The initial outlay on such mulching materials as pulverized bark may seem high, but the return will be enormous in time saved on weeding and watering.

Before planning your labour-saving garden, ask yourself not only how much time you can spare throughout the season but also how that time is distributed between the days, weeks and months of the year.

See also:
Paved areas pp 28–9
Water plants in small garden p 32
Modern herbaceous borders
    pp 54–5

Good bulbs to naturalize p 68
Shrubs for weed suppression p 87

Can a small garden be designed so that it will look bigger than it really is?

The art of creating an illusion is very much a part of garden design and planning. Whether it is a semblance of a natural woodland, a lakeside, a forest glade or an alpine mountain top, an environment that suits the plants you wish to grow must bear some relationship to the habitat in which they grow naturally. There is, however, another aspect to the creating of illusions that has less to do with the plants than with the human inhabitants of the garden.

We all hanker for something we do not have, and inside every gardener with a small area in which to work there is a frustrated Capability Brown. Indeed, the ability to make a small garden appear larger has become so much an essential feature of garden design that certain designers specialize in it and write books on the subject. Some of the major considerations in creating the illusion of space are summarized in the next column.

☐ Remember that you recognize a large area by your ability to see a long way. Avoid planting large trees and shrubs so that it is impossible to see farther than a few metres and impossible, therefore, to judge how much space lies beyond them.

☐ Fill as little as possible of the space with plants while giving the impression that there are a great many of them. One way of doing this is to keep the centre of the garden open and to confine most of the planting to the periphery.

☐ By using plants of appropriate size, ensure that the boundaries to your garden cannot be seen and, most important, ensure that neighbouring gardens are not visible.

☐ If there is open space, such as fields and woods, beyond your garden, arrange your planting so that, although the boundary is obscured, the vista appears as if it is merely an extension of your property. This was part of the reasoning behind the use of ha-has (ditches with sunk fences) that divided English country-house gardens from the estates beyond.

☐ Make use of curves in lawns, hedges and shrubberies to suggest the presence of something beyond what can actually be seen. Try to convey, by a slight hint of mystery, that there is more to the garden, quite literally, than meets the eye.

An illusion of size can be created by keeping planting to the periphery of the garden, *above*. Curved lines, which partially conceal what lies beyond, stimulate interest and give a feeling of depth and extent.

A focal point, such as a garden seat, glimpsed through a gap in shrubs or a hedge, adds visual interest. It has the advantage, too, of providing a place to sit and view the garden from a different angle, a subtle way of making it seem bigger than it actually is.

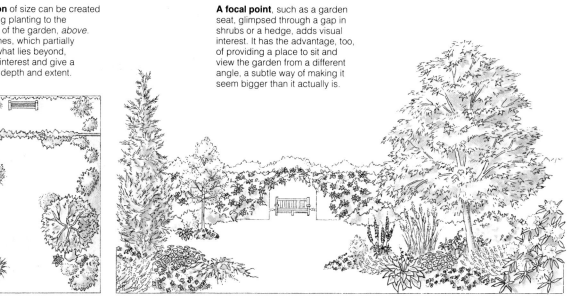

Can I use vegetables ornamentally in the garden?

Yes; a more unusual and adventurous notion is not to attempt concealment at all but to bring the vegetables out into the open. Indeed, some gardeners surround the house with brassicas, peas, beans and root crops (I know of one garden where a plot of leeks occupies all the space in front of the house). Most, however, prefer to integrate them with the rest of the garden.

This may be done to varying degrees and reaches the ultimate in the ornamental kitchen gardens, always more popular in France, where the bulk of the ornamentation is supplied by the vegetables themselves, with roses and other flowers used simply to fill in. The finest example of this approach to be seen in Britain is probably that at Barnsley House in Gloucestershire. A great deal can, however, be achieved without going to such extremes, although tucking the vegetables in among the beds and borders is unlikely to create self-sufficiency.

The real barrier to overcome is that of thinking of vegetables *en masse*. Look at an individual lettuce, carrot, Chinese cabbage, beetroot or onion and see it as a foliage plant, to be used in small groups in borders with more

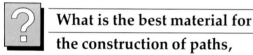

What is the best material for the construction of paths, patios and courtyards?

As with many aspects of gardening, the choice of materials for paths and other 'hard' areas of the garden will, in the end, almost always depend on their cost. The relative merits (reflecting a deliberate element of personal bias) of some of the more commonly used materials are touched on here.

Concrete At its most unimaginative, concrete is a dismal material, providing unrelieved monotony when used for patios, although perhaps slightly more acceptable in restricted form as paths, or where the surface is roughened by adding coarse gravel. Compared with many other materials, it is cheap, especially when bought for home-mixing.

Tarmac Nothing ruins the appearance of any garden as much as an expanse of this dreadful black monotony. Resist the persuasive powers of people who arrive uninvited at your door, just happening to have a load of steaming tar with them, and offer to 'do' your drive.

Gravel and stone chips Available in many different grades and colours, those with angular particles tend to be more expensive and are capable of being compacted when heavy-rolled, while those of the pea gravel type remain loose but give that appealing crunching sound when walked on. The loose types of gravel are among the cheapest materials but do need to be confined by raised edges to prevent them from spilling on to lawns. They are always attractive but are less practical where they are likely to be walked on with muddy boots.

Wood Wood? Yes; wood can be used for paving and is less widely seen than it might be. Short lengths of hardwood trunks, set vertically, can produce an extremely pleasing appearance, a fact known to the gardeners of

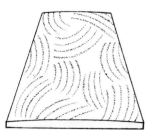

The **appearance** of concrete can be improved by brushing the surface with a stiff broom while it is still wet; an operation that also results in a less slippery surface.

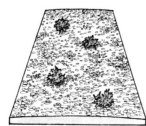

Gravel is cheap and easy to obtain, but it does shift and needs frequent raking to keep it level. Many plants — and weeds — will grow in gravel, which acts as a mulch and conserves water.

Wooden paths and patios look attractive, but wood plays a more useful role as edging.

Tree trunks, sawn horizontally and laid flat face inward, are good for confining loose gravel on paths; use planks vertically to edge bricks. Old railway sleepers make excellent steps.

See also:
Garden design p 22
Screens and hedges pp 23, 91, 114
Children in gardens p 31
Evergreen creepers pp 80–1

conventional ornamentals. Look also at those vegetables that are already grown for their flowers or fruit or that produce them incidentally during the course of the season — tomatoes, potatoes, globe artichokes, beans and peas, marrows and cucumbers.

One cannot pretend that vegetables grown in this way will match in either quality or quantity those produced in a purpose-managed vegetable garden. But a group of globe artichokes or sweetcorn at the back of the herbaceous border, three or four plants of one of the attractively flowered maincrop potato varieties and small groups of red lettuce, Chinese cabbage and carrots near the front, certainly bring a new dimension to vegetable growing. They will introduce novel foliage colours and patterns into your plantings, and they will serve as a talking point among your visitors.

What is the best way to hide a vegetable plot when the garden is viewed from the house?

It is remarkable how gardeners' attitudes vary over admitting to the presence of a vegetable plot. For many, it is a matter of pride and joy that they should be growing food for the family. Other people seem to treat vegetables as the poor relations of gardening, consider the growing of them as a matter for concealment, if not shame, and consign the entire plot to the farthest and most obscure corner.

The most usual approach is to screen the whole area from the rest of the garden by a hedge, a fence or some form of climber-clad trellis. Bear in mind, though, that the screen should be evergreen or at least equally efficient in winter and summer — which allows the choice of beech for hedging. There must also be sufficient space between the screen and the vegetables to prevent the plot from being shaded and drained of nutrient. So make the screen as low as possible, and, if space is limited, use a fence or trellis, since they will not deplete nutrient and moisture in the way that a hedge will.

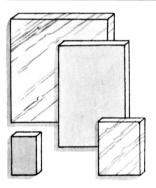

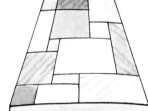

Slabs of different shapes, sizes and colours can be combined for variety. They can be set in a surround of flat pebbles or even used alternately with bricks to make patterned paths.

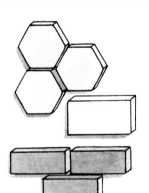

Bricks are difficult to lay well, on sand or mortar, but they can look magnificent in traditional patterns of basketweave or herringbone. Patterns not needing half-bricks are easier to lay.

Japan for centuries. Unfortunately, such areas are better looked at than walked on, for they can be extremely slippery when wet. Large fragments of shredded bark, such as are used for mulching, can also make attractive and functional paths.

Concrete and stone slabs Concrete slabs are the cheapest and most readily available, and although they look pretty dreary when first laid, they can mellow surprisingly well. Slabs of genuine York stone, while beautiful in appearance, have become almost prohibitively expensive. Many of the artificial substitutes now available are well worth considering, but do not be tempted by some of the cheaper ones that flake badly after a few years.

Lay all slabs on a bed of compacted sand and do not cement between them. Instead, fill the gaps with compost, and mat-forming plants tolerant of being trodden on, such as thymes and *Dianthus neglectus*, will root happily, softening the effect and adding colour and perfume. Slabs set in grass should be slightly below the level of the lawn, so the mower will pass over the top.

Brick Although brick looks right and good in some gardens, particularly where the house itself is built of brick, it looks out of place in others. Old bricks can be obtained fairly easily, but they often require cleaning and are usually unsuitable for paving, since they soon tend to crumble. Some of the modern, hard-wearing bricks are unattractive and to obtain a combination of durability and pleasing appearance can be expensive.

Other materials Proprietary blocks are now available in a vast range of colours, sizes and textures. Some simulate natural materials, others are unashamedly artificial. Most are expensive, many prohibitively so for all except for small areas. Stone cobbles, granite setts and tiles can all have a place in the garden. Always try to see a sample area laid, for the end result can be very different from the appearance of individual pieces.

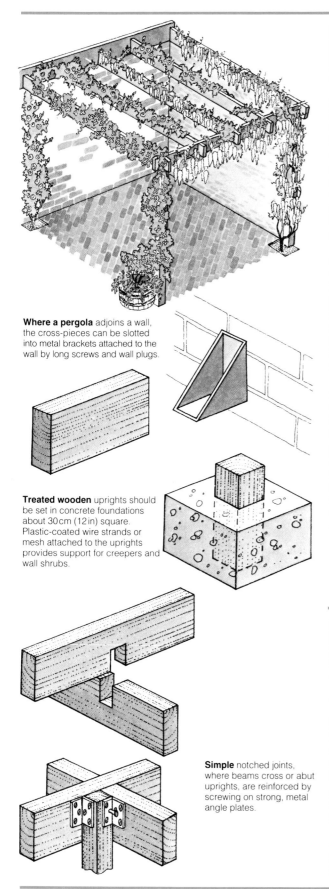

Where a pergola adjoins a wall, the cross-pieces can be slotted into metal brackets attached to the wall by long screws and wall plugs.

Treated wooden uprights should be set in concrete foundations about 30 cm (12 in) square. Plastic-coated wire strands or mesh attached to the uprights provides support for creepers and wall shrubs.

Simple notched joints, where beams cross or abut uprights, are reinforced by screwing on strong, metal angle plates.

How is a pergola constructed and where should it be placed?

Pergola is an interesting word, having its roots in the Latin name for a shed, although a well-constructed and well-planted pergola in the full glory of early summer has about as much resemblance to a shed as a camellia does to a cabbage. It can also mean a balcony; but, in its normal gardening sense, it is what poets call an arbour: an open framework with no sides and no roof, over which climbers and wall shrubs are trained. A pergola creates space for growing climbers additional to that on house walls and fences, while, at the same time, providing an elegant area in which to sit and sip tea or pink gin.

Although rather grand pergolas with spiral brick uprights look splendid adjoining stately homes, upright wooden posts 10 cm (4 in) square with 15 × 5 cm (6 × 2 in) cross-pieces for the top are much better for a more modest garden. Pergolas are often most effective as linking features where you already have two walls at right angles, such as the corner between the house and a boundary wall. Ensure that the position is sunny, however, for no one will want to sit out under a pergola that faces north.

The choice of plants is as wide as the choice of climbers available. Roses will form part of most people's choice, but remember that the structure can look rather bare in winter unless at least some of the climbers are evergreen. They may be planted directly into the ground at the foot of the uprights or, in some instances, in tubs. Do remember to use some wall shrubs as well as true climbers and, if you have the patience to wait for the results, plant wistaria or laburnum and train it over the entire structure. A pergola displays the pendant blossoms as nothing else can, and the effect, when the whole is established, can be magical.

Is there really a place for ornaments such as gnomes and statuary in a garden?

I do not like garden gnomes and their kind and I do not know any other professional gardener who does either, although I am aware that they give pleasure and amusement to many. I suppose that, more than anything, it is the strident colours I find objectionable, both with gnomes and certain combinations of flowers, for I can certainly see a place for the more traditional, unpainted garden ornaments and statuary.

As with much in gardening, generalizations are dangerous and misleading, for one has only to think of some of the classic gardens of all periods to realize the important part that statuary can play in a design. The

See also:
Beds for acid-loving plants p 17
Garden seating p 23
Pruning wistaria p 79
Climbing plants pp 80–1

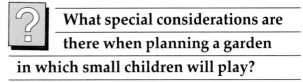

What special considerations are there when planning a garden in which small children will play?

All gardeners who are also parents will have their own views on the concessions that the one role is prepared to make to the other. It is important, though, to make children feel a part of the garden and not that they are allowed into it on sufferance; if for no other reason than that we want gardeners in the next generation, and it is never too early to start introducing children to the wonders that gardening can offer.

Give them a small area that they can call their own and encourage them to understand that plants will die if they are neglected, walked on or pulled up. A children's garden is doubly important if, for reasons of intrinsic value, delicacy or potential danger, the children must not stray into certain beds, borders or other parts of the main garden.

No matter how keen a gardener and no matter how many plants he wants to cram into his allotted space, no garden is so small that part of it cannot be used as a play area. With a little ingenuity and labour, the space can be transformed for family living when the children have grown beyond the tree house stage.

Two more general points should be made. Children must be discouraged from eating any plants in the garden. While a great many garden plants will cause stomach upsets if eaten in modest quantities, two plants, the yew and the laburnum, really are sufficiently poisonous and visually attractive to warrant their exclusion from any garden where young children will play. Additionally, a garden pool, delightful though it is, can be a death trap for the young. A small child can drown in a few inches of water, and, if an existing pool cannot readily be filled in and converted, perhaps to a bed for special acid-loving plants, it should be covered with strong netting.

A tree house, sand pit and courtyard in which balls can be bounced and cycles ridden, provide young children with hours of happy, constructive play and parents with peace of mind, knowing their youngsters are safe.

The space can later be converted to family living by dismantling the tree house, turning the sand pit into a bed for plants needing special conditions and adding bright, aromatic plants in pots.

modern patio or the tiled Italianate courtyard may well be enhanced with an abstract work of art that would appear utterly incongruous in a cottage rose garden. There, a stone sundial or bird bath could provide just the focal point that the garden needs. Moderation in all things is a useful maxim to follow and, often, even a large garden needs only one, carefully chosen item.

Whatever ornament you choose, it should suit the garden not only in style but in size. For a small garden, seek a small piece of statuary which can be set by a pool, perhaps, or against the backdrop of an essential hedge or screen planting. Alternatively, a large decorative urn will serve a dual purpose, for it can contain some treasured plant that needs specialized growing conditions, while the classical shape and the colour and texture of the stone will provide a welcome foil to the leaves and flowers.

Sadly, as with stone troughs for alpines and York stone for paving, the cost of genuine carved stone statues or other ornaments puts them far beyond the reach of most gardeners. But some of the concrete replicas are now excellent, and only close examination will reveal the difference from the real thing once the object has 'matured'. Many concrete ornaments betray their nature because concrete does not weather in the way that stone does, but some of the surface textures now available mimic this weathering most convincingly, and, once algae and lichen begin growing on the surface, the effect is pleasing.

There are several ways in which colonization of the bare surface can be encouraged and among the best are painting with milk or sloppy cow's manure. Do not be taken in by the 'spray-on' algae and lichen that has made its appearance on some of the ornaments offered for sale in garden centres; it is not durable and should be brushed off.

POOLS AND STREAMS

Success with

water gardens

Is it worthwhile constructing a pool in a small garden?

Someone once said that, as an aid to achieving genuine peace of mind, we would all benefit from seeing a large expanse of water at least once a day. Whether this means that people who live on the coast are more placid than those inland might be hard to prove, but the presence of water in a garden does seem to have a soothing effect. Even a small pool is better than none at all, but bearing in mind the minimum size of pool that can function satisfactorily, there must be a question mark over the feasibility of having a pool in an extremely small garden, especially when siting constraints are taken into account.

Where these factors can be met or countered, once it has been built and planted, the maintenance of a pool is an easy matter compared with some of the other choices — beds, borders, or tubs for instance; a factor of significance if time is limited. It also seems that most gardeners, when they have had a pool, would not willingly be without one again, for pools give enormous rewards in terms of visual pleasure and functional interest as well as attracting wildlife.

What is the most satisfactory material with which to construct a garden pool?

Pools can be built in the ancient, the traditional, or the modern way: the three representing increases in both ease and cost. The traditional way for a pool to be constructed, which was used long before people thought of having them in gardens (or, indeed, of having gardens at all), is of clay. Where a garden lies on a firm clay subsoil, this method could still be used. It is hard work, however, for the clay must be puddled, that is, pounded with a wooden mallet and then a spade until it is solid and smooth. A minimum thickness of about 30 cm (12 in) of clay is needed and a firm edge to the pool must be built of rocks or flagstones.

Although it is sometimes suggested that the sole ingredient is clay, traditional puddled pools were usually lined with a mixture of clay, straw and some lime, which was stirred or kneaded together before the pure clay was hammered on top. Above all, the clay must be kept thoroughly wet throughout the operation; all in all, a messy, rather difficult, but satisfying exercise.

Puddled clay was replaced as a pool liner by concrete. It, too, is not easy to apply and, before embarking on an adventure with a concrete pool, you should read a specialist book. Account must be taken of the nature of the underlying soil, of the difficulties of forming vertical walls, of the need to incorporate a water-proofing agent and of sealing the finished pool.

See also:
Garden design p 22
Paved areas pp 28–9

What should I consider when deciding where to site a pool?

Perhaps the most important factor is that the pool should not be overhung by large deciduous trees, which will deposit vast amounts of foliage into the water every autumn. If the leaves are allowed to remain and decay, they will foul the water by using up oxygen at a time of year when oxygenating plants are unable to replace it. This will have serious harmful effects on plant life in general and also on fish.

Although the difficulty can be overcome by stretching nylon netting over the pool during the weeks of autumn leaf-fall, this is time-consuming and unsightly. Actually removing submerged leaves from the water is an equally time-consuming, and also messy, operation. Remember, too, that tree roots can undermine a pool as easily as they can any other structure and cause cracks and leaks.

Sunlight is the most important single requirement for the correct functioning of a pool. There are almost no surface-living water plants that are shade tolerant, while water-lilies are especially light-demanding. Six, or preferably more, hours of direct sunshine a day are essential if water-lilies are to thrive. Don't worry about the effect of direct sunshine on fish; they will find shelter beneath plants and in the deeper parts of the pool.

The slope of the land is another factor to take into account. Clearly, the pool itself must be on level ground, but if it is sited at the base of a steep slope, water draining from the rest of the garden will end up in the pool, which will constantly overflow and create boggy conditions in the surrounding area. This is excellent if you plan to have a bog garden but infuriating if you want a formal pool and like to sit near the water's edge.

Remember that you will almost certainly want to drain the pool at some time (although not as a matter of routine), so you should plan some means of doing this. It can be a lengthy operation to empty even a small pool with buckets; with a large one it can be almost impossible. A pool measuring 7 × 4m (23 × 13ft) and with an average depth of 50cm (20in) will contain over 11,000 litres (2,420 UK gallons) of water. A pump will be essential if the pool is not sited so that a drain can be opened, allowing the water to run out naturally.

Finally, don't forget the important aesthetic aspects of siting a pool. A formal pool requires formal surroundings, and while it is perfectly at home in a paved courtyard it would look incongruous as the focal point of a rock garden, where what is needed is a pool that resembles as closely as possible a natural one in such surroundings.

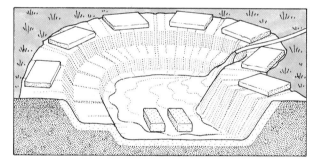

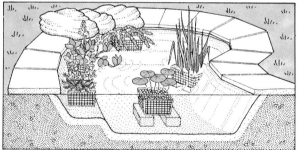

Excavate a pool with sloping sides and rounded corners, leaving some shallow planting ledges. Remove stones and line the pool with about 5cm (2in) of sand to prevent the rubber wearing. Drape the sheeting over the pool, with twice as much extra around the edges as the pool is deep, and anchor it with heavy stones. Fill the pool with water to the level of the ledges.

The weight of the water will stretch the rubber, and it will take up the shape of the pool. Cover 20–30cm (8–12in) of sheeting at the edges with earth and rocks or paving slabs. Cut away any surplus material. Put plants in containers in position on the pool bottom and ledges and fill the pool. Always keep the water well topped up; sunlight can rot the rubber.

Finally, to the simplest method — with modern plastic liners. Polythene sheet, the most obvious choice, is rarely satisfactory since even the heaviest gauge tears easily. At a somewhat higher cost, vinyl sheet is much better; but best of all is butyl rubber. This is quite costly but extremely tough — commercial reservoirs are lined with butyl rubber — and it is well worth the expenditure. All good aquatic suppliers stock it and will give details of how best to lay it. One important thing to remember is to leave a good overlap at the top so that earth and rocks can be used as anchorage around the pool's edge.

Ostensibly the simplest pool liners of all are the pre-formed glass fibre creations that look more like oversized and carelessly made baby's baths than anything horticultural. In my opinion, they can never be sufficiently well disguised as to make them acceptable, and I have never yet found one that was anything like deep enough for growing many water plants satisfactorily. They do, however, seem to satisfy many gardeners' requirements and certainly, with glass fibre, you can decide today that you want a pool and virtually realize your ambition by tomorrow; and you cannot say that for puddled clay.

Is there a minimum size below which a pool does not function properly?

A pool must be treated as an entity, with a careful balance between all its living components, plant and animal; and the larger the pool, the easier it is to achieve this balance.

As a rule of thumb, the minimum dimensions should be about 2 × 1 m (6½ × 3¼ ft), although moulded glass fibre linings are sold even smaller than this. By the time you have allowed for marginal shallows into which planting baskets are placed, the volume of water of sufficient depth not to freeze solid in winter (and able, therefore, to maintain a fish population all year round) will be miniscule in these tiny structures.

Those people who hanker after a few water-lilies or other aquatics but have very little space, perhaps only a terrace on which to garden, might consider a tub garden. After being thoroughly scrubbed inside, wooden half-barrels may either be sunk to the rim in the soil or kept free-standing and filled with water. If the barrel has dried out, it will leak for a while but should seal tightly as the wood swells.

It is then possible to grow some of the smaller water plants, including miniature water-lilies. Plant them in plastic containers, covering the soil as usual with gravel. Remember to add half a dozen bunches of submerged oxygenating plants, and you should find that a pair of small fish and a few water snails will live in such a tub garden quite happily.

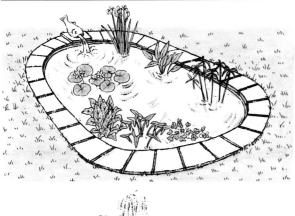

Does a fountain help to keep a pool in a healthy condition?

A fountain is largely ornamental, although it may improve the oxygenation of the water in warm weather. A display incorporating several fountain jets in a fairly small pool can, however, be detrimental to the plant life by overcooling the water. The style of the pool must be borne in mind too, for a fountain has no place in a semi-natural pool, even though it may enhance the appearance of a more formal one.

In larger gardens, with large pools, it may be possible to use a pump to create a system of waterfalls. This can be most effective, done well, although you will need a powerful pump; done badly, in too small a water garden, it looks ridiculous. When installing a fountain in

A cascade can be made on a natural slope or on one formed from the earth excavated when you make your pool. Use bricks and concrete, with a firm base of hardcore, for the course of the 'stream', and butyl rubber for pools on various levels. Hide these materials with earth and rocks, making it look as natural as possible. The gradual colonization of the rocks by lichens and moss and skilful planting of water-loving plants will help to reinforce the illusion.

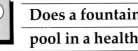

A formal pool in a small garden looks best if water movement is unobtrusive, limited perhaps to a horizontal jet. Exuberant fountains are out of place and can even overcool the water.

Water flowing down a cascade can be returned to the top by a submersible electric pump in the lowest pool. This type is easy to install and, with modern hermetic sealing and magnetic couplings, is extremely safe.

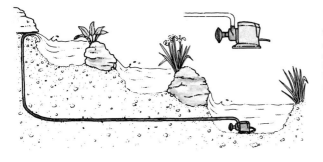

See also:
Statuary in gardens p 30
Frost protection for plants p 19

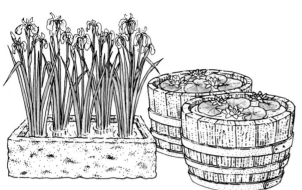

Waterside plants, such as the beardless *Iris laevigata*, will thrive in a stone trough on a patio, provided the soil is peaty and there is always 5–8cm (2–3in) of water covering their roots.

Miniature water-lilies can be grown in plastic planting baskets in a wooden half-barrel. Add some oxygenating plants, a pair of small fish and a few water snails to make a viable tub garden.

a more formal situation, consider having a low-powered jet arranged more or less horizontally, with the effect of simply rippling the water surface.

Once your heart is set on installing some form of water movement, remember that the provision of an electricity supply to a pool and the connecting of cables that will be in contact with water is definitely a task for an electrician. A large range of suitable pumps is now available; select one of appropriate power, if possible one of the modern, low-voltage models that operates through a transformer.

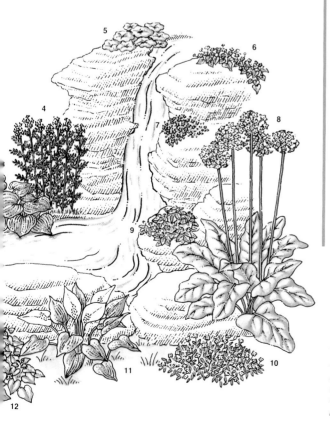

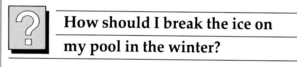

What is the best time of year to set up a new pool?

The best time to plant a pool and then introduce the fish is in the spring and early summer. Plants put into a pool during the autumn will almost always fail to establish themselves before the water temperature drops, and they will then rot away during the winter. Building a pool of even moderate size can be a lengthy operation, and there is an advantage in having the excavation made during the autumn so that construction will be completed in time for planting in the spring.

Bear in mind that most general garden centres will have only a limited number and range of aquatic plants and will soon sell out. It may be worth your while to decide well in advance exactly what plants you need and to place an order for them.

How should I break the ice on my pool in the winter?

It is important that you do not break the ice at all; at least that you do not take a hammer and smash it. Action as vigorous as this will send severe shock waves through the water and can seriously harm fish. But at least part of the surface should be kept free from ice to allow oxygen from the air to dissolve in the water and any harmful gases that may have built up in the water to escape.

The best method, and a fairly easy one to arrange if you have available an electricity supply for powering a pump, is to fit a small, thermostatically controlled heater in one corner of the pool. Some pool owners routinely disconnect and remove the pump during the winter and connect the heater to the same supply. Such a heater should be set to maintain the temperature over a small area of the surface at just above freezing.

Floating a small can in the water and then removing it once ice forms, in order to leave a small patch of free water, is sometimes recommended; but prising the can from the ice can itself cause quite severe shock waves. More effective is to half-fill a can with boiling water and stand it on the ice, replacing the water with more boiling water as it cools. The hot can will then slowly sink through the ice and open up a small area.

Plants pictured left are: **1** *Iris pseudacorus*; **2** Drumstick primula, *Primula denticulata*; **3** Plantain lily, *Hosta sieboldiana*; **4** Jacob's ladder, *Polemonium caeruleum*; **5** *Peltiphyllum peltatum*; **6** Marsh marigold, *Caltha palustris*; **7** *Campanula muralis*; **8** Giant cowslip, *Primula florindae*; **9** Water mint, *Mentha aquatica*; **10** *Arabis caucasica*; **11** Bog arum, *Calla palustris*; **12** *Houttuynia cordata*.

Which plants should I buy to stock a new pool?

The first thing to understand about stocking a pool is that the overall attractiveness of the plants is not the most important factor to bear in mind. Try to think of a garden pool as a sort of corporate being, a complete organism. Like any other organism, it is made up of many components, each performing a particular task.

Among the components that a pool needs are a source of oxygen and a means of disposing of waste substances. Without these, the obvious features of the pool — the water-lilies and other ornamental plants, and the fish — will not survive. Not only do you need the correct components, you need them in the correct proportions; and these are closely related to the size of the pool and to the volume and surface area of the water it contains.

The essential water plants are the submerged, oxygenating plants; not much of them will be visible, but they help to keep everything else alive. It is also important to choose a balance between so-called marginal plants that have their roots in the mud at the edges of the pool but their heads up in the air (some of the aquatic irises for example); those true pond plants, such as water-lilies, that root in the bottom of the pool but whose leaves float on the surface of the water; and, finally, those plants, such as water soldier, that float.

The table gives the type and quantities of plants suitable for pools of different sizes. A small pool is taken as measuring 1.75 × 1.25 m (5¾ × 4 ft), with a depth of 30 cm (12 in); a medium pool, 3 × 1.75 m (10 × 5¾ ft), with a depth of 45 cm (18 in); and a large pool, 4.25 × 3 m (14 × 10 ft), with a depth of 55 cm (22 in). Depths are those in the centre of the pool; much shallower water is needed at the edges for marginal plants to establish themselves successfully.

Type of plant	Suitable plants	Small pool	Medium pool	Large pool
Oxygenating plants	*Elodea canadensis* — Canadian pondweed *Ceratophyllum demersum* — Hornwort *Myriophyllum spicatum* — Milfoil *Hottonia palustris* — Water violet	10 bunches	25 bunches	80 bunches
Marginal plants	*Alisma plantago aquatica* — Water plantain *Butomus umbellatus* — Umbrella rush *Caltha palustris* — Marsh marigold *Iris laevigata* — Bog iris *Menyanthes trifoliata* — Bog bean *Myosotis palustris* — Water forget-me-not *Pontederia cordata* — Pickerel weed *Sagittaria sagittifolia* — Arrowhead *Veronica beccabunga* — Brooklime	6	8	20
Other pond plants	*Aponogeton distachyum* — Water hawthorn *Sagittaria natans* — Arrowhead *Orontium aquaticum* — Golden club *Villarsia bennettii = Limnanthemum peltatum* — Fringe lily	1	2	6
Floating plants	*Azolla caroliniana* — Fairy fern *Hydrocharis morsus-ranae* — Frogbit *Stratiotes aloides* — Water soldier	4	7	20
Water lilies	Requirements vary too much and are detailed separately on p.39			

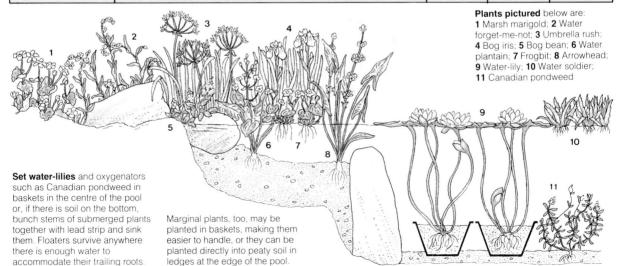

Plants pictured below are:
1 Marsh marigold; **2** Water forget-me-not; **3** Umbrella rush; **4** Bog iris; **5** Bog bean; **6** Water plantain; **7** Frogbit; **8** Arrowhead; **9** Water-lily; **10** Water soldier; **11** Canadian pondweed

Set water-lilies and oxygenators such as Canadian pondweed in baskets in the centre of the pool or, if there is soil on the bottom, bunch stems of submerged plants together with lead strip and sink them. Floaters survive anywhere there is enough water to accommodate their trailing roots.

Marginal plants, too, may be planted in baskets, making them easier to handle, or they can be planted directly into peaty soil in ledges at the edge of the pool.

See also:
Tub gardens p 35
Water-lilies p 39
Marginal plants pp 40, 41

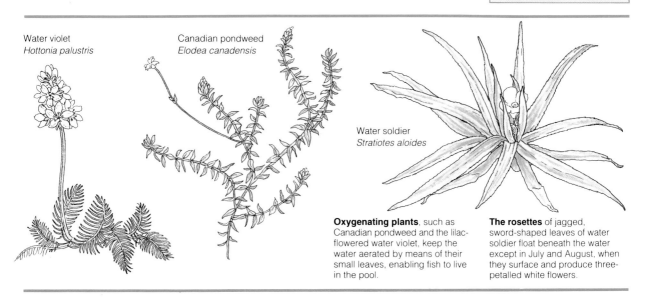

Water violet
Hottonia palustris

Canadian pondweed
Elodea canadensis

Water soldier
Stratiotes aloides

Oxygenating plants, such as Canadian pondweed and the lilac-flowered water violet, keep the water aerated by means of their small leaves, enabling fish to live in the pool.

The rosettes of jagged, sword-shaped leaves of water soldier float beneath the water except in July and August, when they surface and produce three-petalled white flowers.

Should I put fish into my pool at the same time as the plants?

No; it is important that the plants and the water are given ample time to settle down before the fish are introduced — three or four weeks at the least. This also gives the plants time to root properly; new fish are remarkably inquisitive and can easily dislodge plants before they have established.

Choose lively fish with firm, well-expanded fins. However healthy fish may seem, it is a good idea to quarantine them in a proprietary solution for the control of fungus diseases before they are put into the pool. Plants should be dipped in a weak solution of permanganate of potash before planting, to avoid transmitting pests and diseases from one pool to another.

Remember that, as with plants, it is important to have the right quantity of fish for the size of the pool. You will need some bottom-living scavengers among the fish, too, and a small population of water snails (preferably ramshorn snails or freshwater winkles). The following numbers of fish, such as goldfish, golden orfe and shubunkins, should be adequate for pools of roughly the sizes indicated.

What about the actual method of planting?

Apart from the floaters, water plants need something to root in just as much as any other plants do, but there are certain rules that apply specifically to water plants. Always plant them into damp soil, not into organic compost, manure or leaf-mould, for this will rot in the water and deplete the pool of oxygen. And always put a layer of gravel over the soil, since otherwise the fish will happily stir up the soil in the water and make the whole pool cloudy.

Planting is best done between April and mid-August into loam-filled ledges built into the sides of the pool or, more conveniently, into planting baskets. Formerly, wicker baskets were used, but modern plastic baskets available in a range of sizes are perfectly satisfactory if lined with fine nylon mesh to prevent the soil from washing out. Spread the roots out well, don't cover the crowns completely, and position the baskets at the recommended planting depth for the particular species.

If, after receiving your plants, you are unable to deal with them promptly, make sure that they are kept in buckets of water and never allowed to dry out.

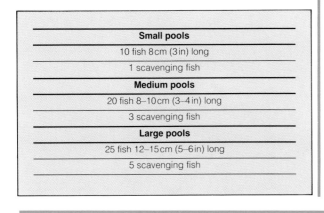

Small pools		
10 fish 8cm (3in) long		
1 scavenging fish		
Medium pools		
20 fish 8–10cm (3–4in) long		
3 scavenging fish		
Large pools		
25 fish 12–15cm (5–6in) long		
5 scavenging fish		

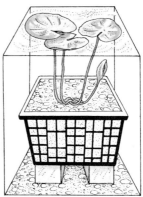

Baskets of water-lilies should be placed on bricks and only gradually lowered to the bottom of the pool, otherwise the plants may not flower in their first season.

The water in my pool often turns murky; what causes this and how can I remedy it?

The water in all pools turns cloudy at some time, so don't worry unduly. With a newly planted pool, the murkiness is usually due to the presence in the water of particles of mud. These will settle out in time, although sometimes clay particles can cause problems; in general, it is wise to avoid a clayey loam when choosing a soil for planting baskets.

If suspensions of clay particles prove persistent in a new pool, liming may be tried, *before* fish have been introduced. Add one or two small lumps of burnt lime to 9 litres (2 UK gallons) of water in a plastic bucket. This will produce a clear liquid that contains slaked lime. Gently water this over the surface of the pool with a watering can fitted with a fine rose.

Once a pool is well established, the water, which may have remained crystal clear throughout the winter, will suddenly turn cloudy in early summer and will periodically continue cloudy throughout the season. This is almost always due to the natural build-up of micro-organisms. But provided a careful balance of plants, including adequate oxygenators, has been chosen, no organic matter, such as manure, has been introduced and leaves have not been allowed to accumulate, there is no cause for concern. In time, clarity will return.

It may be possible to hasten this by adding a chemical algicide, but unless the water has become very green, let nature takes its course. If an algicide is used, be sure to dilute it as directed before adding it to the water; and do not confuse floating green duckweed with algae. The problem is to persuade yourself that garden pools are quite different from swimming pools and that fish and plants have different requirements in terms of water clarity from people. Take a good look at your nearest natural pond and then decide how 'abnormal' the water in your garden pool really is.

How can I remove the green growths that appear in my pool during the summer?

The 'green growths' are the water equivalent of weeds. The two commonest problems are those caused by duckweed, a minute species of flowering plant with leaf-like growths which give it buoyancy, and the masses of green filamentous algae, rather like green wool, that grow below the surface and can rapidly block up a pool. Neither is easily dealt with.

Duckweed is difficult because the presence of fish and other plants in a pool precludes the possibility of using a chemical weedkiller of any sort. It reproduces at a prodigious rate, simply budding off new plants without producing seed. In moderation, duckweed is rather attractive, and physically scooping it up with a net once it begins to take over is the best you can hope to do. It is impossible to remove all of it, and even one plant left behind will soon start up the colony afresh. If your pool is large enough, you could always try introducing a pair of ducks, who will, as the name suggests, greatly enjoy it. Unfortunately, they are quite likely to stir up the rest of the pool and uproot all your other plants too.

The growth of filamentous alga (or 'slime' as most people call it) is rarely satisfactorily controlled with chemical algicides, and even if it is killed off, you will be faced with the problem of removing the dead material before it rots. It is better to scoop it out regularly with a wooden rake; at least, any left behind will still be living and will not decay and foul the water. Be sure not to use a sharp metal tool, however, especially in a pool with a plastic lining. One injudicious swipe can be disastrous.

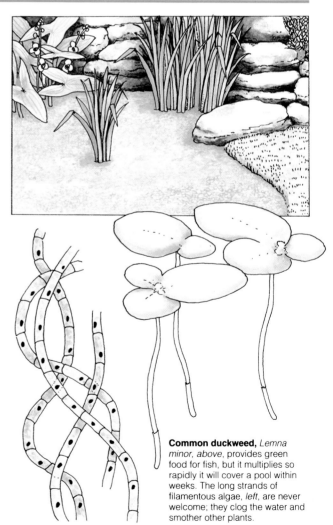

Common duckweed, *Lemna minor, above,* provides green food for fish, but it multiplies so rapidly it will cover a pool within weeks. The long strands of filamentous algae, *left,* are never welcome; they clog the water and smother other plants.

See also:
Water-lilies in tubs p 35
Planting water-lilies pp 36, 37
Slime moulds on lawns p 104

Which types of water-lily will give the best colour?

There are many different varieties of water-lily, varying not only in colour but also in vigour of growth, preferred depth of water, flowering time and length of flowering season. How many plants and which varieties you choose depend, primarily, on the size and depth of your pool. In a small pool, there will probably be room for only one or two plants of the less vigorous varieties. Some plants suitable for the size and depth of water of different pools are given below; but remember that there are dozens of different water-lily hybrids and that to obtain a particular one you may have to order from a specialist nursery.

RECOMMENDED VARIETIES OF WATER-LILY (NYMPHAEA)

White varieties

V	*alba*	medium-sized flowers; needs really deep water
M	*marliacea* 'Albida'	huge waxy flowers with yellow stamens
S	*odorata* 'Alba'	pure white flowers; strong scent
T	*pygmaea* 'Alba'	the smallest water-lily

Pink varieties

V	'Colossea'	long flowering season
M	*marliacea* 'Carnea'	white flowers with a pink tinge
S	'Pink Opal'	star-shaped flowers; strong scent
T	*laydekeri* 'Rosea'	deep rose-coloured flowers; strong scent; not a vigorous grower

Red varieties

V	'Conqueror'	masses of flowers with white flecks; vigorous
M	'Escarboucle'	the finest of all water-lilies; crimson-red with orange stamens; free-flowering
S	'James Brydon'	rich red with orange stamens; excellent and tolerant of some shade
T	*ellisiana*	vivid, dark red flowers contrast with dark green leaves

Yellow varieties

V	'Col A.J. Welch'	star-shaped flowers; marbled leaves
M	*marliacea* 'Chromatella'	free-flowering; soft yellow
S	'Sunrise'	dark green leaves; probably the largest flowers — up to 30cm (12in)
T	*pygmaea* 'helvola'	marbled leaves and soft, sulphur-yellow flowers

V	Vigorous:	surface spread 1.5m (5ft) diam. water depth 30cm–1.5m (12in–5ft)
M	Fairly vigorous:	surface spread 1m (3¼ft) diam. water depth 20–60cm (8–24in)
S	Small:	surface spread 60cm (24in) diam. water depth 15–45cm (6–18in)
T	Tiny:	surface spread 30cm (12in) diam. water depth 10–30cm (4–12in)

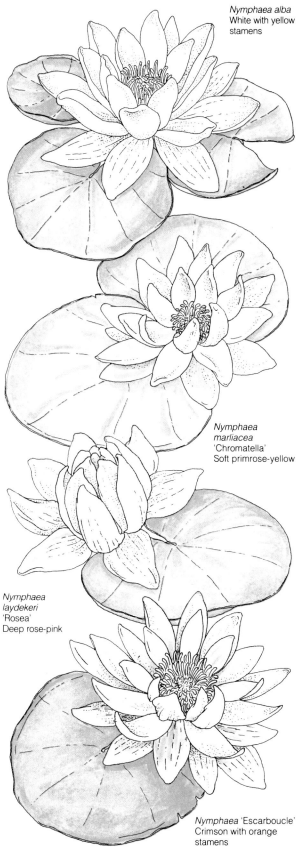

Nymphaea alba
White with yellow stamens

Nymphaea marliacea 'Chromatella'
Soft primrose-yellow

Nymphaea laydekeri 'Rosea'
Deep rose-pink

Nymphaea 'Escarboucle'
Crimson with orange stamens

There is a small stream flowing through my garden; how can I make the most of it?

Lucky gardener! Most experienced gardeners of my acquaintance hanker more for a stream through their land than for almost anything else. A small stream permits you to grow plants that you would otherwise find difficulty in accommodating, while the sound of gently running water adds to the enjoyment of any garden — and how much better when it is natural than when it originates with an artificial fountain.

Stream gardening is not, however, without its problems, the biggest being legal rather than horticultural. When a stream runs along one boundary of your property, you are usually the owner of the stream bed as far as the centre. When the stream runs wholly through your property, you are usually the owner of the whole of the bed. But normally, in neither instance are you the owner of the water that flows in the stream, nor are you necessarily the owner of the fishing rights or the right of access to the water.

In gardening terms, this means that you should give up any idea of damming the stream to form a lake and should avoid doing anything to cause erosion of the banks, or planting plants in such a way that they might impede the flow of the water. Where any doubt exists, discuss the matter with your local water authority.

Once the legalities are clear, there are one or two other matters to consider. The pretty little brook that trickles so peacefully through your garden in summer may be a torrential drainage channel in winter. Ensure, therefore, that you know how much the water course widens in winter before you begin work, and bear in mind the ability of the stream to tear out delicate waterside plants before they have had time to become established.

Unlike a formal garden pool, a stream-side habitat will have a natural vegetation of its own. This has two implications. There may already be many beautiful plants adorning the water's edge that it would be folly to remove — purple loosestrife, marsh marigold and meadow sweet, for example. These may not be apparent in winter, so before you start planning in detail, wait for a summer to pass and reveal what is there already. The summer will also reveal what waterside weeds are present. Water dock, butterbur and willowherb may have their attractions, but unless your garden is large and fairly wild, species such as these will assert themselves to the detriment of more choice plants. Do remember not to use weedkillers at the waterside; any weeding will have to be done by hand.

Despite the ease with which some plants establish naturally in running water, it is usually difficult to persuade them to do so. You may be successful with the water buttercups if you anchor them firmly, but it will usually be more rewarding to confine your planting to the water's edge and the banks. Suitable plants can be bought from any large aquatic stockist (don't uproot them from natural river banks). You should choose a range to include those that prefer to be in shallow water at the stream's edge, through those that like wet soil but not actually to be immersed, to those that need somewhat drier conditions, farther away from the water, but can tolerate a drenching in winter. The marginal plants suggested for planting in the water at the edge of a pond may be used at the side of a stream too, but there are many others.

See also:
Plants for pools pp 34, 36
Irises pp 36, 73

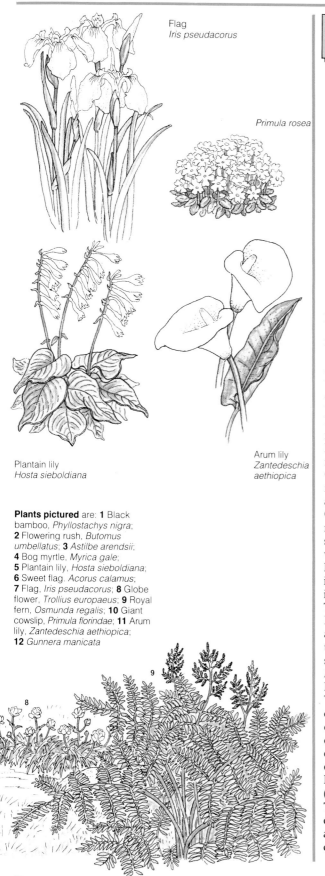

Flag
Iris pseudacorus

Primula rosea

Plantain lily
Hosta sieboldiana

Arum lily
*Zantedeschia
aethiopica*

Plants pictured are: **1** Black bamboo, *Phyllostachys nigra*; **2** Flowering rush, *Butomus umbellatus*; **3** *Astilbe arendsii*; **4** Bog myrtle, *Myrica gale*; **5** Plantain lily, *Hosta sieboldiana*; **6** Sweet flag, *Acorus calamus*; **7** Flag, *Iris pseudacorus*; **8** Globe flower, *Trollius europaeus*; **9** Royal fern, *Osmunda regalis*; **10** Giant cowslip, *Primula florindae*; **11** Arum lily, *Zantedeschia aethiopica*; **12** *Gunnera manicata*

What should I plant in a boggy part of the garden?

The small area half a metre away from the edge of the stream, where the soil is permanently wet, is the ideal habitat for a wonderful range of bog plants, but a bog garden can be constructed anywhere that water is continually available. This might be close to a garden pool (provided it is not a formal pool with paved edges); in a low-lying hollow that does not dry out or at the foot of a slope if drainage water can be directed to it; but not, please, somewhere made wet simply by leaving a garden tap permanently dripping.

When choosing bog plants, use the same criteria as you would when planting any mixed grouping. Be aware just how big some of these species can grow — *Gunnera manicata* is the extreme, having leaves more than 3 m (10 ft) in diameter — and ensure they will not shade out more modest plants. Try to select for continuity of flowering and try to avoid colour clashes here just as you would in the herbaceous border.

There are dozens of plants to choose from; the following is a personal selection:

Astilbe A wide range of hybrids is now available of these invaluable plants with feathery flowers. The pinks are sometimes rather 'shocking' and not to everyone's taste, but the whites are beautiful. Up to 1 m (3¼ ft).

Dodecatheon Shooting Stars. These are delightful, if rather expensive (less so if raised from seed), cyclamen-like members of the primula family. *D. maedia* is the one most often seen. Up to about 60 cm (24 in).

Geum The wild water avens has a number of cultivated forms, including some doubles. The variety 'Leonard' is a good single pink. About 30 cm (12 in).

Gunnera For the biggest gardens only, but quite magnificent in the right place. An entire family could shelter beneath some of the leaves. The crowns need winter protection. Up to 3 m (10 ft).

Hosta There is an ever-increasing range of these indispensable foliage plants, with many shades of green in the leaves and many different patterns of variegation. The flowers are disappointing. Up to about 50 cm (20 in).

Iris Many species are suitable for the bog garden, in addition to those at the water's edge. They all have the typical iris flowers, mostly blue and purple, and range in size from the 15-cm (6-in) *I. cristata* to the 1.5-m (5-ft) *I. delavayi*.

Primula Where do you start with such a valuable genus? There is an enormous choice among the bog primulas of colour, size and form. For a start, among dozens of different forms and species, try *P. rosea*, 15 cm (6 in) with deep carmine-red flowers, *P. florindae* — imagine a cowslip 60 cm (24 in) tall — and *P. bulleyana*, with tiers of orange-yellow flowers. Up to 60 cm (24 in).

Rodgersia An extraordinary foliage plant, up to 1.5 m (5 ft) tall and like a horse chestnut, without the tree.

Trollius There are wild globeflowers in Britain, but cultivated varieties in various colours, including white, are widely available. Up to 1 m (3¼ ft) in height, depending on the species.

ANNUALS AND BIENNIALS

Creating a profusion of colour

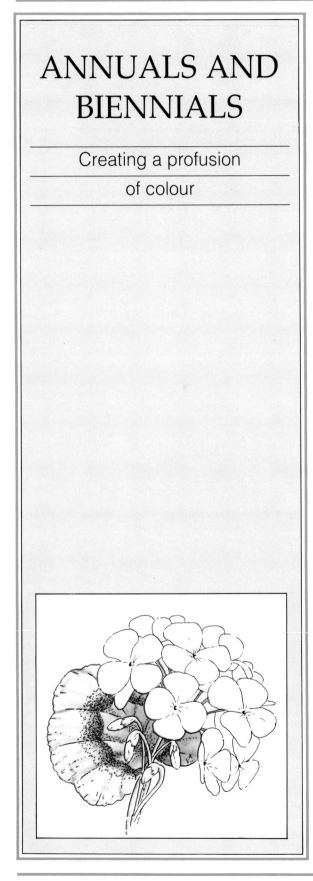

What do the terms annual, biennial, half-hardy and so forth mean?

Seed companies vary in the terms that they use in their catalogues, and a plant described in one as 'summer bedding' will be listed in another as 'half-hardy annual', causing unnecessary confusion. Although, in practical terms, most of these plants are accorded similar treatment, there are important distinctions that gardeners should be aware of.

An annual is a plant that completes its life cycle from seed to seed within the space of one season. Thus, although this usually means that gardeners will need to sow a fresh batch of seed or buy a fresh batch of plants each year, some annuals will be perpetuated in a garden by self-sowing — while each individual plant will survive for only one year, the stock will continue. However, some plants, although potentially perennial and capable of lasting for many years, perform better in a garden if they are sown afresh each season.

A biennial is a plant that requires two seasons in which to complete its life cycle; it establishes itself in the first year, to flower and set seed in the second. The best-known biennial garden flower is the wallflower, but foxgloves and sweet williams are others. (To add to the confusion, wallflowers, sweet williams and some foxgloves are actually perennials but are usually grown as biennials.)

Superimposed upon the annual/biennial distinction is the division into hardy and half-hardy. A hardy plant is one capable of surviving outdoors in a particular climate with no artificial protection. Applied to annuals, it includes those species, such as calendulas, cornflowers, godetias, larkspurs, nasturtiums and sweet peas, that can safely be sown outdoors early in the season or even, in some instances, at the end of the preceding season to obtain the earliest start of all.

A half-hardy annual, by contrast, is one that is capable of growing outdoors during the summer but cannot be placed, or sown, outside until the coldest part of the early spring and the danger of frost have passed. Many of the most popular bedding plants come into this category; African marigolds, antirrhinums, busy lizzies, nemesias, petunias, salvias and tagetes, for example.

Nonetheless, several of the most important of the plants grown as 'half-hardy annuals', such as pelargoniums and begonias, are not annuals at all but half-hardy perennials. This was perhaps more apparent with pelargoniums when they were all lifted at the end of the summer and stored until the following year, but now that so many are raised from seed each season, they are thought of more as annuals than as perennials. All biennials are either hardy or completely tender; a half-hardy biennial is horticulturally impossible.

See also:
Disinfecting soil p 14
Propagators pp 43, 142
Cold frames pp 44, 45

Germination of seeds p 44
Saving seeds p 45
Sweet peas pp 52–3
Disinfecting greenhouses p 143

Are annuals and biennials better sown into seedboxes or straight into the garden?

The answer to this question lies largely with the resources at your disposal, the rapidity with which you want results and the time you have to spare. Half-hardy annuals cannot be placed in the open garden until the danger of cold and frost has passed; so to obtain the earliest flowering, it is essential that they are put out as plants rather than as seed. Even with fast-growing, half-hardy annuals, such as helichrysums and asters, there can be several weeks' difference in the time of

Loosely fill a seedbox with compost, brush it off level with the top of the box and firm it down with a board to about 1 cm (⅜ in) below the top. Shake the seeds evenly from the packet. Dribble compost through your fingers or a fine sieve to cover the seeds, but check with the packet — some may not need covering. Water with a fine rose on the can or stand the seedbox in shallow water for about 10 minutes.

A heated propagator may be useful if you have no greenhouse. It consists of a glass fibre tray, containing a thermostatically controlled heating element, and a plastic cover to create a closed environment.

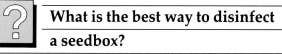

coming into flower between transplanted and direct-sown plants. With many others, such as petunias, salvias, tagetes and pelargoniums, you will be extremely fortunate if direct-sown individuals reach the flowering stage before the autumn frosts intervene.

The general rule with most half-hardy annuals is, therefore, to sow the seeds under protection earlier in the year. If you have a warm greenhouse or frame, a heated propagator in an unheated greenhouse or even a warm window-ledge, a start may be made at the end of January with some of the plants that need the longest growth period (pelargoniums especially). Others may be sown sequentially, according to the directions on the seed packets, through until April. If you do not have any heated raising space, wait until late March before sowing; and plant seedlings outside in late May or early June.

Hardy annuals can be sown outdoors as soon as the soil begins to warm up, toward the end of March in most areas; there is no need to wait until the danger of frost has passed. Even so, it is possible to achieve an earlier start and the earliest flowering by sowing some seeds in boxes or pots in the same way as half-hardy varieties. Sweet peas are among the special instances in which sowing in the previous autumn may be tried.

Biennials, such as wallflowers, tend to be big, bulky plants and cannot be sown in seedboxes; nor is there any real advantage in doing so. They should be treated differently and sown outdoors, in a seedbed, in May or June. Once the plants are about 5 cm (2 in) high, they should be transplanted 15 cm (6 in) or so apart in a lining-out bed. Here they will grow substantially during the summer, ready for planting into their flowering positions during October and November.

Because wallflowers take up so much space for so long, gardeners often prefer to buy them as plants each autumn. If you choose this option, ask if the plants have been freshly lifted, for commercial growers tend to lift early and keep the plants in cold stores. Kept for too long in such conditions, they deteriorate rapidly when planted out.

What is the best way to disinfect a seedbox?

Clean, fresh seedling compost and a more or less sterile seedbox are essential if you are not to incubate pests and diseases along with your tender young seedlings. The best way to clean seedboxes is to scrub them thoroughly with a stiff brush and hot, soapy water. Ensure that all traces of old compost and fibrous roots have been removed. Then soak the boxes in a solution of a proprietary disinfectant for an hour or so.

Finally, rinse them again in clean water and allow them to dry thoroughly before storing them. This is an operation best done as soon as the boxes are finished with each season, rather than leaving them dirty until the following spring.

What does hardening-off mean and how do I do it?

When plants are grown under conditions of artificially high warmth and moisture, their cells tend to be relatively large, the tissues as a whole contain an abnormally high amount of water, and the outer surfaces of the plant are thin. If such plants are then placed outside, they will be prone to desiccation, to cold damage and, because of their cell structure, to be physically unstable. Hardening-off is the process by which plants grown under protection are accustomed gradually to outside conditions in order that new cells, as they form, are smaller, thicker walled and generally more able to tolerate the harsher conditions.

The best way of hardening-off plants is by using a cold frame — an unheated, usually wooden enclosure with a removable, glass-panelled cover. The glazing ensures some enhancement of the outside temperature and helps to trap some warmth for night-time protection, but it is less cossetting than a greenhouse. During the daytime, the cover may be raised or removed completely (depending on the weather), until, after two or three weeks, the plants can safely be exposed fully to the outside environment.

Although the daily attention to the cold frame, and the care needed to ensure that it is closed up at nights until the danger of frost is passed, might seem laborious and unnecessary, hardening-off is almost the most important aspect of raising seedlings. Having spent money on compost, seeds and the warmth to germinate and raise them, to pay inadequate attention to ensuring that they are equipped to face the rigours of a British summer is folly indeed.

Why do some seeds germinate so much more successfully than others do?

It surprises many people to realize that plants do not exist simply to be grown in gardens at the whim of gardeners. Gardening is not a discipline in isolation from nature; it is the harnessing of nature and the bending of it to man's will. Nowhere is this more true than with the sowing and germination of seeds. It is sometimes forgotten that they had an existence before the seed packet and that those few brown grains represent not just the raw material for colouring gardens but the media for the survival of entire species.

Obviously, therefore, nature takes special care of seeds and builds into them intricate mechanisms to ensure that their resources are not wasted. It is particularly important that seeds have a means to prevent or inhibit germination from occurring at a time when the general environment is unsuitable for the resulting young seedlings to grow. Thus, there would be no merit in the seeds of most plants germinating as they fall from the parent in the autumn if the subsequent winter temperatures would kill the young plants.

Similarly, the seeds of many plants that originate from extreme climates require hard, thick coats to enable them to survive especially high or low temperatures. Even more subtle is the adoption of a thick coat by the seeds of plants that live in climates with marked seasonal rainfall. Clearly, a single shower of rain provides insufficient moisture for a seedling to live for long; but a thick seed coat, softened and penetrated only by a prolonged downpour, ensures that the seed will not germinate until the environment contains enough moisture for the survival of the resulting plant.

Thus it is that some seeds germinate easily with moderate moisture and warmth, others require prolonged exposure to the same conditions, while yet others require special treatment. Among the commonest tricks that gardeners will find suggested on seed packets or in gardening books are: placing seeds in a fridge or freezer (or leaving them outside in the depths of winter) in order to mimic a natural cold spell; and even scorching some seeds to simulate either baking summer temperatures or brush or forest fires.

Although rather different, it is worth mentioning also the treatment of some tiny seeds such as those of lobelia and fibrous-rooted begonia. These seeds contain insufficient food reserves to enable the seedlings to reach the light if they are buried, even slightly, in compost, and they should be scattered thinly on the surface and then carefully kept moist.

Mix extremely small seeds with sand or brickdust before sprinkling them on the surface of the compost, **1**, or shake them off a sheet of paper. Don't cover them with compost. Soak large seeds, such as broad beans, for 12 hours before sowing or, better, bury them in damp peat overnight, **2**. Hard seeds, such as sweet pea, will germinate more easily if the seed coat is nicked with a sharp knife on the side opposite the 'eye', **3**.

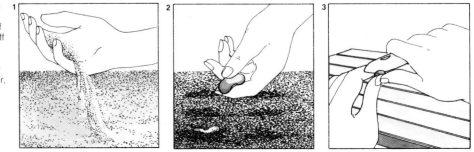

See also:
F₁ hybrids pp 118–19
Seedlings shrivelling and
damping-off p 129

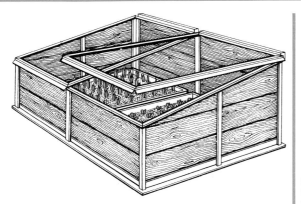

Seedlings raised in a greenhouse or propagator must be hardened off before being planted in the garden. This is best done in a cold frame, which can be made from planks of wood screwed together to form a box shape, with the back higher than the front. Make the cover of glass or plastic sheet and raise it during the day to expose the seedlings to air and sunlight.

Gather seed heads and pods when they are not quite dry and spread them out on trays in the sun or bunch the stems and hang them up with their heads in a paper bag. Shake the bag now and again so the seeds drop into it as they dry.

Store seeds in a cool, dry place or a fridge in clearly marked envelopes or in paper or cellophane bags. Do not use plastic bags; any moisture still in the seeds will be retained and may encourage fungus to grow.

Should I save seed from annuals to plant next year?

Although it still represents remarkably good value for money, seed is not cheap, and the annual investment on garden seeds runs into millions of pounds. Can the individual gardener cut costs by saving seed from his own plants, and, more pertinently, should he? The answer must be both yes and no. There are few more satisfying aspects of gardening than collecting seed from a plant in your garden, cleaning it, storing it during the winter and then sowing it the following year to produce a fresh crop.

For anyone interested in crossing one variety with another in the hope of producing improved hybrids, seed collection is, of course, essential. Such deliberate crossing of varieties provides a quite addictive challenge, but the many natural hybridizations that occur in the garden during the course of the summer mean that anyone sowing seed from their own plants always stands a chance of finding something new. You do, however, need to follow certain guidelines.

☐ Never save seed from a variety that is described as an F₁ hybrid, for the resulting plants will be a genetic hotch-potch and will bear little resemblance to their parent. F₁ hybrid seed must be raised afresh from new crossings each year, which is why it tends to be more expensive than other seed.

☐ Never save seed from plants that are in any way sickly or abnormal; they may well be diseased and the affliction could be passed on to their progeny.

☐ Always store seed carefully; for one year, it can be kept most easily in small paper packets in a fridge.

☐ Never offer for sale any seed that you have saved; it is possible that the variety has Plant Breeders' Rights protection, which means that only the breeder who owns these rights is legally entitled to sell it.

Is it possible to introduce diseases into my garden with poor seed?

Yes, it is; but with modern methods of commercial seed production, it is unlikely you will introduce any serious problems in this way. Vegetable seed especially is tested to ensure that certain defined standards of purity are attained. The risks are much higher for anyone saving seed from their own plants, and it is sensible to take certain precautions.

Poor or sickly plants should not be used as a source of seed. Although this is partly because the seed may, like the parent, lack general vigour, it is also possible that virus contamination is responsible for the poor growth, and many plant viruses can be transmitted from one generation to the next within the seed. The commonest problem with home-produced seed is probably damping-off of the seedlings, for many species of microscopic fungi can adhere to the seed coat and show themselves when the seeds are sown and incubated. Before sowing, all seed from home-grown plants should be dusted routinely with a combined insecticide and fungicide seed dressing.

Which annuals or biennials will give early colour to beds and borders?

The early part of the bedding-plant season is, above all, the domain of the biennials. They have been well established since the previous year and so have a head start in producing flowers.

RECOMMENDED BIENNIALS

Wallflower Two main types are grown in gardens, the common wallflower, *Cheiranthus cheiri*, and the Siberian wallflower *C. allionii*; flowering is from April through to June. The former is the type grown by the million for planting in municipal parks and gardens, and, if you simply ask for 'wallflowers', this is the one you will be sold. There are dozens of varieties in a wide range of colours and they fall into three groups: the Intermediates, which grow to 40 to 45cm (16 to 18in); the Dwarf Bedding types (usually given the name 'Bedder') which attain about 35cm (14in); and the compact 'Tom Thumb' varieties, especially useful for small areas, fronts of borders or for windy sites where early season gales can ruin larger plants.

The Siberian wallflower reaches approximately the same size as the Dwarf Bedding forms but is later flowering, tends to be grown more as a true perennial and is available only in gold and yellow.

Sweet william Although they flower a little later than most wallflowers, and are early summer rather than spring plants, sweet williams have long been cottage garden favourites. They may be grown in the same way as wallflowers, although, being of more manageable size, can be sown in boxes. Most varieties reach 45 to 60cm (18 to 24in), and the auricula-eyed forms, with red or pink flowers and a white eye, are especially attractive. 'Indian Carpet' is a dwarf strain in a range of colours.

RECOMMENDED ANNUALS

The types of annual bedding plant to choose for the earliest display are the hardy varieties that can be sown outside in late August or September of the previous year. Those that cannot be sown until March will be correspondingly later coming into flower. Half-hardy annuals, raised under protection and planted out after the frosts have finished, will not provide much colour until late June. Sown outdoors, they will be later still. Recommended hardy annuals for early colour are:

Alyssum Dwarf and compact, use them for edging, crevices in paving, window boxes and formal bedding. 'Snow Carpet' and 'Minimum' are the most compact whites; 'Little Dorrit' is slightly taller; 'Oriental Night' a good deep purple and 'Rosie O'Day' the best lilac-pink.

Asperula This is a less well known, good pale blue or lilac-blue plant for the front of the border and for cutting. It is about 25cm (10in) tall and tolerates some shade. It is usually sold as *Asperula orientalis* or *A. azura setosa*.

Calendula (pot marigold) Familiar yellow or orange, double or semi-double cottage garden flowers, they are self-seeding to the extent of becoming weeds if not checked, but are pretty and good as cut flowers, too. They range from about 30cm (12in) in height, with 'Baby Gold' and the 'Gitana' range, to 60cm (24in) with 'Orange Cockade' and the 'Pacific Beauty' varieties. 'Mandarin' is the first F_1 hybrid, an early and free-flowering double.

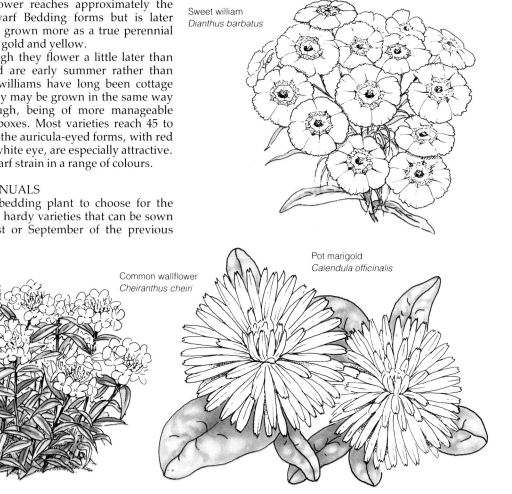

Sweet william
Dianthus barbatus

Common wallflower
Cheiranthus cheiri

Pot marigold
Calendula officinalis

See also:
Hardy and half-hardy plants
pp 42, 43
New varieties of annuals pp 48–9
Wallflowers p 48

Candytuft Another pretty and popular cottage garden flower, 20 to 30cm (8 to 12in) tall, with flattish heads of white, pink and lilac blooms; this is quick growing and suitable for any soil. The best-coloured varieties are 'Red Flash' and 'Pink Queen'; pure whites are usually obtained only from a mixture sold as Fairy Mixture.

Clarkia Like miniature hollyhocks, 30 to 60cm (12 to 24in) tall in shades of pink, purple, red and white. There are several mixtures available, but the *pulchella* forms are smaller. Some of the taller types may need support.

Cornflower This was once a common cornfield weed, hence the name. The tall-growing varieties, such as 'Blue Diadem', reach 60cm (24in); the smaller ones, such as 'Dwarf Blue', 'Polka Dot' and 'Jubilee Gem', 30 to 45cm (12 to 18in). Mixtures are available with pinks, reds and white, in addition to the more familiar blue.

Echium Sometimes known as annual borage, the foliage is somewhat coarse, but the 30-cm (12-in) spikes of blue, white and pink flowers make a contrast with most of the other early flowering annuals. Hybrid mixtures are available, but the best blue is the old 'Blue Bedder'.

Eschscholzia Although the individual single, double or semi-double flowers last for a short period only, they continue to appear for a long time in all shades of orange, yellow, red, pink and white. Grow them in large groups in the poorest soil in the garden and in full sun. Most seed companies offer only mixtures called 'Harlequin', 'Ballerina' or 'Art Shades'.

Godetia Some are called azalea-flowered varieties, for they resemble single and double azalea blooms and occur in similar colours. The tall varieties, up to 60cm (24in), may need staking, but smaller types are available also.

Gypsophila One of the best early annuals for flower-arrangers, the masses of tiny, long-lasting white flowers of the 'Monarch' or 'Covent Garden' strains are especially welcome in spring and early summer. They grow from 30 to 45cm (12 to 18in) tall and truly fit the description of 'frothy' that is often applied to them.

Larkspur These are annual delphiniums and fill a similar role, giving height to the early season border. They reach 1 to 1.25m (3¼ to 4ft) and are usually sold as mixtures of white, pinks, purples and lavender. There are smaller 'hyacinth-flowered' forms, such as 'Dwarf Rocket', with especially compact blooms.

Poppy Taken for granted, perhaps, but still very beautiful, if short-lived, poppy flowers are now available in a wide range of brilliant colours. The old single red is hard to beat, but the Shirley mixtures that include doubles add delicacy to early summer beds.

Virginia stock Probably the easiest of all annuals to grow. These pretty little plants are available in mixtures of reds, pinks, mauves, blue and white; sow them almost anywhere and let them self-sow for ever.

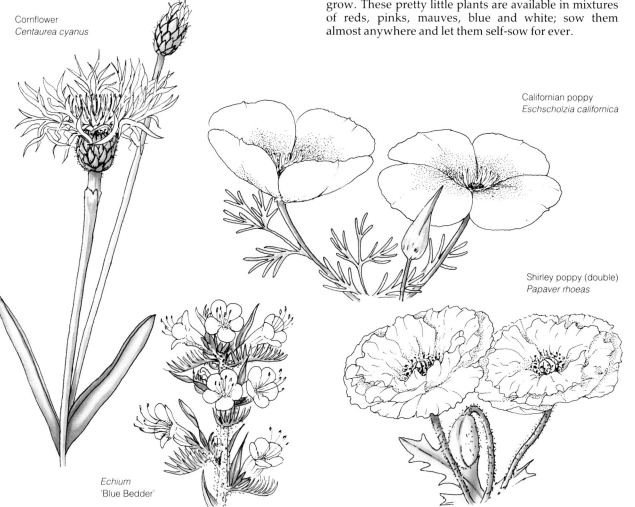

Cornflower
Centaurea cyanus

Californian poppy
Eschscholzia californica

Shirley poppy (double)
Papaver rhoeas

Echium
'Blue Bedder'

Some of my wallflowers have yellow stripes on the petals; have I created a new variety?

It is remarkable how certain abnormalities become accepted as a part of everyday life, and, in gardening, the yellow stripes on wallflowers are probably the most common example. This is a feature of a large proportion of the dark red wallflowers to be seen in gardens all over Britain and yet, despite the fact that it is a colour clearly different from that illustrated on the seed packet, few gardeners remark upon it. They should; especially if they are vegetable gardeners too. The yellow streaks are caused by the presence of a virus infection in the flowers, usually a virus called turnip mosaic virus, and the symptom provides an opportunity for a reminder about the importance of cross infection between plants by viruses in general.

Viruses are never seen by gardeners in the way that fungi or insects are, for they are submicroscopic and occur within the cells of affected plants. Unlike many other organisms that cause disease, viruses can survive only within living cells, where they disrupt the normal cell functions with consequent poor growth of the affected plants. They are transmitted from parent plant to offspring in cuttings and sometimes in seeds and are most usually carried from one growing plant to another by insects, aphids especially. Viruses cannot be controlled chemically (although good aphid control will often help minimize their spread), and destruction of affected plants is usually the best recourse, especially with perennials.

To return to wallflowers. The disrupted flower pattern is rather attractive, there is usually little obvious reduction in vigour of the plants and, since they will be pulled up at the end of the spring, what harm, you may wonder, is done by ignoring the infection? The answer lies with the name of this particular virus, turnip mosaic virus; for not only does it attack wallflowers, but turnips and other brassicas too. In this particular instance, the plants concerned — brassicas and wallflowers — are closely related, but viruses may affect a wide range of plants that are botanically quite distinct.

The extreme example is a virus called cucumber mosaic virus that affects thousands of different plants, representative of most plant families. Significantly, in the present context, infection by turnip mosaic virus on brassicas causes crumpling and disfiguring of the leaves, black spotting and stunted growth. Thus, that attractive embellishment on your wallflowers may be a signal that your Brussels sprouts are already on the slippery slope. The sensible vegetable gardener will uproot and destroy his 'new variety' of wallflowers before aphids transfer the virus to the family's greens.

 ## I am bored with the usual annual bedding plants; are there any new varieties?

Most gardeners are conservative by nature. While there are undoubtedly many who will always turn first to the front of their seed catalogues and automatically order new items, specially promoted for the forthcoming season, they are in a minority. The majority will write out almost a carbon copy of the order they made the previous season and, perhaps, for many seasons past. Not surprisingly, therefore, boredom may set in.

The following personal selection gives some of the more appealing and interesting new annual bedding plants introduced over recent seasons, together with a few plants that, although not new, have been neglected in the past. Most of the new introductions are varietal (and many are F_1 hybrids), for it is relatively infrequently that totally new species make an impact on the bedding-plant market. Many of the new developments are in an improved colour range, are freer flowering and more compact in growth.

Adonis The pheasant's eye is not new, but few seed companies still stock it. Reminiscent of an anemone, with lush, feathery foliage and crimson cup-shaped flowers; about 30 cm (12 in) tall.
Ageratum 'Bengali' is a rose-carmine colour that makes a welcome change from the familiar blue.
African marigold There are many new varieties of compact growth, about 30 cm (12 in) tall, especially the 'Inca' range. Related are the new Afro-French hybrids; the 'Solar' range have compact growth and strong, bright colours.

The sun plant, *Portulaca grandiflora*, originated in Brazil. It is a succulent of prostrate habit, growing 15–20 cm (6–8 in) tall. From July to September, it bears a mass of saucer-shaped flowers, about 2.5 cm (1 in) across, in a riot of colours — white, pink, scarlet, apricot, yellow and mauve; the stamens are bright yellow.

See also:
Clubroot in brassicas pp 14, 127
Growing chrysanthemums p 62
Growing dianthus pp 62–3
Aphid control pp 95, 96

F₁ hybrids pp 118–19
Unusual vegetables pp 122–3
Cucumber mosaic virus p 148

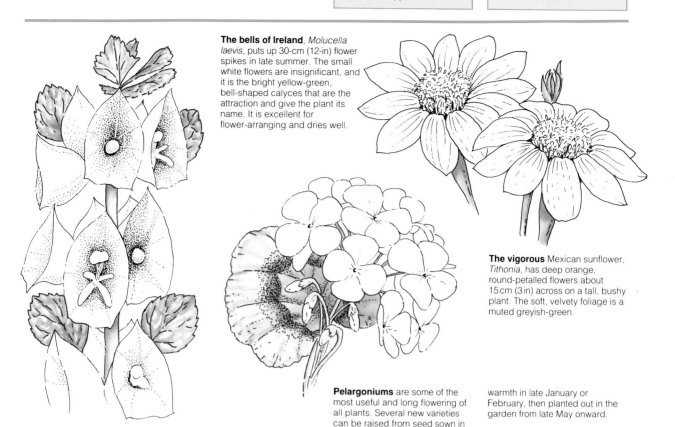

The bells of Ireland, *Molucella laevis*, puts up 30-cm (12-in) flower spikes in late summer. The small white flowers are insignificant, and it is the bright yellow-green, bell-shaped calyces that are the attraction and give the plant its name. It is excellent for flower-arranging and dries well.

The vigorous Mexican sunflower, *Tithonia*, has deep orange, round-petalled flowers about 15 cm (3 in) across on a tall, bushy plant. The soft, velvety foliage is a muted greyish-green.

Pelargoniums are some of the most useful and long flowering of all plants. Several new varieties can be raised from seed sown in warmth in late January or February, then planted out in the garden from late May onward.

Begonia The fibrous-rooted *Begonia semperflorens*, grown as an annual, has given rise to many excellent new hybrids that mix well with the new busy lizzies. 'Pink Avalanche' is a continuously flowering trailing variety.

Cabbage Although certainly not flowers, ornamental brassicas are a useful addition to summer bedding, providing a range of attractive leaf colours on plants ranging from low-growing rosettes to much taller plants of kale form.

Chrysanthemum carinatum There are several annual forms of chrysanthemum, but this one in particular provides masses of flowers for cutting. Ferny foliage and 75 cm (30 in) tall, daisy-like flowers in a good range of colours.

Dianthus Although most people will think only of perennial carnations and pinks, the genus *Dianthus* includes some good annuals too. Among recent introductions is 'Snow Fire', with red centres to white flowers on 20 cm (8 in) high plants.

Impatiens There has been a revolution in recent years with the traditional busy lizzie and many beautiful, compact and subtly coloured varieties are now available. Keep your eye open especially for some gorgeous pinks.

Leptosyne This is a semi-double daisy-like flower of egg yellow with a long flowering season. The plants reach about 45 cm (18 in) and merit far wider attention.

Lobelia The biggest breakthrough has been 'Ruby Cascade', the first truly red trailing variety for use in window boxes and hanging baskets.

Mimulus The new 'Calypso' hybrids are compact, free and early flowering and can be found in a wide range of attractive colours.

Molucella The bells of Ireland has been available for many years but is often neglected, although valuable with its unusual green 'flowers'. They make a useful contrast with other annuals and are good for indoor decoration also.

Nicotiana 'Domino' is a range of hybrids in many colours, all compact — about 30 cm (12 in) tall — long lasting and vigorous.

Pelargonium There are many new varieties for raising from seed. 'Orange Cascade', 'Sprinter', 'Snow White', 'Scarlet Diamond', and the 'Breakaway' range are among the best.

Petunia This is one of the most popular garden annuals, but one that has undergone something of a revolution in recent years with many free-flowering and compact new F₁ hybrids being produced.

Portulaca Almost like miniature roses, but ignored by many gardeners, the new mixture called 'Fairy Tale' offers unique compactness with a range of bright colours.

Sweet william When considering the well-known biennials, do not forget the annual mixtures, such as 'Roundabout', which give much quicker results.

Tithonia One of the most neglected of the larger annuals, this produces big bushy plants about 1 m (3¼ ft) tall, with masses of rich orange flowers — like daisies or single dahlias — over a long season. 'Goldfinger' is a particularly worthwhile new variety.

Line a plastic-covered wire basket with sphagnum moss, *above*, or with green or black plastic, *below*, punctured for drainage.

Put a few lumps of charcoal in the basket, *above*, to help retain moisture, and then fill the basket with compost, *below*.

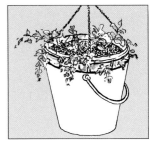

Plant up, with trailing plants on their sides; firm in the compost and water well. Keep the basket in a sheltered spot until the plants have settled down.

If you go away for a few days, set the basket in the shade on top of a bucket of water with the bottom just touching the water, which will be drawn up by the compost.

What annuals will give colour all summer through in hanging baskets?

It is important that hanging baskets contain a blend of plants that will give continuity of colour, without the need for any replanting during the course of the season and with the minimum of dead-heading or other routine attention. They should also be compact in form and include a range of types covering upright, possibly climbing, prostrate and trailing habit; it is important that a hanging basket should appear attractive from all angles.

Although the question relates specifically to annuals, it is almost essential to include at least one or two perennials to obtain a balance of colour, texture and habit. Annuals will, however, be the mainstay for many people who do not wish to spend too much on a basket, and the old faithfuls most frequently found are lobelia, alyssum and dwarf petunias.

Many people forget the potential offered by the chains that support the container, but twining plants can be used to wend their way upward. The best for this is one of the types of plant sometimes called black-eyed susan, *Thunbergia alata*, a most appealing half-hardy annual that blooms continuously with rather uncommon, rich orange-cream flowers with a dark centre. It is easily grown from seed, but needs full sun and may not be successful in colder areas.

Thunbergia can also be allowed to trail downward, but that role is more usually filled by trailing lobelia, such as one of the 'Cascade' varieties (among which there is now a real red, 'Ruby Cascade') and by ivy-leafed pelargoniums. Among the latter, which must still be raised from cuttings (unlike F_1 hybrid zonal varieties), the biggest impact in recent years has been made by the red and white bicoloured forms.

Nasturtiums can also be used to trail, but they sometimes fail to produce their best because the compost in the basket is too good. The liquid feeding and constant attention to watering that are so important for successful hanging baskets are not really to their liking. Other useful trailing plants are pendulous begonias and some of the trailing campanulas.

Remember the value of foliage plants in adding interest to the basket; there are now many attractive variegated

See also:
Colour from annuals pp 46–7
Foliage plants pp 64–5
Growing tomatoes p 146

ivies that will trail over the edge and can be replanted year after year. The greyish-leafed, trailing ground ivy, *Nepeta hederacea*, is also valuable, for it grows faster and longer than many of the other trailing forms and will almost reach the ground in favoured situations.

In the centre of a hanging basket, pride of place is usually given to a compact zonal pelargonium or to one of the dwarf cascading fuchsias; 'Cascade' or 'Swingtime', for example. Around it may be planted almost anything that takes your fancy, provided it meets the criteria of compactness and tidiness. Here too, in the 'body' of the basket, foliage plants, particularly grey or silver varieties are valuable; try using *Cinerarea maritima candicans* 'Dwarf Silver', which you can raise from seed.

Many of the plants used in hanging baskets can also be used for window boxes, but some more substantial types, such as salvias, the more robust fuchsias and additional zonal pelargoniums can be included. Experiment also with most of the compact annuals.

Partly because they are so expensive to buy ready made but also because of their intrinsic interest, many gardeners are turning to setting up their own baskets. Many others are put off by difficulty in obtaining the traditional lining material, sphagnum moss. Although this is an excellent lining, plastic sheet with drainage slots cut in it works almost as well. Use a good potting compost; a John Innes No2 is preferable to a peat-based one, which tends to go rapidly from the extreme of being soggy to that of being dry — when it is almost impossible to rewet.

And don't forget that the constant watering needed by hanging baskets during the summer results in nutrients being leached out almost more quickly than in any other gardening situation, so regular application of a liquid feed is essential. Lastly, do have a secure bracket from which to hang the basket; they can be extraordinarily heavy when full and wet.

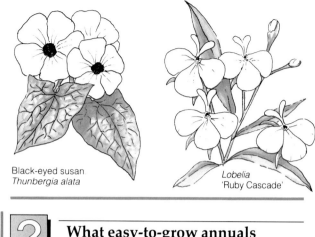

Black-eyed susan
Thunbergia alata

Lobelia
'Ruby Cascade'

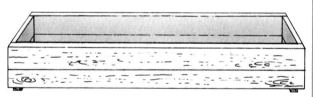

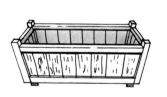

Wooden window boxes must be treated against rot and must have drainage holes in the bottom. They should have feet or be raised on bricks to prevent the wood underneath from rotting. Plastic troughs can be used on their own or they can be planted up and put inside wooden boxes, enabling you to prepare batches of plants to flower in succession.

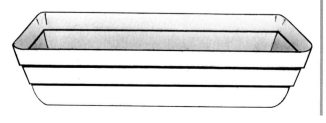

What easy-to-grow annuals can be recommended for a child's first garden?

There is no better way to introduce a child to the joy of gardening than to let him do it himself. Best of all is to give him his own small garden, where, under supervision, he can experiment with almost anything he chooses. The one virtue that most children lack is patience, and almost all soon become bored; so guide them toward trying plants that grow quickly and give results as dramatically and rapidly as possible.

Especially for younger children, choose plants with fairly large seeds that can be sown directly into their flowering positions. There will be plenty of time later for children to be introduced to seedboxes and pricking-out. This is where some of the annuals come into their own. Few have larger seeds or grow as rapidly or as dramatically as sunflowers; but put a limit on the number of seeds that are sown, since a dozen or more sunflowers can leave little room for anything else.

Almost as satisfying and certainly producing big plants from single seeds is *Tithonia*, the Mexican sunflower, a plant that is grown far too little. It produces masses of rich-orange, daisy-like flowers over a long period on a 1m (3¼ft) high bushy plant. Another good choice is borage, a big, bushy annual herb that, once established, will self-sow for years and has masses of flowers of quite fascinating shape and electric-blue colour.

Among smaller-growing species, calendulas, or pot marigolds, can always be relied on, as can nasturtiums, nigella (love-in-a-mist) and nemesias. For something different, try annual hibiscus, the flower-of-an-hour, which, as its name suggests, has short-lived individual flowers but blooms over a long period and also produces attractive inflated seedpods.

Don't forget to include some of the quick-growing vegetables. Lettuce is always a good bet, as are radishes; but a helping hand to raise one or two tomatoes and marrows from parentally supplied plants will also be well rewarded.

What is the secret of growing sweet peas successfully?

Sweet peas really do represent outstanding value and return for time and effort. Few other summer annuals produce so much bloom, such delightful perfume and such a range of colour for so long, while also supplying a continuity of cut flowers for the house. They are not difficult to grow for normal 'domestic purposes' provided their basic requirements are understood and catered for.

SOIL AND SITE

Sweet peas like the sunshine; always choose a site in the garden that affords them as much light and air as possible, and avoid any position overhung by trees or shaded by buildings. But combine these requirements with shelter, for sweet peas are not happy in a windy position. Try to choose a spot with a good depth of topsoil and good drainage; sweet peas appreciate an extensive root run and are prone, as are the rest of their family, to root rotting in waterlogged conditions.

If the plants are to be grown in rows, rather than in clumps, try to ensure that the rows run north–south in order to maximize the amount of sun they will receive. Provided there are no problems with disease or waterlogging, there is no need to change the site for sweet peas every year; in many gardens this is impossible, for there is only a limited number of ideal positions.

Prepare the soil as early as possible, preferably in the autumn; dig in well-rotted farmyard manure to a depth of 45 to 60cm (18 to 24in) and, as it is incorporated, add two good handfuls of bonemeal to the square metre (yard). As always when adding manure, ensure that it is distributed evenly through the soil and not deposited in layers like a sandwich. Many gardening books advocate

Sow sweet peas into pots early in October, using a soil-based rather than a peat-based compost. Sow two seeds to each 7.5cm (3in) pot at a depth of about 1.5cm (½in). Water after sowing and cover with newspaper. Put the pots in a cold frame with slug bait and some mousetraps near by.

Once the seedlings emerge, remove the newspaper and leave the frame open in all but the wettest and coldest winter weather. After the seedlings have produced two or three pairs of leaves, pinch out the top of each seedling to encourage bushy growth. Plant out from the end of March onward.

Pansies refuse to grow in my garden; what is wrong?

Many people find this problem when they move to a new garden and attempt to grow pansies or some of the other species of *Viola* for the first time. Varieties that grew well in a previous garden simply fail to establish themselves satisfactorily and eventually the plants fade away and die. If the plants are pulled up, the roots are usually seen to be decayed and blackened. The same symptoms sometimes occur after pansies or violas have been grown for many years in the same bed or border. Where they grew well previously, they now fail.

This problem is often called pansy sickness, and it is rather similar to the difficulties sometimes experienced when an old rose bed is replanted with fresh stock. Because pansy sickness is confined to pansies and violas, it is clearly not a simple nutritional difficulty but is thought to be the result of the build-up in the soil of certain parasitic micro-fungi, able to attack this group of plants specifically.

Unfortunately, there is no fungicidal treatment that will eliminate the problem, but there are two ways around it. As with roses, one way is to replace the soil where the pansies are to be planted with fresh soil from a site that has not previously grown them. If this is impracticable, it may be possible to raise each plant individually in a peat pot containing fresh potting compost. A pot of about 10cm (4in) diameter should suffice and, once well established, the plant may be planted out in the pot. This should provide a disease-free base in which it can grow.

See also:
Germination of seeds p 44
Hardening-off seedlings p 44
Mulching p 57

Clematis wilt p 87
Rose sickness p 91
Tomato wilt pp 146–7

putting manure in the bottom of a trench. This is bad advice; a trench is fine, but add manure to the soil as the trench is filled to obtain uniformity of soil conditions.

Allow about 60 cm (24 in) width for each row of plants and a circle of the same diameter if they are to be grown in clumps. At worst, dig to half this depth and fork in manure or compost, but try to have the job completed before Christmas, especially in heavy soil.

SOWING SEED AND RAISING PLANTS

There are several different ways of raising sweet pea plants, which causes confusion. The seeds may be sown outdoors in the autumn; they may be sown in pots or boxes in the autumn and overwintered in a cold frame for spring planting; they may be sown under protection in the early spring for transplanting later; or they may be sown directly into the garden in April. The latter is generally the least satisfactory and should be a last resort.

Autumn sowing into pots is my recommendation, with spring sowing under protection as second choice; but this is advisable as first option in colder areas. Germination of the black-seeded varieties especially may be improved by nicking the seeds on the side opposite the 'eye' with the tip of a sharp knife. Alternatively, soak all seed in water for twelve hours before sowing.

The young sweet peas may be planted out in most areas toward the end of March; allow a spacing of 20 cm (8 in) between them. There are several ways in which the plants may be supported; exhibition growers will have a semi-permanent framework of posts, but bamboo canes, 2.5 m (8 ft) long, either in a double row or a wigwam for clumps of plants, are the most popular. For simple garden culture, within a mixed border for instance, sweet peas look most effective when they are allowed just to scramble up twiggy branches. Allow one cane or branch per plant.

Here are a few more hints that will help you to ensure your sweet peas thrive and produce masses of bloom:

☐ Never allow the plants to dry out; a mulch of leaf-mould may, with advantage, be applied once the flower buds form.

☐ Remember to tie in plants to canes as it becomes necessary, although with twigs, plants usually find adequate support.

☐ Cut the flowers regularly; the flowering season will be shortened if the plants are allowed to set seed.

Finally, a personal choice of varieties from the many now available: white, 'Royal Wedding'; pink, 'Fiona', and 'Sally Unwin'; mauve, 'The Doctor'; blue, 'Blue Danube'; lavender, 'Southampton'. No red recommended, you will notice; I believe it is really not a suitable colour for such a delicate flower.

A permanent framework of metal or wooden poles with wires stretched between them and down to the ground provides the most satisfactory support for sweet peas if you have a large garden or plan to show them. The plants need to be tied in.

A wigwam of 2.5-m (8-ft) tall bamboo poles takes up less room, while still permitting the free circulation of air and allowing the plants plenty of room to spread. Sweet peas allowed to scramble over twiggy branches will find sufficient support and will need no tying-in.

HERBACEOUS PERENNIALS

Plants for beds

and borders

To answer this question, a little must first be said about the history of the herbaceous border. It has always been a curiously English garden feature, its invention usually credited to a curiously English personage, the writer and horticulturist Gertrude Jekyll (1843 – 1932). Miss Jekyll and her contemporary, William Robinson, were largely instrumental in popularizing the reaction against the rigid formal bedding schemes which were common in the early Victorian garden.

Having seen the natural associations of different species of plants growing in the wild in various parts of the world, Robinson realized that it would be possible to mimic these natural blends in a garden, but with the added advantage that plants from different countries could be brought together. He advocated 'wild gardens', closely reflecting alpine meadows and similar habitats. But Jekyll, with an eye for colour and harmony, concentrated on what is now called the herbaceous border: a blend of plants of varying heights, spreads, flowering seasons and colours, usually in a relatively long and fairly narrow bed.

The objection to formal bedding was financial as much as aesthetic, for the plants were enormously costly to raise and plant out. Ironically, the herbaceous border at its grandest was also extremely labour intensive, necessitating routine attention to staking and dead-heading and regular replacement of plants as their flowering seasons ended. Sometimes, plants in pots were moved into and out of the borders during the course of the season, and the plants were often so widely spaced that weeds were able to grow up between them, and weeding was a constant chore. If the herbaceous border is 'out of fashion', therefore, it is due in great part to this labour intensiveness, and the original concept has now been modified in several ways to make borders more manageable.

Modern herbaceous plants are predominantly hardy perennials, not needing annual removal, and even the routine attention to staking is less with some of the shorter and more robust modern varieties. Plants now tend to be placed close together, and the value of this groundcover in terms of weed suppression is widely recognized; modern chemical weedkillers have been of value too.

The herbaceous border itself has largely evolved into the mixed border, in which shrubs of varying sizes form a permanent framework within which herbaceous perennials are planted. Nor is the border always a long, narrow area, confined to the periphery of the garden; the popularization during the past fifty years of the island bed, usually within an area of lawn, has added a new dimension to herbaceous gardening. With careful planning and choice of plants, the mixed border should be the mainstay of year-round appeal in most gardens.

See also:
Plants to attract butterflies p 60
Dividing bulbs p 75
F_1 hybrids pp 118–19

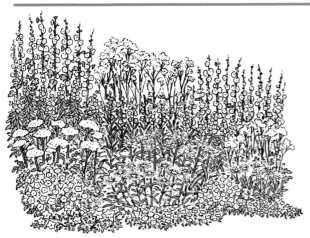

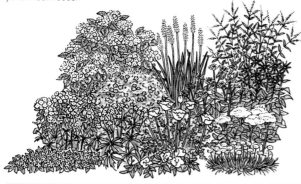

A typical border as designed by Gertrude Jekyll, *above*, might have contained hollyhocks and thalictrum to give height, with purple phlox, dark blue Canterbury bells, spiraea, golden-yellow yarrow and shasta daisies. Lower-growing plants would have included blue and mauve *Campanula carpatica*, and erigeron, with deep purple flowers. In front would have been gentian, candytuft and red, pink and yellow rock roses.

A modern, mixed border, *below*, will have a framework of shrubs, such as hydrangea, buddleia and potentilla, interplanted with perennial red hot poker, rudbeckia, phlox and heliopsis. Other easy plants are crane's bill, scabious, oriental poppy and sedum. In the front are masses of blue-purple *Campanula muralis*, yellow *Oenothera missouriensis* and pink pincushions of thrift — all good groundcover plants.

Is it better to grow herbaceous perennials from seed or to buy plants?

A glance through the catalogues of the large, commercial nurseries that offer herbaceous perennial plants for sale indicates that stocking a garden in this way can be expensive. The high price per plant means that most gardeners can afford only a few each season. And with a fairly large section in seed catalogues devoted to perennials, it would seem that, provided you have a greenhouse and a cold frame, you can achieve the same results for a fraction of the price. Unfortunately, this is not so.

The major drawback to raising herbaceous perennials from seed is that only a limited range of varieties of each type of plant, and often not the best, is available. This is because many plants do not come true from seed and must be propagated by cuttings. Moreover, most of the perennials offered as seed are hybrid mixtures, which will give rise to plants in a range of colours and of varying quality. If you want to know exactly how a plant will appear when mature, therefore, don't raise your own from seed; but if you are happy to embark upon this horticultural lottery, you stand a good chance of producing at least some good individuals.

The second major advantage of buying herbaceous perennials as plants is that they take a shorter time to flower. Few raised from seed can be guaranteed to flower in the first season, whereas most bought as plants will. Remember, too, that having paid for a single initial plant, you will be able to increase your stock by cuttings or division. And there are few more satisfying and enjoyable ways of increasing your range of perennials than by exchanging cuttings and divisions with gardening friends and neighbours.

When should I divide and plant herbaceous perennials?

If you buy herbaceous perennials in containers, you can fairly safely plant them at any time. Removing an established plant from open ground is a different matter, for it will experience extensive root disturbance. If it is lifted during the period of active growth, the plant will lose water through its leaves faster than its disturbed roots are able to replace it, and the plant will wilt and fairly soon die. During the winter, damage will be caused to the roots if herbaceous plants are dug up, and the broken tissues will encourage rot to set in, which may bring about the demise of the entire rootstock. This is why moving and dividing are best confined to the spring and autumn.

With most types of perennial, it matters little which season is chosen, and the general principle of selecting the time furthest from their flowering season holds

good. With those perennials, such as peonies, which resent disturbance (usually because they have thick, fleshy roots), moving in spring shortly before growth recommences is probably safer. Division of peonies, helleborus and the few other types resentful of disturbance should be performed infrequently and cautiously.

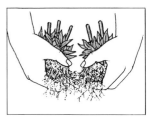

Divide an overgrown clump of fibrous-rooted perennials by plunging two garden forks back to back into the crown and forcing the handles apart to lever out the roots. Pull the clump apart and clear out any dead divisions before replanting young rootstocks.

Is it possible to grow herbaceous perennials satisfactorily in a poor, shady site?

Shady, certainly; poor, with severe limitations. The ability of many herbaceous perennials to tolerate shade is an important aspect of mixed border design, for the taller-growing plants will inevitably take some light from the lower-growing ones. In a naturally shady situation, it is perfectly possible to select and plant simply those that are happy in such conditions, although the range of colour and form will be more limited than in the ideal position for a mixed border, which is where it will receive maximum sunlight. The list gives some suggestions for shade-tolerant herbaceous perennials, but in a modern mixed border some shade-tolerant shrubs will be needed also.

Aconitum Partial shade. Rather reminiscent of delphiniums, with spires of blue, purple, yellow or white. *A. arendsii* (blue), *A. napellus* 'Bressingham Spire' (deep violet) and *A. orientale* (white, tinged yellow) are reliable. Late summer/autumn. Up to 1.25 m (4 ft).

Alchemilla Partial shade. Invaluable for its fresh green, ground-covering foliage and greenish flower sprays in summer. 45 cm (18 in).

Aruncus Partial shade. Similar to, but taller than, *Astilbe. A. sylvester* (white) is widely available. Summer. Up to 1.5 m (5 ft).

Asarum Full shade. Useful front-of-border plant with thick, rounded leaves. 15 cm (6 in).

Astilbe Partial shade with moisture. Feathery plumelike flowers in white, red or 'shocking' pink. 'Bressingham Beauty' (pink), 'Snowdrift' (white), 'Rheinland' (deep pink) and 'Fanal' (red) are recommended. Summer. Most are up to 60 cm (24 in).

Cimicifuga Partial shade. Narrow, graceful spikes of tiny white flowers. Late summer/autumn. 1.5 m (5 ft).

Digitalis Partial shade. 60 cm–2 m (24 in–6½ ft). Many of the foxgloves are shade tolerant. For a change from the common species, try the 1-m (3¼-ft) tall *D. lutea*, with spikes of long yellow flowers in late summer.

Euphorbia Full shade. Many spurges tolerate shade; the most useful are *E. cyparissias* and *E. robbiae*, both with green flowers and narrow, dark leaves. They grow 30–45 cm (12–18 in) tall.

Filipendula Partial shade. The cultivated forms of *F. ulmaria*, meadowsweet, are worth trying in moist shade. The form known as *aurea* is grown for its golden foliage more than for its flowers. 45 cm (18 in).

Geranium Full shade. Although most geraniums like the sun, three species do well in shade. *G. phaeum* produces tall wands of dark purple flowers (and exists also in a white variety, *alba*), while *G. maculatum* and *macrorrhizum* are lilac and pink respectively; both have beautiful variegated forms too. Summer. Up to 45 cm (18 in) in height.

Helleborus Partial or full shade. Most of the Christmas rose family, *H. foetidus* especially, enjoy some shade. Its apple-green, pink-tinged bells appear early in January and continue for weeks. 30–60 cm (12–24 in).

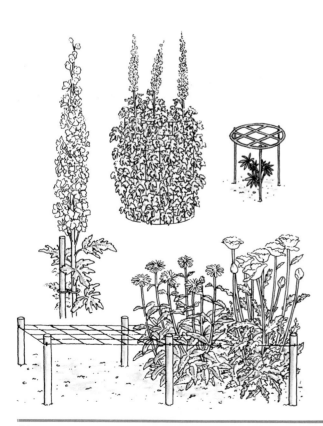

Is there an easy way to tie in and stake herbaceous perennials?

Almost every gardener faced with this problem has asked himself how such plants survive in the wild, where there is no green-fingered human with a ball of green twine to keep them upright. The answer to this is three-fold. First, many of the cultivated varieties of plants grown in gardens have been bred deliberately with larger-than-normal flower heads and so are less stable than their wild counterparts.

Second, most natural plant communities do not have bare spaces between the plants, which are held upright and protected from wind by their neighbours. And, third, toward the end of the season, many wild plants do actually fall over, spilling their seed as they do so. With no fastidious gardener's eye to offend, they thus perform their natural function perfectly well.

What does this tell gardeners about the management of herbaceous perennials? It tells them to look carefully

The least obtrusive way to stake a plant is to use a cane or to make a cage of canes around the stems and tie them in. A metal ring on tripod legs or a cat's cradle of netting stretched between stakes allows a plant to grow around and through the support.

See also:
Difficult sites pp 20-1
Shrubs to grow in shade p 79
Climbers for a north-facing wall
    pp 80-1

Shrubs for groundcover p 87
Growing grass under trees
    pp 101, 106

Monkshood
Aconitum

Bugbane
Cimicifuga

Christmas rose
Helleborus

Gladwyn iris
Iris foetidissima

Lamium Partial shade. Groundcover. The cultivated forms of dead nettle are useful at the front of the border. *L. galeobdolon* has yellow flowers and *L. maculatum*, pink. Summer. 15–60 cm (6–24 in). ·

Omphalodes Full shade. One of the most beautiful, useful and neglected of plants for the shady border. *O. cappadocica* has electric-blue flowers, somewhat reminiscent of, but immeasurably better than, forget-me-nots. *O. verna alba* is white. Spring and autumn. 15 cm (6 in).

Trachystemon Full shade. Another useful but neglected plant. *T. orientale* produces spikes of rich purple-violet flowers. Spring. 25 cm (10 in).

And what about poor soil? The simplest answer is to say, improve it, for herbaceous perennials are not really happy unless the soil is reasonably fertile. The plants most tolerant of poorer soils are probably the euphorbias and the lamiums, but it would be a pretty miserable border that had nothing other than these. Dry shade is less easy to correct, although, even here, generous applications of organic matter will be beneficial.

Plants from the list that are fairly tolerant of dryness include alchemilla, digitalis, euphorbia, geranium, helleborus and lamium. Although it will scarcely be a herbaceous border in the familiar sense, these, together with such plants as bergenia, cyclamen, epimedium, hypericum, ivy, *Iris foetidissima*, pachysandra, symphytum, teucrium, vinca and *Viola labradorica*, will at least bring life and colour to an otherwise extremely difficult habitat.

before selecting varieties that appeal to them, for modern hybridists are well aware of the instability of many of the older forms and are constantly trying to improve their robustness. It explains why borders should be designed so as to achieve the optimum density of· planting consistent with good growth, and why isolated tall and weak individuals should not be planted among much lower-growing species. Finally it explains why dead flowering stems must be promptly removed from the plant.

Despite all this, many taller, flowering perennials will still need some form of support. The traditional way has been with canes, preferably green; but even here, the appearance can be improved and labour saved with many species by placing three, four or five canes around a group of stems and tying twine around the whole, rather than staking each stem individually. With some really dense clumps of massed stems, twigs, inserted around the clump before the flowering stems have elongated, will sometimes be found effective, without any need for tying-in.

In recent years, several proprietary supports have appeared on the market, comprising metal rings or tripod structures, sometimes with adjustable heights and diameters. Many gardeners use them and find them satisfactory, but it is almost impossible to hide them adequately while still restraining all the stems.

How important is mulching for herbaceous perennials?

Extremely; for even the species mentioned earlier as tolerant of fairly dry conditions will benefit from the improved moisture retention that mulching imparts to the soil. The golden rule with mulching is to remember that a surface mulch will maintain the soil in its existing condition — mulch a dry soil, and it will remain dry. So always mulch after a good fall of rain or after giving the soil a thorough soaking.

Spring is generally the best time to apply a mulch, for it will help to conserve moisture during the summer, although a mulch in autumn has the benefit of protecting the crowns of perennials from penetrating winter cold. The best overall mulching material is well-rotted manure, compost or leaf-mould, though peat is useful too. The aesthetic appeal of the pulverized bark now sold for the purpose is considerable — until you discover the cost.

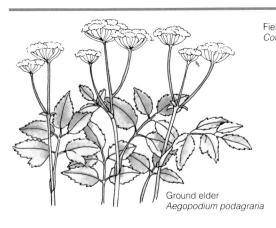

Field bindweed
Convolvulus arvensis

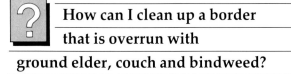

Ground elder
Aegopodium podagraria

How can I clean up a border that is overrun with ground elder, couch and bindweed?

These three are the commonest deep-rooted and widely spreading perennial weeds that you are likely to come across. They are not the most difficult garden weeds to control (that dubious distinction must belong to oxalis and horse tail), but it is these that are most likely to invade and subjugate a herbaceous border. There is no truly satisfactory way to tackle them without resort to modern weedkillers. Although, by back-breaking persistence, couch can be eradicated with digging and/or rotavating in an open bed, this is scarcely feasible in an established border. Bindweed, with roots that can penetrate to a depth of at least 6m (19½ft), will resist even the most stubborn and energetic of gardeners.

One general point should be made regarding the removal of these problem weeds. Although couch can be eradicated fairly easily with a highly specific modern chemical that is harmless to almost all other vegetation, and even bindweed and ground elder can, with care, be controlled *in situ*, this does not make thorough digging of the bed unnecessary. A border overrun with perennial weeds probably has a compacted and impoverished soil in need of opening up and feeding. Moreover, even when killed, couch in particular will leave a residue of tough roots and rhizomes that decay slowly and limit the penetration of water into the ground. The rule, therefore, should be to use chemicals to kill, but the fork to cultivate.

Couch Spray thoroughly, when the couch is growing vigorously, with a weedkiller containing the systemic chemical alloxydim-sodium. This is almost specific for killing couch and can safely be sprayed over most other vegetation. It is, as a result, invaluable in tackling couch where it grows among other plants without the need to dig them all up. Alloxydim-sodium can damage some other ornamental grass species and should not be used on them; nor, of course, should it be used on lawns.

Although the weedkiller can be either sprayed or watered on with a watering can, the former will be found much more economical and effective. If a can is used, don't forget to wash it out thoroughly.

Bindweed This weed seems to strike more fear and loathing into gardeners than any other; perhaps because of the way it actually strangles other plants, rather than merely competing with them for soil space. The answer to bindweed is another systemic weedkiller, glyphosate, the only substance capable of travelling sufficiently far within the plant's tissues to be able to eradicate its extremely deep roots. Glyphosate is best applied as a spray, but remember that it is a total weedkiller and will kill all forms of green plant life. Where bindweed is entangled among other plants, its leafy stems should be pulled away and laid on the ground where they can be sprayed.

Glyphosate is absorbed through green tissue, and the more leaf area the weeds have, the better they will take up the chemical. Spray when bindweed is well grown and again every two to three weeks during the summer; six hours without rain must elapse after spraying for the glyphosate to be properly absorbed. It may at first seem to be having no effect, but gradually the weeds will yellow and shrivel. Any regrowth will need further spraying, but, with persistence, a badly infested border can be cleaned within two seasons. Glyphosate does not remain in the soil, and treated areas can be replanted immediately.

Ground elder The treatment of ground elder is essentially the same as for bindweed, although it does not twine around other plants. It reaches a well-leafed stage early in the season and, in a mild spring, spraying can begin in April.

Bindweed entwined with other plants can be treated with glyphosate, without affecting them, by spraying down a short length of 19mm (¼in) diameter plastic pipe directly on to a leafy shoot of the bindweed.

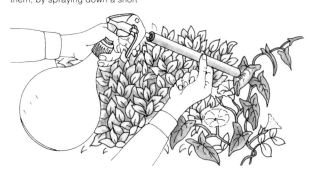

See also:
Designing a minimal maintenance
   garden p 26
Modern mixed borders p 54
Naturalizing bulbs p 68
Pruning clematis p 85

What plants will give all-season colour in a minimal maintenance border?

It is an essential feature of any good herbaceous border that it should give continuity of colour, but the minimal maintenance aspect means that plants requiring the least amount of staking and dead-heading and with as long a flowering season as possible must be used. It is important, in order to limit the time spent on weeding, that good ground coverage is achieved with weed-suppressing foliage.

For this reason, dahlias are included, although they need planting out at the beginning of each season and lifting at the end of it, they do provide good weed suppression. Similarly, although peonies have a fairly short flowering season, their large and attractive foliage lasts well into the winter and provides an excellent foil for other plants.

The suggested plan is for a one-sided border (against a wall or fence, for example) but it could be doubled up, back to back, for an island border. It would require an area of about 15sqm (18sqyds), but larger or smaller beds could be planted by adjusting the numbers of plants. Where individual varieties are suggested, they have been chosen on the basis of personal experience, but this does not mean that other, similar varieties would not work as well.

Key to plants in the scheme for a modern mixed border:

1 *Bergenia cordifolia purpurea*; **2** *Cimicifuga racemosa*; **3** *Lilium henryi*; **4** *Echinops ritro*; **5** *Aconitum napellus* 'Bressingham Spire'; **6** *Delphinium* Pacific Hybrids; **7** *Digitalis*, foxglove; **8** *Achillea filipendulina* 'Gold Plate'; **9** *Paeonia*, peony; **10** *Chrysanthemum maximum* 'Snow Cap', shasta daisy; **11** Dahlias; **12** *Helenium* 'Copper Spray'; **13** *Helleborus orientalis* Hybrids; **14** *Euphorbia polychroma*; **15** *Hosta* 'Krossa Regal'; **16** *Geranium* 'Claridge Druce'; **17** *Doronicum* 'Harpur Crewe'; **18** *Gladioli* Butterfly varieties; **19** *Phlox* 'Pinafore Pink'; **20** *Ceratostigma plumbaginoides*; **21** *Polygonum affine* 'Dimity'; **22** *Sedum spectabile* 'Autumn Joy'; **23** *Geranium rectum album*; **24** *Lavandula nana alba*; **25** *Aster* 'Little Pink Beauty'; **26** *Hosta sieboldiana elegans*; **27** *Geranium grandiflorum plenum*; **28** *Calamintha nepetoides*; **29** *Alyssum saxatile compactum*

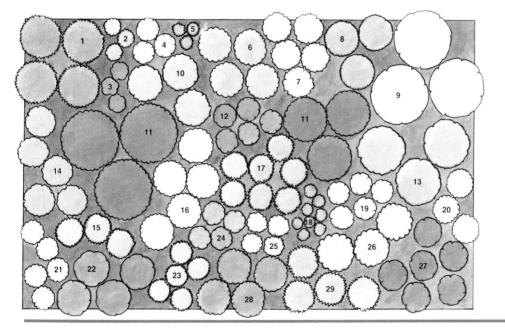

What are herbaceous clematis and how should I grow them?

It is a pity that more forms of clematis are not grown, for even among the climbing types, only a small fraction of the hundreds of existing species and varieties will be found in most nurseries and garden centres. Most clematis are climbers, but there is a small number of excellent herbaceous types that mix well with other plants in the border. Four herbaceous species in a total of about twelve varieties are likely to be found at specialist clematis nurseries, but more general suppliers may have only one or two. The commonest are *C. heracleifolia* and its varieties, such as 'Crepescule', 'Côte d'Azur', and 'Wyevale', with blue, hyacinth-like flowers in late summer on stems of 60 to 120cm (24 to 48in); *C. integrifolia*, July flowering and blue in 'Hendersonii' but a pretty pink in 'Rosea', up to 60cm (24in); and *C. recta*, the most vigorous species, with masses of small, sweet-scented flowers on rather lax 1.5-m (5-ft) stems.

The herbaceous clematis will thrive in similar conditions to the climbing types and prefer alkaline soil; other plants in the border provide the shade at the roots that they enjoy. The biggest mistake in growing herbaceous clematis is to try and stake them; this is never really successful and they are much better allowed to scramble over and through other bushy plants. Pruning is performed by simply removing all top growth during the winter.

I want to attract butterflies to my garden; what plants should I choose?

My pampas grass is enormous but never flowers. Why?

One of the saner features of the present vogue for 'wild gardening' has been an interest in conserving our diminishing native butterfly population. There has, though, been a tendency recently for gardeners to be presented with the options either of gardening in the accepted sense, which involves cultivating hybrids or alien species, or of abandoning cultivation and allowing 'nature' to take over the garden completely.

The latter option is supposed to be good for conservation, the former, bad; but there is no reason why cultivation should be harmful to native wildlife and the subject of butterflies well illustrates this point. It also provides an opportunity to demonstrate the difference between merely attracting adult butterflies to flowering plants by virtue of their nectar and actually providing them with somewhere to breed.

Almost everyone knows *the* butterfly bush, *Buddleia davidii*, in its numerous varieties, although butterflies find other buddleia species appealing too. Many other plants also attract butterflies:

Candytuft	Honeysuckle
Golden rod	Ice plant (*Sedum spectabile*)
Hawthorn	Lady's smock
Lavender	Pinks
Lilac	Sweet violet
Michaelmas daisies	Thyme

Having attracted the butterflies, it is then possible to go some way toward helping them increase their numbers without turning the entire garden into a wilderness. If a garden is large enough, a clump of stinging nettles can surely be accommodated somewhere, for this will provide food for the caterpillars of small tortoiseshells, red admirals and peacocks. A buckthorn somewhere in the hedge will be appreciated by brimstones, while even the smallest garden has room for a clump of jack-by-the-hedge, *Alliaria petiolata*, which will provide food for the butterfly that, for me, is the real harbinger of spring, the orange tip.

These butterflies occur throughout much of Britain, but in certain areas many other species are likely to live in the surrounding countryside and could be persuaded to breed in your garden. Vetches, trefoils and other legumes will encourage common and chalkhill blues; plantains will attract fritillaries, and many of the taller-growing grasses will bring in some of the browns.

Moths should not be forgotten either, although many species are small and insignificant. There are few more thrilling sights on a warm summer evening than to watch hawk-moths visiting night-scented flowers — and that pleasure is compounded by the knowledge that they are assisting in pollination. Honeysuckle, white summer jasmine, night-scented stock, petunias and tobacco plants are attractive to some of the larger species.

You either adore pampas grass or you cannot stand it. Judging by the thousands of clumps that adorn suburbia, like so many over-sized shaving brushes, most people fall into the former category. I like it too, in the right place — especially as a feature in a really large garden, where its towering size does not appear incongruous.

Its assertive form can be softened by planting around it with other, shorter ornamental grasses of contrasting form, colour and size. *Miscanthus sinensis zebrinus*, about 1.5 m (5 ft) tall and with golden-yellow striped foliage is one such, and it could be accompanied by groups of the even shorter *Avena candida*, a steel-blue relative of the oat. It is worth considering, too, the rather shorter-growing forms of pampas grass. *Cortaderia selloana pumila* has plumes less than 2 m (6½ ft) tall and is very compact;

Orange tip butterfly on jack-by-the-hedge, *Alliaria petiolata*

Small tortoiseshell butterfly on stinging nettle, *Urtica dioica*

See also:
Plants for water gardens and
    boggy areas p 41
Grasses and bamboos p 65
Pruning buddleia p 85

the form known as 'Silver Comet' is shorter still, reaching only 1.25m (4ft), and has most attractively variegated leaves.

The non-flowering of pampas grass is most often explained by the owner having bought a plant grown from seed. Many of these seedling forms are extremely shy flowerers and a plant of selected strain should always be chosen. If an established clump is failing to flower, a generous feeding with sulphate of potash in the early spring may be sufficient to persuade it to burst into life.

Remember to clear out as much as possible of the old foliage in the autumn; setting fire to the clump is the method usually recommended, but although it is generally satisfactory on large plants, there is always the risk of killing a small one. A stout pair of gloves provides a safer means of achieving the objective.

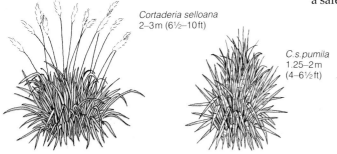

Cortaderia selloana
2–3m (6½–10ft)

C.s.pumila
1.25–2m
(4–6½ft)

C.s. 'Silver Comet' under 2m (6½ft)

Pampas grass originates in South America, as its name suggests. It makes an excellent specimen plant, and the silky plumes look particularly effective against a dark background, such as a yew hedge.

What varieties of fern should I choose for the garden; do they need special care?

It is a great shame that for many gardeners ferns begin and end with maidenhair in the house and bracken, if they are unlucky, in the garden, for there are many hardy ferns that can be grown outdoors and are not invasive. They occur in a wide variety of size and leaf shape, and some are evergreen. Most ferns are not fussy plants, although almost all will thrive best in cool, moist conditions and with at least partial shade.

Increasingly, garden centres are offering 20 to 30 different forms, while some specialist nurseries have even more. The following represent a wide range of those offered most frequently.

Adiantum venustum A hardy maidenhair that forms good green groundcover. 30cm (12in).
Asplenium scolopendrium The hart's tongue is unusual among ferns in having entire, not toothed, fronds. Crested forms exist with tassels at the tips. 45cm (18in).
Athyrium nipponicum-pictum The Japanese painted fern needs some shelter but is particularly beautiful, with silver-edged fronds and dark red stems. Good against a moist north wall. 70cm (28in).
Blechnum penna-marina A tiny, evergreen fern with deeply dissected fronds, it grows well in the crevices in damp walls. 20cm (8in).
Matteuccia struthiopteris The ostrich feather fern is especially beautiful as the featherlike fronds uncurl in spring. 60cm (24in).
Osmunda regalis The royal fern. A giant species for the water's edge, with magnificent fronds. 1.25m (4ft).
Polypodium vulgare This has almost entire fronds; it is tolerant of dry conditions and really at home on dry limestone walls. 30cm (12in).
Polystichum setiferum The soft shield fern; the best form is *divisilobum*, with finely divided fronds. 50cm (20in).

Is there such a plant as a blue poppy, or is it just a myth, like the blue rose?

There is nothing mythical about the plant often called the blue poppy of the Himalayas, but it is still not as well known as it should be; or, to be precise, as they should be, for there are several different species and varieties. All belong to the genus *Meconopsis* and are true members of the poppy family, closely related to one of the most handsome of our native flowers, *M. cambrica*, the Welsh poppy.

Most of the larger, better nurseries will supply the blue poppy under the names *M. baileyii* or *M. betonicifolia*. It is also possible to raise it from seed, although many gardeners experience problems with damping-off before the seedlings are well established. There is, moreover, a great deal of variation within the species and not all plants are truly perennial, some dying after a single season's flowering; additionally, some strains do not have the rich kingfisher-blue that is the great attraction. The best plan is to buy plants from a specialist nursery and to ascertain that one of the specially selected forms is being offered.

The blue poppy prefers light shade and a well-drained soil, although with plenty of moisture at the roots; the ideal site would have a light, preferably lime-free soil in which plenty of peat has been incorporated.

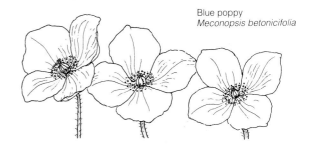

Blue poppy
Meconopsis betonicifolia

Is growing chrysanthemums and carnations in a garden as complicated as it appears to be?

As with most hobbies, the growing of some types of flower can be simple or as involved as you choose to make it. There is, however, a mystique about growing chrysanthemums and carnations that puts off less-experienced gardeners. But if you are not planning to produce blooms that will take prizes at specialist shows, the guidelines given here for growing the easiest types of chrysanthemum and carnation should bring some of the pleasure and enjoyment of these lovely plants to your garden and house.

Chrysanthemums

The easiest to grow of all types of chrysanthemum are the garden sprays, of which there are singles, doubles and pompons in a wide range of colours. They require no disbudding, usually no staking, and can be left in the bed over winter. They produce splendid displays well into the autumn and, given feed and water, a mass of bloom for cutting.

Prepare the ground well in advance of the spring planting time by incorporating plenty of farmyard manure or compost in the autumn. Plants are available from nurseries and garden centres in April and, since they will have been raised under protection, should be hardened off in a cold frame. About two weeks before planting them out, rake blood, fish and bone fertilizer into the soil at a rate of 100 g/sq. m (3 oz/sq. yd). Space the plants 30 to 40 cm (12 to 16 in) apart.

Although most garden sprays do not need staking unless they are in a particularly exposed position, it is advisable to provide each with a bamboo cane for tying-in during the first season. Thereafter there will be little to do other than to ensure that the plants are well watered during the summer. Once the autumn frosts have taken their toll, the dead stems should be cut down to about 2.5 cm (1 in) above ground level. In most areas, the crowns will benefit during the winter from a protective mulch.

The range of varieties is now extensive. The 'Pennine' range of singles and doubles can all be recommended and, together with the 'Margaret' doubles and the pompons such as 'Bright Eye', 'Fairie', 'Glow' and 'Bunty', should provide a colour to suit everyone.

Carnations

Carnation is liberally interpreted here to include those other, superb members of the genus *Dianthus* generally classed as pinks. The best true carnations to grow outdoors are those called border carnations. Many gardening books suggest that a special carnation border should be established for them, but I believe that few

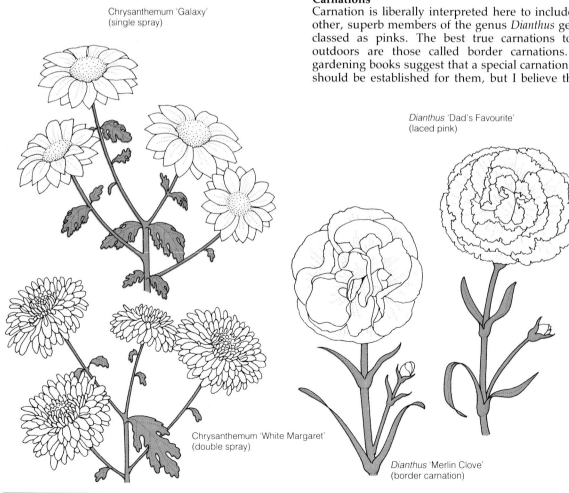

Chrysanthemum 'Galaxy' (single spray)

Chrysanthemum 'White Margaret' (double spray)

Dianthus 'Dad's Favourite' (laced pink)

Dianthus 'Merlin Clove' (border carnation)

See also:
Bedding plants p 60-1

Once planted, border carnations should be tied carefully to the stake and, although it is not essential, better blooms will be obtained if some disbudding is performed, leaving the terminal bud only of the main stem and at the tip of each side shoot.

Pinks may be treated in exactly the same way as border carnations, but since they tend to be lower growing, they generally do not need staking. If the heads do loll unacceptably, a group of four or five green split canes may be placed discreetly around each clump, and a strand of thin, dark twine looped around the whole. Disbudding of pinks is never necessary.

Many varieties of border carnation are available in a wide range of colours. There is also a large choice of pinks, but these fall into several different groups. The *allwoodii* pinks are hybrids between the old, fringed white pink and the perpetual flowering carnation (a non-hardy plant for the cool greenhouse). They have the merit of continuity of flowering from spring to autumn and the distinction of almost all bearing boys' or girls' names; 'Doris', with pale pink petals and dark red eye, is the best known.

The old, or Tudor, laced pinks are the modern survivors or equivalents of a group popular in the seventeenth century. They are extremely beautiful, having a pale overall colour with darker edging and lacelike markings. Among the best known are 'Dad's Favourite', white with a deep red centre and brown-red lacing, and 'Laced Romeo', which is white with dark red lacing. 'London Glow' is crimson with a white edging; 'London Lovely', white with a deep red centre and mauve lacing, and 'London Poppet', pinkish-white with a dark red centre and lacing. 'Laced Prudence' is white with crimson lacing; and 'Laced Joy', pink with crimson lacing and centre.

The Show Pinks are the so-called aristocrats of the group, having large double flowers on tall stems. Although longer flowering than border carnations, they do not last for as long as the *allwoodii* pinks. Most have the prefix 'Show' before their names.

All other pinks of this general 'border' type are called Old World, Old Garden or Village pinks. They vary in the length of the flowering period, but almost all are blessed with the heavy, clovelike scent that pervades the traditional cottage garden. Among the best known are the double white 'Mrs Sinkins', 'Sam Barlow' a double white with a black-red centre, and the crimson 'Red Emperor'. There are, however, several other excellent old pinks: the pure white 'White Ladies' is older but stronger growing than 'Mrs Sinkins'; 'Inchmeri' is a pale shell pink and 'Messine's Pink', a double salmon; 'Earl of Essex' has double rose-pink flowers. Most of the other pinks fall into the group known as rock pinks and are low-growing, almost alpine forms for the rock-garden.

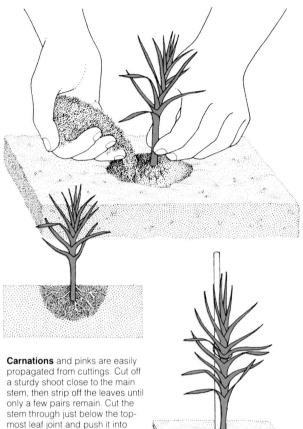

Carnations and pinks are easily propagated from cuttings. Cut off a sturdy shoot close to the main stem, then strip off the leaves until only a few pairs remain. Cut the stem through just below the top-most leaf joint and push it into seedling compost, mixed with sand. After 18–21 days, plant out rooted cuttings with a short length of stem showing above the ground and, as you plant, insert a short stake for support.

garden plants look their best when massed together to the exclusion of other types. Plant groups, certainly, but intersperse them with groups of other plants or you will have a monotony of shape and flowering season that does no justice to the plants and will give you little satisfaction.

Both carnations and pinks revel in the sun and much prefer a light, well-drained soil; on moderately heavy land, they do best if the bed is raised slightly. The other prime requirement is that the soil is not acid, and lime should be added if it is. A moderate amount of organic matter may be incorporated well in advance of planting, and bonemeal should be raked in about a week before the plants are set out.

The commonest problems gardeners encounter are caused either through planting too deeply or by using organic mulches close to the plants; both will induce rotting at the stem base. The temptation to treat carnation plants like heathers and bury them up to the lower leaves is understandable because they tend to lie down when planted; the answer is to provide them with a short, split-cane stake. The other common problem is that induced by too liberal use of nitrogenous fertilizers, which can give rise to split calyces (flower bases) and also to sappy foliage that later turns strawy.

Can you suggest some foliage plants to give a range of colours and leaf shapes in the garden?

Although the value of foliage plants in the house is widely acknowledged, they are generally not given the recognition in the garden they merit. There is, nonetheless, a wide variety to choose from and some nurseries even specialize in them. Almost all foliage plants produce flowers too, and sometimes these are appealing in their own right. In some instances, attractively leaved varieties can be chosen of what are basically flowering plants; the fuchsia *magellanica aurea* is a good example. The following selection, however, is primarily made with leaf colour, form, shape and availability in mind:

Artemisia These are valuable silvery-foliaged plants. Some older forms were invasive but 'Powys Castle', 'Silver Queen', both about 60 cm (24 in) tall, and the smaller *frigida*, are trustworthy.

Bergenia These have always been valuable for their shade tolerance and their big, rounded, leathery leaves, but the older forms had straggly, disappointing flowers. *Bergenia cordifolia purpurea, B. schmidtii* and the newer hybrids such as 'Bressingham Salmon', 'Bressingham White' and 'Ballawley' are great improvements. Up to 30 cm (12 in).

Hosta sieboldiana elegans

Hosta crispula

Hosta lancifolia

Hosta The range of hostas has never been greater and there is even a society specializing in their cultivation. Although usually considered plants for a moist bed, they will put up with a surprising level of dryness. Those listed are representative of the main types. *Hosta fortunei*; bluish-green leaves, no variegation; *fortunei albo marginata* and 'Thomas Hogg', cream edge to the leaves; *fortunei picta*, cream leaves, edged green; *fortunei aurea*, golden leaves; *sieboldiana elegans*, bluish-green leaves but a bigger plant, up to 1 m (3¼ ft); *crispula*, dark green leaves, white margins; *undulata*, wavy leaves; *tokudama*, puckered leaves; *lancifolia*, narrow leaves. Some hostas have purple, and some have white flowers.

Lamium Because the cultivated lamiums are relatives of the dead nettle, many gardeners scorn them. They make attractive groundcover, however; *maculatum aureum* has golden leaves, 'Beacon Silver', silver leaves, while 'Chequers' is a pretty marbled form.

Mentha Many of the mints occur in attractively leaved forms and, although they are invasive, they can be contained by growing them in large plant pots sunk to the rim. Among the best for foliage are 'Eau de Cologne', dark purple; variegated 'Bowles' or apple mint, with woolly green and white foliage; and *gentilis aurea*, with a delightful green and gold variegation.

Ophiopogon The form known as *planiscapus nigrescens* is a grasslike member of the lily family. It is not to everyone's taste but is invaluable as almost the only plant with black leaves.

Phormium These plants, sometimes called New Zealand flax, are tall — up to 1.5 m (5 ft) — tough (although not all reliably hardy in colder areas), grasslike plants in a range of attractive leaf colours with red, purple, gold and cream stripes. 'Maori Sunrise', 'Cream Delight' and 'Sundowner' are among the best. But the flower spike on some varieties can tower up to 5 m (16½ ft), so choose your spot with care.

Yucca It needs a special border to make a Yucca look right, for they have an assertive presence and usually look best in a large tub or pot in the more formal garden. The foliage is strap-like and spiky (sometimes quite viciously so). *Yucca filamentosa* is the species seen most often, and there are variegated types.

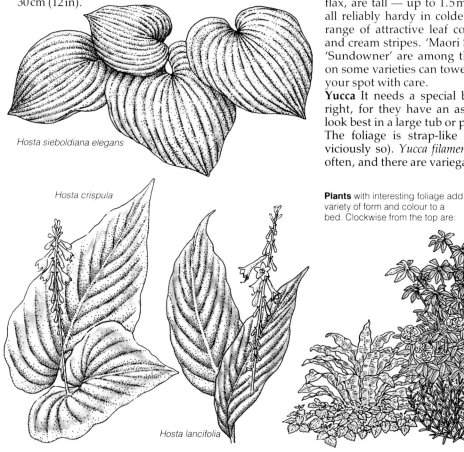

Plants with interesting foliage add variety of form and colour to a bed. Clockwise from the top are: *Fatsia japonica*; bearded iris; hosta; oenothera; old English lavender; dead nettle; *Asplenium scolopendrium* and peony.

See also:
Perennials for shade p 56
Pampas grass pp 60–1
Ferns p 61
Controlling mildew on roses p 95
Mildew resistant roses p 97

Grasses and Bamboos The real danger with both these groups of plants (they belong to the same family; bamboos are merely woody), is that many are invasive, for they are all related to couch. They are, nonetheless, valuable in introducing some unique colours and shapes to the border. Relatively few garden centres stock more than a couple of each type, so you may have to shop around to find them. The following selection is based solely on personal experience and preference:

Grasses

Alopecurus pratensis aurea This is the gold and green variegated form of common foxtail grass. 50 cm (20 in).
Festuca amethystina A low, tufted grass with truly blue leaves. Good for edging. 30 cm (12 in).
Hakonechloa macra albo-aurea A bronze leaved plant, with gold and buff variegation. 25 cm (10 in).
Milium effusum aureum Produces beautiful soft clumps of golden yellow. 45 cm (18 ft)

Miscanthus sacchariflorus Few gardens can accommodate a grass that grows 3 m (10 ft) tall in a single season. Still, it is not invasive and has its uses; as a windbreak, for example, for the dead stems persist throughout the winter months.

Bamboos

Arundinaria murieliae This has green canes and lush green leaves, but reaches almost 4 m (13 ft).
Arundinaria viridistriata One of the best variegated bamboos, although it can look a little ragged toward the end of the season. Pale green canes and white stripes on the leaves. 1 m (3¼ ft).
Shibataea kumasasa Not the best colour, being more or less uniformly pale green, but compact. 50 cm (20 in).

My Michaelmas daisies are devastated by mildew every year; can this be prevented?

Mildew is probably the commonest garden disease, affecting an enormous range of plants. Usually it takes some weeks for a mildew attack to develop to significant proportions, but it always spreads most rapidly in hot, dry conditions. Not surprisingly, therefore, those mildew-prone plants that mature toward the end of the summer consistently suffer the most severe damage; and Michaelmas daisies usually top the list.

There are three main ways to tackle the problem. The first is to select those varieties that are inherently more resistant to attack. All Michaelmas daisies are forms of perennial aster, most of the older varieties belonging to *Aster novi-belgii*, a species that is particularly prone to mildew. But among the taller-growing types, the following are fairly reliable: 'Coombe Rosemary' (double purple), 'Freda Ballard' (semi-double red) and 'Patricia Ballard (semi-double pink). Even better is to select varieties of quite different species, such as *Aster novae-angliae* or, perhaps best of all, those derived from *Aster amellus*. The hybrid form *frikartii* has the classic Michaelmas daisy lavender colour and is a superb plant. 'Pink Zenith' and 'Violet Queen' are related varieties in other shades. Finally, a recommendation for the form known as 'Nana', an outstanding lower-growing lavender-coloured variety of *Aster thomsonii*, the species that is the other parent of *frikartii*.

Having selected a good variety, it is important to minimize the impact of mildew by careful cultivation. The disease is favoured by dryness, so water regularly and mulch generously between the plants. The sprays that give the most long-lasting protection are those containing a systemic chemical such as benomyl or thiophanate-methyl.

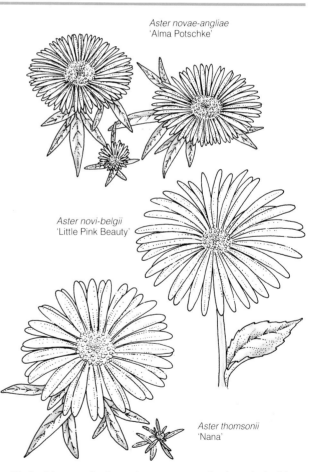

Aster novae-angliae
'Alma Potschke'

Aster novi-belgii
'Little Pink Beauty'

Aster thomsonii
'Nana'

The best low-growing types of *Aster novi-belgii* include 'Little Pink Beauty' (semi-double pink), 'Jenny' (double purple) and 'Snow Sprite' (white). There are some beautiful pink and red forms of the 1–1.25 m (3–4 ft) tall *Aster* *novae-angliae*, in particular 'Alma Potschke' and 'Harrington's Pink'. Among the best dwarf types is *Aster thomsonii* 'Nana', with clear lavender flowers and hairy, grey-green foliage.

BULBS, CORMS AND TUBERS

Flowers from
underground stores

How deeply should bulbs be planted?

There are thousands of different types of bulbous plant and, as with any grouping so large, generalizations regarding treatment can be misleading. It is often suggested that you should plant with the base of the bulb or corm at a depth equal to two and a half times the average diameter. This system works reasonably well with most bulbous plants, but if you stick rigidly to it, you will make a few serious mistakes, especially with those bulbs that should be planted close to the surface and will perish if they are buried deeply.

Lilium candidum is the outstanding example of this and is the only lily that needs shallow planting. There is also an obvious temptation to plant nerines deeply, in the same way as narcissi, for the bulbs appear similar, but they prefer to have their necks just protruding, as do shallots. Apart from these few rather expensive mistakes that can be made, experience with plant and soil conditions will teach you how to vary the general rule.

The small, spring-flowering bulbous irises are a case in point. To plant *Iris reticulata* at two and a half times its diameter would place its base at about 5 cm (2 in). At this depth, although it may flower for one season, it may well be washed or pulled from the soil or produce only leaves in future years. It is commonly suggested that it should, therefore, be planted at 10 cm (4 in), but even then many people find they have to treat the plant as an annual and replace with fresh stock every season. I now plant mine at a depth of 15 cm (6 in), which seems cruel to such a small bulb, but they always reach the surface. And while *Iris reticulata* and its yellow relative, *Iris danfordiae*, are not reliable perennials, they do last much longer when treated in this way.

The chart depicts the best general planting depths for some common bulb species.

1 *Lilium candidum*; **2** Puschkinia; **3** *Cyclamen persicum*; **4** *Galanthus nivalis*; **5** *Acidanthera bicolor*; **6** *Scilla sibirica*; **7** *Narcissus* 'Trevithian'; **8** Muscari; **9** *Iris reticulata*; **10** *Lilium auratum*; **11** *Fritillaria imperialis*;

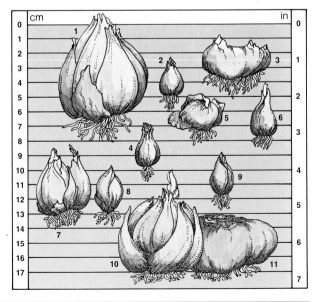

See also:
Naturalizing bulbs in grass p 68
Feeding bulbs p 70
Treating bulbs before planting p 71
Irises p 73
Cutting foliage after flowering p 74

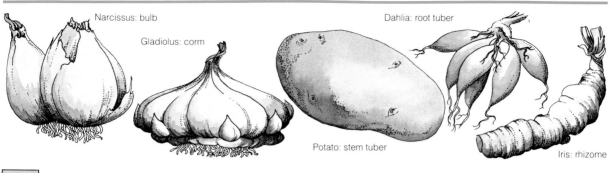

Narcissus: bulb

Gladiolus: corm

Dahlia: root tuber

Potato: stem tuber

Iris: rhizome

What is the difference between a bulb and a corm?

For many gardeners, the terms bulb and corm are virtually interchangeable. The two are certainly grouped together in most gardening books because they give rise to similar types of plant, generally require similar treatment and serve a similar purpose in the plants that produce them. Botanically, however, they are quite distinct structures.

A bulb is a specialized form of shoot in which the leaves are closely folded over each other and swollen in order to store food reserves for the young plant. The stem on which the leaves are borne is reduced in size and shape to a flattened, platelike structure at the base, and from this modified stem, the roots arise. Therefore, even though no roots may be present when bulbs are planted, it is important to place this flat plate downward in the soil.

Some bulbs (onions, narcissi, and tulips, for example) have swollen leaves closely covering the entire structure, with the outermost leaves reduced to papery scales. In other bulb types, of which lilies are the best-known example, the swollen scales are more loosely overlapping and have no papery outer layer. From the base of the parent bulb, small buds form, and from these, daughter bulbs develop. In narcissi, for example, the old and new bulbs remain attached, and eventually a large mass develops. In other plants, the old, parent bulb dies, leaving one or two slightly smaller offspring.

Structurally more simple than a bulb, a corm is a solid, swollen stem that serves the purpose of storing food. Superficially, some corms (those of crocus, for instance) look much like bulbs, but they have a bud at the top, not within. One or more (sometimes, as in gladioli, many more) daughter corms are formed below the parent during growth. These should be carefully separated if the corms are lifted at the end of the season.

Some plants, such as potatoes, produce swollen storage organs that are neither bulbs nor corms but stem tubers. These should, in turn, be distinguished from root tubers (of which dahlias are the best-known example); they bear buds over a large part of the surface (potato 'eyes' are buds) whereas root tubers have buds only at the top.

Finally, among the 'bulbs' in your gardening catalogues will be lily-of-the-valley and irises. Although some irises do produce genuine bulbs, all the large, familiar, bearded forms, as well as lilies-of-the-valley, develop swollen rhizomes, fleshy stems that creep horizontally below the surface of the soil.

Now, having, I hope, cleared up some of the confusion, I shall refer to all plants of the types that produce swollen food storage structures as 'bulbous plants', irrespective of whether the storage organ is a bulb in the botanical sense.

What soil preparation is needed before planting bulbs?

One of the most satisfying features of almost all bulbous plants is that they will give a good display of flowers in the season after planting, with the absolute minimum of soil preparation. This is largely because their food reserves are already contained within the swollen storage tissues. After flowering, that food reserve will, however, be depleted, and if the plants are to repeat their show the following year, a fertile soil is essential.

There are two aspects of soil preparation to consider: it must be well supplied with fertilizer and it must also be in a condition to minimize the likelihood of the soft, fleshy tissues succumbing to rot. For this reason, bulbs must have a well-drained soil. If there is any tendency for waterlogging, the soil should be lightened and opened up generally, and the individual bulbs placed on a bed of sand, lightly mixed with bonemeal. With the most rot-susceptible bulbs such as those, like lilies and fritillaries, with overlapping scale leaves, pack sand around the bulb as well as underneath it.

While a heavy soil should be opened up and its drainage improved with organic matter in advance of planting, care should be taken to ensure that no manure comes into contact with the bulbs, for this will encourage rotting. Manure may, with advantage, be placed below the planting depth, however. A general light application of bonemeal, well raked in before planting, will aid root establishment.

A bulb planter is the best tool for planting single bulbs in grass or moist soil. Thrust the planter into the ground to the required depth to remove a core of earth; set the bulb in the hole and tidily replace the soil and grass above it.

What are the best bulbs for naturalizing in grass?

The main advantage of growing bulbs among grass is that they do not occupy bedding space needed for other plants when their flowering season is over; and once they have finished flowering, their foliage does not look nearly as unsightly as it does in a border. In any event, masses of bulbs among grass look spectacular and can be used to add interest to areas under trees that are otherwise pretty bleak early in the season.

The chief consideration in selecting species and varieties is that they should not be in competition with the grass. This means that many of the bulbs that naturalize successfully are fairly large and favour being planted quite deeply, below the level at which the grass roots deplete the nutrients in the soil. Second, planting into established grass is laborious and is something you will want to do only once in a garden, so the bulbs should be capable of flowering for many years without any need to replant. To achieve an impressive display, you will probably want to plant mostly large-flowered bulbs, although a few notable exceptions are also suggested.

Daffodils and narcissi are the most important and obvious choice for naturalizing, but some varieties are much more successful than others when grown in this way. Try to resist buying the relatively cheaply priced mixtures often advertised as suitable for naturalizing. Usually this is just a means whereby companies dispose of left-over bulbs and, although cheap, the resulting hotch-potch display does not stand comparison with spaced out groups of carefully selected varieties, chosen to provide a range of colour, size and flowering time. The better nurseries will sometimes offer their own selections of groups of individual varieties for naturalizing, and provided you are willing to accept their choice, savings can be made in this way.

Daffodils and narcissi are the mainstay of grass planting, but many other bulbous plants also look excellent in this setting. The autumn-flowering *Colchicum autumnale* (often wrongly called crocus) produces its tall flowers after the leaves have died down and needs the support of tall grass around it, both physically and to set off the rich lilac colour. The same is true of the genuine autumn crocus, *Crocus speciosus*.

Colchicum autumnale 'Album'

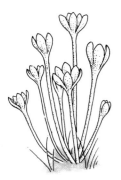

Cyclamen hederifolium

Snake's head fritillary
Fritillaria meleagris 'Poseidon'

GOOD VARIETIES FOR NATURALIZING

The following daffodils and narcissi can be relied on to naturalize well and to give a good range of flowering season and colour.

Variety	Colour
'King Alfred'	golden yellow
'Mount Hood'	white
'Spellbinder'	greenish-yellow
'Carbineer'	orange-red cup/yellow frill
'Duke of Windsor'	cream cup/white frill
'Green Island'	greenish white cup/white frill
'Semper Avanti'	orange cup/cream frill
'Mrs R.O.Backhouse'	pale apricot cup/white frill
'Ice Follies'	pale yellow-white cup/white frill
'Irene Copeland'	double; creamy white-apricot
'White Lion'	double; white-cream
'Actaea'	yellow eye, edged red/white frill

If small bulbs are planted in grass, it should be among short turf, which must be trimmed carefully around them and mown only when they are dormant below ground. The tiny, hoop-petticoat daffodil, *Narcissus bulbocodium*, looks delightful grown this way (choose the form known as *vulgaris conspicuus*), and many of the spring-flowering crocuses naturalize exceedingly well.

Among the large-flowered Dutch types, choose 'Jeanne d'Arc' (white), 'Queen of the Blues' (silvery-lilac); 'Yellow Giant' (egg-yellow) and 'Striped Beauty' (white, streaked purple). Among the species, try the more vigorous of the early-flowering types, such as *Crocus laevigatus fontenayi* (lilac, streaked purple) and *C. ancyrensis* (orange). As with daffodils, crocuses are best planted in groups of each variety rather than mixed indiscriminately, although they may be interplanted with another good plant for turf, the golden-yellow winter aconite, *Eranthis hyemalis*.

Cyclamen always look pretty (both in flower and leaf) in short grass beneath trees; *hederifolium* is the best and most easily available of the autumn-flowering types, with *coum*, which unfortunately is rather expensive, for spring. But to bring a touch of class to your grass planting, you need look no further than one of Britain's rarer native plants, the snake's head fritillary, *Fritillaria meleagris*. Don't uproot it from its ever-diminishing home in the water-meadows, for most specialist bulb nurseries stock it in a range of delightful colours.

There will inevitably be some competition between bulbous plants and the grass, and, as with any other flowering plant, additional feeding is desirable. A balanced general liquid fertilizer should be applied after flowering, and the foliage of the lower-growing bulbous plants allowed to die down naturally. Daffodils and narcissi may be mown six weeks after flowering finishes.

See also:
Lifting dahlia tubers pp 19, 77
Design for naturalizing bulbs p 26
Soil preparation before planting
  bulbs p 67
Feeding bulbs p 70

Treating bulbs before planting p 71
Cutting foliage after flowering p 74
Planting hyacinths after indoor
  flowering p 75

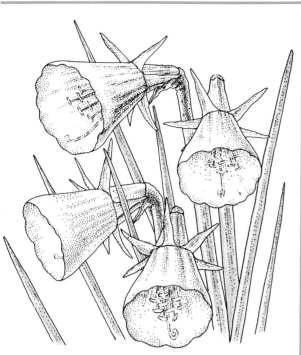

*Narcissus bulbocodium vulgaris
conspicuus*

Winter aconite
Eranthis hyemalis

? Should bulbs be lifted every year or can they be left from season to season?

It is evident from what has been said about naturalizing bulbous plants in grass that many will survive and proliferate if left more or less indefinitely. By inference, it may be assumed that the same holds true for plants growing in borders. Some gardeners do, however, routinely lift almost all their bulbs each season, but, apart from the non-hardy plants, such as gladioli, it seems doubtful if this repays the time and effort spent on it. The two strongest candidates for annual lifting are lilies and tulips but, given a good surface mulching with leaf-mould and a well-drained soil, most lilies will survive and multiply for many years. If they do ultimately decline, it is most likely to be through the build-up of virus in the stock, and annual lifting will make no difference to this.

The argument with tulips is that the foliage takes a long time to die down and the plants take up an inconvenient amount of space and appear unsightly well into the summer. Usually, therefore, bedding tulips are lifted and replanted temporarily elsewhere (a corner of the vegetable garden is ideal), before finally being lifted and dried off toward the end of the summer. This is probably a sound course of action, although it is not necessary with the species tulips, which are mostly smaller and neater plants. There are so many gardening tasks to perform and, among the half-hardy subjects, so many plants that *must* be lifted each season, that to add to the work load by removing hundreds of additional bulbs smacks of horticultural masochism.

The endearing little deep yellow, hoop-petticoat *Narcissus bulbocodium vulgaris conspicuus* blooms in February and March. Its narrow, cylindrical leaves and widely flaring trumpet show to best advantage when it is grown in short grass. The stems of winter aconite, *Eranthis hyemalis*, are naked, with only a ruff of pale green leaves around the base of the cup-shaped golden-yellow flowers. Plant them in drifts with snowdrops and early flowering crocuses.

Sweetly scented *Crocus laevigatus* is completely hardy and blooms from November to January; it can often be seen poking up through the snow. Its flowers range from white to pale blue-lavender, with deep purple veining and bright orange centres and stamens.

Is it possible to have bulbs flowering in succession right through the year?

Yes, and it is a great pity that more gardeners are not aware of the possibilities that bulbous plants offer. It is true that they really come into their own in the months when there is little else in flower, but it tends to be for the spring, rather than the pre-Christmas period, that gardeners think of them. For it is then that the masses of daffodils and tulips burst forth in such obvious and dramatic fashion, and there is no way that this abundance can be matched at other seasons.

Even so, it is possible to have a tulip season that begins in March and extends into late May, and a crocus season for the six or seven bleakest months of the year. Species tulips are discussed elsewhere, so here I shall suggest crocuses for continuity of flowering and also offer other suggestions for the bleak weeks before and just after the end of the year, when almost anything is welcome.

You should not expect to be able to obtain all the suggested crocus varieties from your local garden centre; for some you will have to contact a specialist nursery, but the selection should be wide enough to enable you to find representative plants for each month reasonably easily. Remember that the precise months of flowering will vary slightly in different parts of the country, in different parts of a garden and, to a lesser extent, in different years.

A SEASON OF CROCUSES

Month	Species/Variety	Colour
September	C. cancellatus cancellatus	lilac/purple lines
	C. cartwrightianus albus	cream white/yellow
	C. nudiflorus	deep purple
October	C. banaticus	lilac
	C. longiflorus	lilac
	C. medius	lilac
	C. sativus	lilac
	C. speciosus	lavender/violet
	C. zonatus	lilac/yellow
November	C. ochroleucus	white
	C. laevigatus fontenayi	lilac/purple
	C. longiflorus	lilac
	C. speciosus	lavender/violet
	C. tournefortii	violet
December	C. ochroleucus	white
	C. laevigatus fontenayi	lilac/purple
January	C. ochroleucus	white
	C. laevigatus fontenayi	lilac/purple
	C. ancyrensis	orange
	C. imperati 'de Jager'	violet/brown
February	C. korolkowii	golden yellow
	C. etruscus 'Zwanenburg'	lavender
	C. sieberi 'Bowles' White'	white
	C. sieberi atticus	blue/gold
	C. sieberi (other varieties)	lilac/pink/purple
	C. tomasinianus 'Whitwell Purple'	purple
	C. biflorus alexandri	white/purple
March	C. biflorus biflorus	white/purple
	C. corsicus	lilac
	C. minimus	violet/purple
	C. susianus	golden yellow
	C. tomasinianus albus	white
	C. chrysanthus (many varieties)	white/gold/purple
	Dutch crocus (many varieties)	white/gold/purple

Bulbs for the bleakest months

Most snowdrops appear toward the end of January and in early February, but the season can begin as early as the New Year with *Galanthus graecus*. The winter-flowering iris, *Iris unguicularis*, will flower as early as November in some situations and in one or other of its forms can be relied on well into the early spring. Liriope, the so-called evergreen grape hyacinth, will flower until fairly late in the autumn and is rewarding, for its attractive foliage persists throughout the winter.

Cyclamen, too, are excellent value for both flowers and leaves. In some years, *hederifolium* will flower until October. *Cilicium* is later still and, in a sheltered spot, *mirabile* is a delightful plant that will flower until just before Christmas, when it overlaps the earliest of the spring-flowering species, *coum atkinsii*. *Anemone blanda* should not be forgotten for February; the easiest and earliest is the familiar 'Blue'. The first daffodils are probably some of the little hoop-petticoats, *Narcissus bulbocodium*, although the earliest ones are not the most free flowering or easiest to naturalize. Perhaps it is better to rely on the *Narcissus cyclamineus* hybrids, such as 'February Gold', for dependable pre-March flowers.

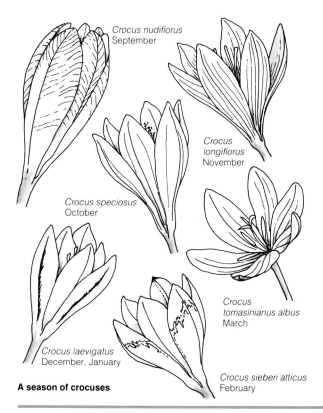

Crocus nudiflorus
September

Crocus longiflorus
November

Crocus speciosus
October

Crocus tomasinianus albus
March

Crocus laevigatus
December, January

Crocus sieberi atticus
February

A season of crocuses

See also:
Weedkiller and fertilizer mixes
   for lawns p 18
Bulbs, corms and tubers p 67
Soil preparation before planting
   bulbs p 67

Feeding bulbs p 70
Species tulips p 72
Weedkillers on lawns p 104

Planted in a large pot set near a window, from October to March the Algerian iris, *Iris unguicularis*, will provide a feast of sweet-scented, lavender-lilac flowers to brighten the dull winter days.

What is the difference between a daffodil and a narcissus?

All the plants we call daffodils and narcissi are either species, varieties or hybrids belonging to the genus *Narcissus*. The genus is divided, for horticultural purposes, into several groups, depending on the species from which the particular plant was derived, its flower type and its flower colour. The name daffodil has no strict scientific meaning but tends to be applied to those plants whose flowers have markedly elongated trumpets, irrespective of size.

Even so, you will find some bulb nurseries habitually refer to any member of the genus *Narcissus* as a daffodil. There is no reason to be disconcerted by this, but it is best to become familiar with the characteristics of each of the different divisions if you decide to specialize in these plants and grow them for exhibition.

Why do the bulbs I plant flower well for a year or two, then produce only leaves?

It is dangerous to generalize, for there are so many different types of bulbous plant, but there are three common reasons for an obstinate refusal to flower. The first is simply that too much has been expected of the plants and that they have not been fed and given the wherewithal to replenish the food reserves exhausted during the first season's growth. This is especially true in a poor soil or one where no advance preparation (cultivation, fertilizing and manuring) was carried out before planting.

A second reason for a failure to flower is that the bulbs have been attacked by a pest or disease — a bulb rot, eelworm or maggots of narcissus fly, for example. Some of these problems will be more serious in certain seasons than others but three general precautions can be taken. *Never* plant bulbs on waterlogged or poorly drained land; *always* soak them for about 30 minutes before planting in a spray-strength suspension of either benomyl or thiophanate-methyl fungicide to lessen the chance of rot setting in, and dust HCH insecticide around the bulbs when planting them to discourage attacks of some soil pests.

A third cause of bulbs failing to flower is unlikely to arise after only one or two seasons but does sometimes occur after several years. This is a build-up in the plants of virus contamination and unfortunately there is no way either of checking with certainty whether this has happened or of curing the problem. If feeding the plants fails to achieve results, and yet, when a few are dug up, there is no sign of rot or pest attack, virus should be suspected and fresh stock purchased.

Is it safe to use weedkillers on an area planted with bulbs when they are dormant?

This depends on the type of weedkiller you plan to use. If it is one of those that is active when absorbed by green plant tissue but not persistent in the soil, then bulbs will not be harmed. If it has some residual soil action, damage may well result. It is perfectly safe, therefore, to use lawn weedkillers on grass during the summer after all above-ground growth of bulbs has disappeared but before any early-flowering species have begun to produce new shoots below ground. Similarly, in beds and borders, foliar-absorbed weedkillers, such as glyphosate, may be used quite safely while bulbs are dormant. Products such as simazine or sodium chlorate should not be used, since bulbs (especially small ones close to the surface) may well be harmed.

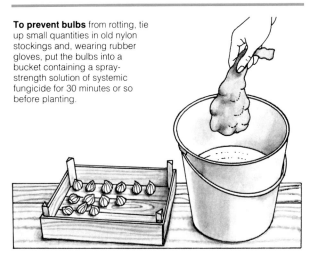

To prevent bulbs from rotting, tie up small quantities in old nylon stockings and, wearing rubber gloves, put the bulbs into a bucket containing a spray-strength solution of systemic fungicide for 30 minutes or so before planting.

Tulipa turkestanica
February, March

Tulipa greigii 'Red Riding Hood'
April

Tulipa tarda
April

Tulipa
sprengeri
May, June

What are 'species' tulips; how do they differ from normal garden tulips?

All plants that grow wild and have not been specially selected, crossed or otherwise bred by horticulturists are natural species. When these 'unaltered' plants are grown in gardens, gardeners use the word species as a prefix to distinguish them, as a group, from hybrids. Thus, species tulips are wild tulips, principally from the western parts of Asia, whereas the Darwins, Parrot-flowered, and other familiar garden tulips are all hybrids, derived over many years of breeding from one or more of the species.

Recently, the species tulips have become increasingly popular as their merits as garden plants have become more widely recognized, and most garden centres now stock a range of them. They have several appealing features. Most are lower growing and have smaller flowers than the hybrids and so are excellent in small beds and rock gardens. They occur in a wide range of flower shapes and colours, and by choosing several species they can be used to increase considerably the flowering period of tulips in general — the earliest will flower in March and the latest at the end of May. In addition, despite their increased popularity, they are still little enough grown to have the appeal of novelty.

About twenty 'pure' species are fairly frequently seen in catalogues and garden centres, together with a small selection of varieties of a few of them and a range of hybrids obtained by crossing *Tulipa kaufmanniana* with *T. greigii* or *T. fosteriana*. It is sometimes suggested that the bulbs must be lifted every year, but I have not found this necessary, although the flower size and quality of some of the *kaufmanniana* hybrids may diminish in time. The selection given here is made largely on the basis of variety in form and flowering season.

VARIETIES OF SPECIES TULIPS (TULIPA)

Species	Colour	Height cm / in	Flowers
acuminata	green and red twisted petals	45 / 18	May
aucheriana	pink with yellow base	10 / 4	April
batalinii 'Bronze Charm'	bronze-apricot	12 / 5	May
biflora	white, two or three per stem	15 / 6	March
clusiana	white with red stripe	30 / 12	April
eichleri	scarlet with yellow and black centre	23 / 9	May
fosteriana 'Red Emperor'	scarlet with black and yellow base	45 / 18	March/April
fosteriana 'White Emperor'	white with yellow centre	50 / 20	March/April
greigii	scarlet (with spotted leaves)	20 / 8	April
greigii 'Red Riding Hood'	scarlet with black base (spotted leaves)	20 / 8	April
kaufmanniana	yellow/pink with white centre	20 / 8	March
kolpakowskiana	red with golden centre	30 / 12	March/April
maximowiczii	scarlet	12 / 5	April
praestans 'Fusilier'	scarlet-orange, up to five per stem	20 / 8	April
pulchella violacea	purple with black or yellow centre	10 / 4	February/March
sprengeri	bronze-red with scarlet centre	33 / 13	May/June
sylvestris	yellow	40 / 16	April
tarda	cream with yellow centre	15 / 6	April
turkestanica	white with yellow centre, up to nine per stem	23 / 9	February/March
urumiensis	bronze with golden centre	15 / 6	March/April
KAUFMANNIANA HYBRIDS			
'Ancilla'	pink with white, red and yellow centre	15 / 6	March
'Heart's Delight'	pink with white, red and yellow centre	20 / 8	March
'Johann Strauss'	cream and red with white centre	15 / 6	February/March
'Shakespeare'	orange, pink, apricot	15 / 6	March
'Stresa'	red and yellow	17 / 7	February/March

See also:
Waterside plants p 35, 36, 40–1
Planting depths for bulbs p 66
Bulbs, corms and tubers p 67
F$_1$ hybrids pp 118–19

I am confused by the many types of iris; which should I choose for my garden?

The genus *Iris* is a large one with more than 200 species. This is bewildering to gardeners because, although an iris is immediately recognizable from its flowers, the plants vary widely in other respects. Some have large creeping rhizomes, others tubers and yet others bulbs. They also cover a wide range in size, from tiny rock-garden species to giant waterside plants. Botanically, the genus is divided into a number of groups, but, for basic garden purposes, a simpler subdivision can be used that reflects fairly well the different ways in which the most useful garden irises are grown.

Small bulbous irises These are the spring-flowering rock-garden species. All are extremely pretty but not all are hardy in colder climates and they are difficult to keep perennially, since, after one season, some tend to produce a small number of daughter bulbs, which never really build up satisfactorily to flowering size. Those that are seen most frequently are the blue *I. reticulata* and its varieties, especially the sky-blue 'Harmony', the blue *I. histrioides* and the yellow *I. danfordiae*. The latter is extremely difficult to maintain after one year, but *histrioides* is reliable, and *reticulata* will survive if it is planted deeply.

Large bulbous irises These are the varieties usually known as English, Dutch and Spanish irises and are derived principally from the species *Iris xiphium* and its relatives. They reach a height of about 60 cm (24 in), prefer a deep, well-drained soil in full sun and flower from mid-May (with the Spanish varieties) through to July (with the English varieties). They are available in a wide range of colours and make excellent garden flowers. Since they produce their leaves early in the autumn before flowering, they should be lifted, moved and divided in late summer.

Bearded irises These are probably the most familiar garden irises. They fall into three groups: the June-flowering tall bearded, which reach 90 to 120 cm (3 to 4 ft); the April- or May-flowering dwarf bearded, which barely reach 30 cm (12 in), and the intermediates, which lie between the two in flowering time and size. All produce thick, fleshy rhizomes, which must always be planted at the surface of the soil with only the fibrous roots buried; and all require an exceptionally sunny, well-drained site. Bearded irises occur in a large number of varieties and a wide colour range.

Californian hybrids This is a group of beautiful rhizomatous irises, all only about 45 cm (18 in) tall, in a wide range of subtle colours. They make excellent garden plants and, although sometimes said to require an acid soil, will tolerate a small amount of lime and also light shade.

Waterside irises Although not closely related to each other, there is a group of moisture-loving irises that is invaluable for bog and water gardens. The best known are the Japanese *Iris kaempferi* and *I. laevigata*, both available in a range of colour varieties; the Siberian irises, which include *I. sibirica*, and a range of hybrids in several colours. *Iris pseudacorus*, the giant yellow flag, belongs in this group also.

The winter-flowering iris, *Iris unguicularis* (or, as it is still sometimes called, *I. stylosa*), is uniquely valuable for its flowering season, which extends through the winter from late November to February. It requires a poor, free-draining soil and a good baking in summer and is excellent in a large pot. The best form is the deep blue known as 'Mary Barnard'.

The Gladwyn iris, *Iris foetidissima*, is another valuable plant. It is evergreen and revels in dry shade. Although its flowers are unexciting, its vivid red seeds, which remain attached within the split pod, are extremely striking and good for flower arranging.

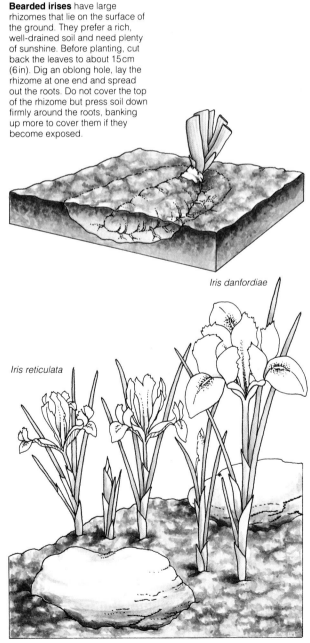

Bearded irises have large rhizomes that lie on the surface of the ground. They prefer a rich, well-drained soil and need plenty of sunshine. Before planting, cut back the leaves to about 15 cm (6 in). Dig an oblong hole, lay the rhizome at one end and spread out the roots. Do not cover the top of the rhizome but press soil down firmly around the roots, banking up more to cover them if they become exposed.

Iris danfordiae

Iris reticulata

Lilium henryi

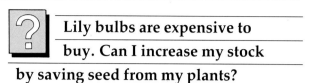

Lily bulbs are expensive to buy. Can I increase my stock by saving seed from my plants?

Lilies are certainly among the more expensive bulbs and they should be bought with care. Transportation and other marketing considerations mean that suppliers cannot make bulbs available for sale for several weeks, if not months, after lifting; so always examine potential purchases from garden centres thoroughly. Check that the bulbs have been carefully packed and that they are plump, with no signs of 'pinching'. If you buy by mail order, avoid cut-price offers and ascertain when delivery will be made. It is important that lily bulbs are replanted soon after they have been lifted in the autumn, before the roots have dried and shrivelled.

Since the bulbs are expensive, you are unlikely to buy many at one time, so it is reasonable to ask if the stock can be increased by seeds. This is not, however, the only way in which to multiply your plants, although with some methods you may have to wait many years for the plants to reach flowering size.

Do not bother to save seed from any of the hybrid lilies, for it will be most unlikely to produce plants resembling those from which it was collected. This is, however, the simplest way to raise large numbers of species lilies, although some seeds may take a long time to germinate, and the rapidity with which plants reach flowering size varies: *Lilium regale* may flower within two years, *L. martagon* may take seven. Sow the seed in a soil-based seedling compost as soon as possible after collecting it. Always sow thinly, for some lilies suffer root damage when disturbed, and the less pricking-on needed, the better. Place the seedbox in a cold frame and be prepared to wait a year for germination to take place.

Should I cut off the leaves of bulbs when they have finished flowering?

A massed planting of daffodils, when flowering is over, is the gardening equivalent of 'after the Lord Mayor's Show'; they look unsightly, increasingly so as the weeks pass and the foliage begins to brown. But you must resist the temptation to cut off the foliage of any bulbous plant immediately the plant as a whole has lost its appeal, for healthy foliage is the key to flowering in future seasons. The bulb must be given the opportunity to replenish its depleted food reserves, and it is the leaves that enable it to do this. Extensive tests with daffodils have proved that a period of six weeks after the end of flowering should elapse before the foliage may safely be cut off or mown, and this should be taken as the rule for all other bulbs.

All, that is, except tulips, which really should be left longer. Large hybrid garden tulips are, therefore, better lifted and temporarily replanted elsewhere to enable

See also:
Lifting dahlia tubers pp 19, 77
Dividing herbaceous plants p 55
F_1 hybrids pp 118–19

Lily bulbs are composed of overlapping scales, which may be removed and used to produce new plants. Press each scale, tip uppermost, into a box containing seedling compost, which must be kept warm while the young plants develop. A good way to do this is to wrap the seedbox in plastic and put it in an airing cupboard. As soon as the first leaf appears, remove and pot up each young plant. Plants grown from scales should flower in 3–4 years.

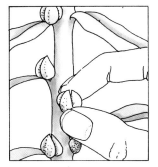

Bulbils are tiny black bulbs produced by some species of lily on the stem or, by stem-rooting lilies, at the base of the stem. Remove them after the flowers have faded and before bulbils on the stem drop to the ground, when they are difficult to find. Sow bulbils with their tips just below the surface in seedling compost in partial shade. Sow thinly to avoid transplanting before the lilies are well grown. They should flower in 3–4 years.

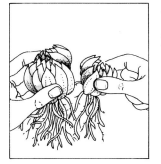

The bulbs of a mature lily that has been in position for a few years should proliferate to produce a fairly large clump. This may be lifted and carefully divided in the autumn and the separated bulbs replanted. Quite often these bulbs will produce flowering plants the following year.

Which are the easiest varieties of lily to grow?

Lilies have a reputation for being difficult to grow, but it is often not justified. Many years ago it was probably more true. Research had not then revealed how to rid lily bulbs of virus contamination; the fungicides available for combatting the fungus diseases were not particularly effective, and many of the species and old varieties lacked vigour. This has now changed, and the average garden shop stocks a good range, especially of the modern hybrids.

Any selection from the many hundreds available will be biased; my personal recommendations are:

Lilium henryi	Deep orange-yellow; up to 2.5 cm (8 ft); August
Lilium hansonii	Rich golden-yellow; 1 – 1.5 m (3¼ – 5 ft); June
Lilium fortunei giganteum	Huge; orange with purple spots; 2 m (6½ ft); August
Lilium monadelphum	Yellow with black spots; 2 m (6½ ft); June
Lilium candidum, madonna lily	White; 1.5 m (5 ft); June
Lilium 'Bright Star'	White with orange centre; 1 m (3¼ ft); July
Lilium 'Green Dragon'	White, flushed green; 2 m (6½ ft); July

their place to be taken by summer flowers. The smaller species tulips can usually be left *in situ*, although their leaves should be removed carefully as they die off to prevent the soil from becoming contaminated with a damaging fungus disease that develops on old foliage. Although some tidying-up of the foliage of daffodils by carefully tying the leaves together with light twine is permissible after flowering, actually knotting them damages the leaves so that they cease to function properly, and it is grotesquely unsightly.

Can I plant hyacinths in the garden after they have flowered indoors?

Yes; waste not, want not is as useful a philosophy in the garden as anywhere else, but don't pitch your expectations too high. Most of the hyacinth bulbs that are grown in pots indoors for flowering at Christmas or shortly afterwards have been pre-treated by carefully controlled temperature conditions to induce them to flower in this unseasonal manner. They will, however, oblige only once in this way and when grown subsequently, either indoors or out, they will flower later and less impressively.

Although some gardeners feel that hyacinths are, by then, little better than bloated bluebells, there is nothing wrong with a bluebell. After flowering has finished indoors, therefore, liquid feed the plants to enable the bulb to regain some of its vigour, then allow the foliage to die down naturally before drying off the bulb ready for planting outdoors in the autumn.

Which of the less-familiar bulbous plants can be easily grown outdoors?

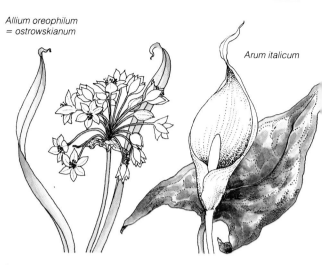

Allium oreophilum
= ostrowskianum

Arum italicum

The increase in the range of bulbous plants on general sale has been one of the most welcome features of gardening in recent years; as, indeed, has the rapidity with which plants newly discovered in the wild are brought into cultivation, multiplied and made widely available. Several unfamiliar species of crocus and tulip have already been mentioned, so I shall suggest here some other types of bulbous plants worth trying.

Allium This is the onion, garlic and chive genus, and although the last, in particular, does have extremely attractive flowers, there are many other highly ornamental species. Two points to watch when choosing alliums are that some have a fairly strong onion smell (although commonly only when the foliage is bruised), and one or two can get out of hand, for they produce large numbers of rapidly dispersed bulbils. The taller species all need staking.

Among the best are *A. oreophilum = ostrowskianum* with deep rose-pink flowers in May, about 15 cm (6 in) high. It establishes well, but the bulbs should be planted close together in order that the flower stems will support each other and not flop. *A. caeruleum* produces deep blue flowers on stems about 60 cm (24 in) tall in June; *A. moly*, a rapidly spreading, but not unruly, and very pretty yellow-flowered species, has flower stems about 25 cm (10 in) tall in June and July; *A. albopilosum* is a striking plant with large, violet flower heads on 60 cm (24 in) tall stems in June. And, for the back of the herbaceous border, *A. giganteum* is an imposing, June-flowering species with large, pale lilac flower heads on stems up to 1.5 m (5 ft) tall.

Arum Most gardeners will be familiar with the native cuckoo pint, or lords and ladies, but there are many exotic species too. Among those hardy in Britain, one of the best is *A. italicum*, a larger plant than the native form with a yellowish-green spathe, or hood.

Chionodoxa A March-flowering genus sometimes known as the glory of the snow. Chionodoxas look a little like bluebells, but with the flowers directed upward and only about 15 cm (6 in) tall. *C. lucilliae* and the larger-flowered *C. gigantea* are the species most frequently seen.

Erythronium This is a genus of beautiful bulbs for moist, shady situations. They have broad, lush, often variegated leaves and almost lily-like flowers in April on stems up to 25 cm (10 in) tall. The bulbs tend to be

Erythronium tuolumnense

Erythronium dens-canis
Dog's-tooth violet

See also:
Lifting dahlia tubers p 19
Bulbs for naturalizing p 68
Crocuses pp 70–1
Species tulips p 72

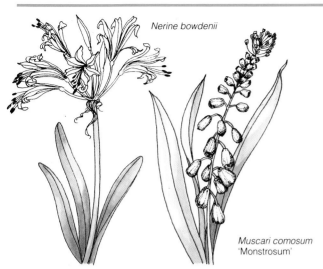

Nerine bowdenii

Muscari comosum
'Monstrosum'

expensive, but among the best and most frequently offered are *E. dens-canis* in a range of white, pink and purple varieties; *E. revolutum* 'White Beauty', which has large white flowers with yellow centres, and *E. tuolumnense* 'Pagoda', with flowers of sulphur-yellow.

Leucojum Best described as large, late-flowering snowdrops, the snowflakes, especially *L. aestivum*, are useful plants for extending the 'snowdrop' season into late April or even May, when they make a very attractive blend with the blue of muscaris and scillas.

Muscari Muscaris, or grape hyacinths, have a reputation for rapidly becoming garden weeds, and they need to be kept in check, although their ability to spread rapidly is useful in wilder parts of the garden. A somewhat different and pretty species is the tassel hyacinth, *M. comosum* 'Monstrosum', which in May has a 20-cm (8-in) spike of purple flowers, topped by a blue tassel.

Nerine Autumn-flowering bulbs in general are valuable, but few more so than the nerines, of which *N. bowdenii* is the one likely to succeed most widely, although it needs a sheltered position against a sunny, south-facing wall. It has a loose head of somewhat onion-like pink flowers in September and October. The bulbs must be shallowly planted and covered with peat or straw for protection in winter.

Scilla The squills have perhaps the most perfect blue of any flower apart from the gentians, and they are invaluable for late spring. The best form of the common *S. sibirica* is 'Spring Beauty', with strong colour and a 20-cm (8-in) flowering stem.

Zephyranthes The romantically named flower of the western wind is unfortunately not very hardy, but in warmer areas *Z. candida* should be tried outdoors. They are autumn-flowering, white, crocus-like flowers, about 20 cm (8 in) tall, with narrow, almost rush-like leaves.

My dahlias are always spindly and have small flowers; how should I grow them?

The key to success with dahlias is to start with strong, healthy stock and then to appreciate that large, lush leaves and big flowers can result only from adequate watering and feeding. It is possible, even in an unsuitable and inadequately prepared bed, to obtain reasonable flowers from tubers in the first year, although from young rooted cuttings it will be difficult to achieve even one season's success unless the site is prepared in advance.

Dahlias always thrive in a sunny position with a deep, moist, but freely draining soil. The addition of well-rotted manure or compost in the autumn always benefits dahlias, for it improves the moisture retentiveness of a free-draining soil, it opens up a heavy one and will provide a modest supply of nutrients. If the soil is light enough not to need further extensive cultivation before planting in the spring, a dressing of bonemeal at the rate of 135 g/sq m (4 oz/sq yd) should be applied with the manure in the autumn; on heavier land, it is better left until the spring.

Although dahlias are surprisingly tolerant of dry spells, the plants will become spindly and develop poor flowers if watering is neglected for long. A mulch of well-rotted manure will be beneficial after a period of rain to maintain the soil in a moist condition. Routine liquid feeding during the summer will also help, not only in producing good plants during the season but also in ensuring that sound tubers are built up for the following year. If the plants are being grown for garden display and for cutting for the house, no disbudding or side-shooting is necessary, although this will be essential if blooms are required for showing.

Dahlias should be left in the ground until the foliage is killed by the first frosts. The plants must then be lifted with a fork, carefully to avoid spearing the tubers. The frosted stems should be cut down to about 15 cm (6 in), the roots dried, dusted with fungicide and stored.

Dahlia tubers should be planted about 15 cm (6 in) deep in mid-April, when they are still almost dormant. Insert a strong stake close to the tuber now; it will be damaged by a cane pushed in later. Allow 1 m (3¼ ft) between tall varieties, down to 45 cm (18 in) with smaller types.

Rooted cuttings should be planted in late May, when danger of frosting has passed. They, too, should be staked and lightly tied between the first and second pairs of leaves. As plants grow, add more ties, being careful not to damage the stems.

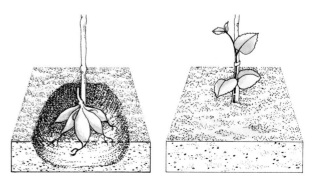

SHRUBS AND CLIMBERS

Year-round interest

for every garden

Mention autumn colour to most gardeners and they think automatically of maples. While maples and, indeed, many other trees do provide beautiful leaf colours in the autumn, so do many shrubs and some are worth growing for this reason alone. With others, it is an added bonus to another major attribute. Leaf colours will be better in some years than others. A mild autumn, with no frosts until late in the season, usually means that colours are less impressive, for the development of vivid reds and yellows is associated with death of the leaves; with the disappearance from them of green chlorophyll and the deposition of other pigments.

Acer Although almost all *Acers* are really trees, some are small and others so slow growing that in many gardens they seldom reach more than shrub size. *A. palmatum dissectum* in its several varieties is the most widely grown of these small forms and is a good species for autumn colour.

Berberis Most berberis colour well, but the numerous forms of *B. thunbergii* are perhaps the best. Many varieties, such as 'Atropurpurea Nana', 'Dart's Purple' and 'Rose Glow' have purple foliage during the summer that later turns fiery red.

Ceratostigma willmottianum The 'shrubby plumbago' is valuable for its late, clear-blue flowers and also for its foliage, which colours rich red in most years.

Cornus Many of the dwarf dogwoods are valuable, but none more so than the varieties of *C. florida*.

Cotinus Many gardeners think that the autumn colours of *C. coggygria*, the smoke bush, are unrivalled among shrubs. If its flowers cause 'smoke' in spring, its foliage certainly sets the autumn border alight.

Cotoneaster Several cotoneasters have good autumn colour, but there are few reds more vivid than that of the much maligned *C. horizontalis*.

Rhus The stag's horn sumach undoubtedly produces a dramatic effect, seen against the autumn sun, but it makes you pay for it with five months of looking like an undressed scarecrow.

Ribes Some of the flowering currants produce good autumn foliage colour; the yellows and reds of *R. americanum* are perhaps best of all.

Roses Shrub roses, too, are excellent autumn plants. After their flowers have finished, they put on a superb display of hips (if the birds allow) and complement this with some glorious leaf colours. The yellows of the many varieties of *Rosa rugosa* are probably the most appealing.

Stephanandra This is a valuable small genus of shrubs. Perhaps the most useful, not least for its autumn colour, is a vigorous, low-spreading plant, providing excellent groundcover, known as *S. incisa crispa*.

Viburnum Another valuable genus and a large one, with many excellent deciduous and evergreen species. Two deciduous viburnums seen commonly and providing good autumn colours are *V. carlesii* and *V. opulus*.

See also:
Herbaceous perennials for shade
pp 56–7
Colour from foliage pp 64–5

Shrubs for year-round interest p 80
Coral spot p 87
Trees for autumn colour p 111

What attractive shrubs will grow in a shady border?

As with herbaceous and groundcover plants, the shady border, especially the dry shady border, always presents problems with shrubs, and the choice of plants is fairly limited. The species list given here offers suggestions for at least some colour all year round; most of the plants are available in a range of varieties.

How can I rejuvenate an ancient and rather rotten wistaria?

Wistarias are, for many people, the queens of climbing shrubs. Once established and gnarled (a term from which they seem inseparable), they display a character that puts them in the same league as yews, with the advantage that wistarias actually appear old and gnarled when they are still fairly young. A 25-year-old plant can look as if it has been there since the dawn of time.

They can be something of a handful: allowed free rein, a wistaria will charge to the top of a house wall and be up the roof and over the ridge before you realize what is happening. It then becomes a menace, for its long, serpentine shoots will inveigle the slates and tiles into giving them access to your loft. From that point on, its management, as you tear metre after metre of rampant greenery from the building, makes you feel you are taking on the entire plant kingdom. And yet, this is so often the state in which people acquire wistarias; planted and bequeathed by some long-gone previous owner, they challenge you to control them.

And control them you can, for a wistaria is all but indestructible. Text books will tell you that a wistaria should be pruned twice a year, in July and December and, although not sacrosanct, these are good times to take one in hand. In summer, be fairly ruthless about cutting back all long green shoots to within 30 cm (12 in) or so of the base. It may be possible, even then, to see which of the woody branches must be removed; either because they are tangled around others, or are rotten or otherwise diseased (coral spot is common on wistaria).

Much of this framework reconstruction is better done in winter, however, for when the plant is leafless its overall shape is much easier to appreciate. Don't hesitate then to untie the branches temporarily from the wall and untangle them on the ground — they are pliable and you are unlikely to do much damage. Once the main framework is established, the long shoots that were pruned back in summer can be shortened further to two buds from the base. The overall objective is to encourage a 'tufted' structure with short shoots arising from nodes, rather than untidy, pliable, long growths. Thereafter, continue with a twice-yearly pruning, shortening shoots to six buds in July and two in December.

SHRUBS FOR A SHADY BORDER

Plant	Noteworthy features
Aucuba japonica	Variegated and female (berried) forms are best
Camellia x williamsii*	'Donation' (semi-double pink) is the hardiest and most free flowering
Daphne laureola	Fragrant yellow-green flowers early in the spring
Euonymus fortunei	Low growing; some good variegated varieties are available
Fatsia japonica	Large, glossy leaves; may be slightly tender in colder areas
Ilex altaclarensis	A large-leaved holly; many beautifully variegated forms exist
Ilex aquifolium	Common holly; numerous varieties with variously coloured leaves and berries
Lonicera nitida	A relative of honeysuckle; stands clipping and is good for low, shaded hedges
Mahonia aquifolium	Yellow flowers in early spring; tolerates dense shade
Osmanthus heterophyllus	Holly-like with scented flowers in autumn; variegated forms are best
Phillyrea decora	Hardy small shrub; fragrant white flowers in spring
Prunus laurocerasus	Cherry laurel; hardy big shrub with large, glossy leaves
Rhododendron* (some)	Enormous range of varieties; the hardy hybrids are among the best for shade
Ribes alpinum (deciduous)	Underrated small, dense shrub with pretty yellow flowers and red berries
Skimmia japonica	Choose female clones with attractive red berries
Viburnum davidii	Low growing, with large, glossy leaves; plant several to ensure that berries form

* = intolerant of limey soil

Summer-prune in late July, cutting long, whip-like growths back to six leaves from the main branches.

In December or January cut the same growths back further, to two buds on each stem.

What shrub can be recommended as a feature for all-year interest in a small garden?

'All-year interest' is a personal criterion by which to judge any plant. It could take the form of evergreen foliage; of variegated evergreen foliage (with or without conspicuous flowers); of moderate attractiveness in summer but something quite stunning in winter, when very little else has colour; of a pervading and alluring scent, or even of a particularly attractive overall shape or leaf form.

These are all important visual aspects to bear in mind, but if the plant is to be a major feature in a small garden, it is also important to choose one that is perfectly hardy in your area, for there is nothing more depressing than to establish a shrub as a crucial feature, only to have it laid low by the first really hard winter. Having once staked everything on two hebes in a small garden, I learned by bitter experience what a disaster one really sharp frost can be.

Consider, too, the rate of growth and ultimate size of the plant you have chosen. If the garden is small, then this feature plant may represent a major part of your capital investment and, although the shrub may be slow growing, it could be worth buying a fairly well-grown specimen to make an immediate impact. Regarding ultimate size, check carefully that the plant will not outgrow its allotted position; there is no firm division between a shrub and a tree, and some shrubs have an enormous spread even if their height is restricted.

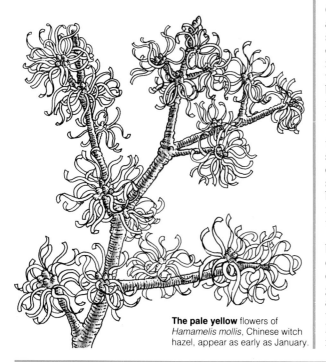

The pale yellow flowers of *Hamamelis mollis*, Chinese witch hazel, appear as early as January.

SHRUBS FOR YEAR-ROUND INTEREST

Plant	Summer features	Winter features
○ Cornus alba 'Variegata'	Grey-green leaves with a cream margin	Bright red leafless shoots
● Elaeagnus pungens 'Maculata'	Dark green, shiny leaves with a central gold blotch	As summer; scented flowers in autumn
○ Hamamelis mollis	Large, grey-green leaves (yellow in autumn)	Grey leafless twigs with vivid yellow flowers in January
● Ilex altaclarensis 'Golden King'	Glossy, dark green leaves with a gold margin	As summer, plus red berries
● Ilex altaclarensis 'Camelliifolia'	Glossy, large, dark green, camellia-like leaves	As summer, plus large red berries
● Mahonia 'Charity'	Large, glossy green leaves with soft spines	As summer, plus long sprays of yellow flowers in early winter
○ Salix fargesii	Dark green, glossy, elongated leaves	Stout, dark red, leafless shoots with red buds

● = evergreen ○ = deciduous

What climbers would be suitable for a north wall?

One of the most difficult aspects of giving gardening advice is to convince gardeners that they should plant some of their most tender plants on the north-facing side of the house. North, understandably, spells cold; but it is important to realize that it is often not the depth to which the winter temperature sinks that causes damage, but the rapidity with which frozen plant tissues thaw. A north wall is protected from rapid thawing because it receives no early morning winter sun.

Naturally, this must be balanced by any requirement that a particular plant may have for sun later in the season; there is little point planting a somewhat tender climber against a north wall, solely to enable it to survive, if it will never flower. As a corollary, it should be said that some plants produce better flower *colour* in a north-facing situation because they are protected from the bleaching action of the sunlight.

There are only two good flowering climbers that can be widely recommended for north walls. The deciduous, climbing hydrangea, *Hydrangea petiolaris*, is a self-clinging climber, with large green leaves and large clusters of greenish-white flowers in June. It is a vigorous plant, attractive enough when in flower but rather dismal in winter, when it is reminiscent of a tangle of old rope. Much more dramatic in flower, but equally nondescript in winter, are the large-flowered hybrid clematis, which

See also:
Difficult sites pp 20–1
Herbaceous perennials for shady
 sites pp 56–7
Herbaceous clematis p 59
Shrubs to grow in shade p 79

? Are there any evergreen climbers that also have attractive flowers?

Not many! At least, not many that are hardy, although there are several quite delectable plants suitable for mild areas or for the frost-free conservatory or cool greenhouse. One of the best of the hardy plants is unfortunately rarely seen, even in specialist nurseries. This is a relative of the hydrangeas, *Decumaria sinensis*, which has gloriously perfumed green and white flowers in the spring.

Holboellia coriacea is hardy but needs sun to flower, when it produces rather pretty little green, white and purple blooms in spring. *Trachelospermum jasminoides*, the star jasmine, is a personal favourite, requiring a modicum of shelter but rewarding with its richly scented, white flowers in late summer. Some of the evergreen honeysuckles have attractive flowers — *Lonicera japonica* is probably the best known, and *Pileostegia viburnoides* is a hardy but slow-growing self-clinging climber, with creamy-white flowers in late summer.

There are, too, a few more or less evergreen members of groups that are usually thought of as deciduous; *Rubus henryi* is an evergreen bramble with pink summer flowers, and the banana-scented, white-flowered climbing rose, *Rosa longicuspis*, is evergreen in most years.

Star jasmine
Trachelospermum jasminoides

Rosa longicuspis

always produce their best colour when facing north. There are many varieties; 'Nellie Moser' is perhaps the best known, but 'Dr Ruppel' is a newer and highly attractive form with pink stripes.

If the absence of attractive flowers is of no concern, the various species of *Parthenocissus* thrive when facing north and more than make up for the lack of bloom with their autumn colours. *P. quinquefolia* is the Virginia creeper, although that name is often applied incorrectly to *P. tricuspidata*, Boston ivy. Both are self-clinging, as is the even more beautiful *P. henryana*. But if you have a wall with old bricks and mortar and are concerned about damage that might result from a self-clinging plant, try *P. inserta*, which has many of the features of its relatives but needs a wire support, since it climbs by means of tendrils.

Although I would never recommend ivy for old walls, it is perfectly safe on sound, modern bricks and mortar, and there are now dozens of attractively leafed forms. 'Buttercup' and 'Goldheart' are aptly named; 'Cristata' has twisted, crinkly leaves, 'Glacier' silvery-grey leaves with a white margin; and there are many more. If a young ivy plant refuses to climb (as 'Goldheart' in particular is prone to do), don't try to force it by pinning it to the wall. Allow it to form a clump at the base of the wall for the first year or two; it will then usually take off of its own volition.

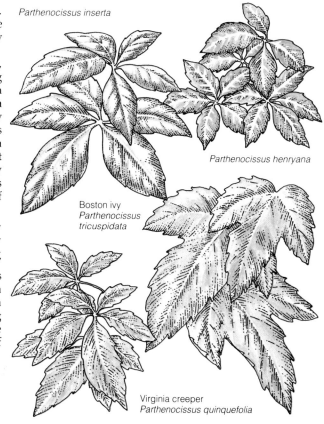

Parthenocissus inserta

Parthenocissus henryana

Boston ivy
Parthenocissus tricuspidata

Virginia creeper
Parthenocissus quinquefolia

What conditions do dwarf conifers need and what varieties can be recommended?

There has been a phenomenal growth of interest in dwarf conifers in the past few decades, and nurseries specializing in these plants may now offer more than a thousand different varieties. It is not easy, from such a bewildering selection, to choose the best for your garden, and choice is made even more difficult by the names of the plants, which seem to increase in inverse proportion to the size of the plant itself.

Dwarf conifers do not, however, present any problem in respect of growing conditions, for there are varieties tolerant of a wide range of soils and situations. Although most prefer a well-drained, peaty soil, they will grow perfectly satisfactorily in all except the most alkaline conditions; and even there, with the aid of sequestrene, many will survive. Most also prefer a sunny situation, but they may be browned by exposure to cold wind. Many dwarf conifers thrive in pots and tubs, where a John Innes No 3 potting compost suits them ideally. A thick mulch of pulverized bark helps to retain moisture, for drying-out of the roots can be a problem when plants are grown in this way.

It is not easy to provide a short list of recommended varieties, mainly because most nurseries and garden centres stock only a small range of the many available. The plants given in the table should all be fairly easily obtained, but a visit to a specialist supplier will reveal the real potential offered by dwarf conifers.

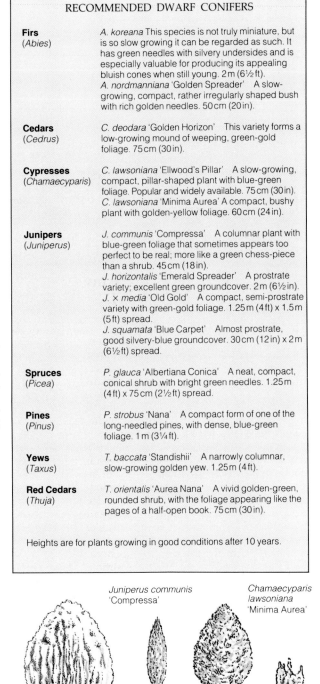

RECOMMENDED DWARF CONIFERS

Firs (*Abies*)	*A. koreana* This species is not truly miniature, but is so slow growing it can be regarded as such. It has green needles with silvery undersides and is especially valuable for producing its appealing bluish cones when still young. 2 m (6½ ft). *A. nordmanniana* 'Golden Spreader' A slow-growing, compact, rather irregularly shaped bush with rich golden needles. 50 cm (20 in).
Cedars (*Cedrus*)	*C. deodara* 'Golden Horizon' This variety forms a low-growing mound of weeping, green-gold foliage. 75 cm (30 in).
Cypresses (*Chamaecyparis*)	*C. lawsoniana* 'Ellwood's Pillar' A slow-growing, compact, pillar-shaped plant with blue-green foliage. Popular and widely available. 75 cm (30 in). *C. lawsoniana* 'Minima Aurea' A compact, bushy plant with golden-yellow foliage. 60 cm (24 in).
Junipers (*Juniperus*)	*J. communis* 'Compressa' A columnar plant with blue-green foliage that sometimes appears too perfect to be real; more like a green chess-piece than a shrub. 45 cm (18 in). *J. horizontalis* 'Emerald Spreader' A prostrate variety; excellent green groundcover. 2 m (6½ in). *J. × media* 'Old Gold' A compact, semi-prostrate variety with green-gold foliage. 1.25 m (4 ft) x 1.5 m (5 ft) spread. *J. squamata* 'Blue Carpet' Almost prostrate, good silvery-blue groundcover. 30 cm (12 in) x 2 m (6½ ft) spread.
Spruces (*Picea*)	*P. glauca* 'Albertiana Conica' A neat, compact, conical shrub with bright green needles. 1.25 m (4 ft) x 75 cm (2½ ft) spread.
Pines (*Pinus*)	*P. strobus* 'Nana' A compact form of one of the long-needled pines, with dense, blue-green foliage. 1 m (3¼ ft).
Yews (*Taxus*)	*T. baccata* 'Standishii' A narrowly columnar, slow-growing golden yew. 1.25 m (4 ft).
Red Cedars (*Thuja*)	*T. orientalis* 'Aurea Nana' A vivid golden-green, rounded shrub, with the foliage appearing like the pages of a half-open book. 75 cm (30 in).

Heights are for plants growing in good conditions after 10 years.

Cedrus deodara 'Golden Horizon'

Picea glauca 'Albertiana Conica'

Abies koreana

Juniperus communis 'Compressa'

Chamaecyparis lawsoniana 'Minima Aurea'

Thuja orientalis 'Aurea Nana'

Taxus baccata 'Standishii'

Pinus strobus 'Nana'

See also:
Use of sequestrene p 12
Dwarf hedges p 116

Honey fungus makes its presence known by the appearance of black bootlace strands of fungus in the soil and toadstools around the base of the affected tree. If loose bark is stripped away, flattened strands of fungal growth can be seen.

How can I prevent honey fungus appearing in my garden and how control it?

Perhaps more than any other garden disease, the thought of honey fungus sends panic through the gardening fraternity. To some extent, this is justified, for the disease affects a wider range of plants (certainly of woody plants) than almost any other. It is often a killer of the established trees and shrubs that form the framework of a garden, and it is exceedingly difficult to combat satisfactorily.

Few gardens, however, are actually devastated by the disease, and it is usually only a problem in gardens that have once been woodland or an old orchard, or have a similar long history of containing deciduous trees. For it is through the stumps of such trees that the fungus usually gains a foothold in the soil, spreading to healthy trees nearby by means of dark strands, like bootlaces.

Indeed, the presence of these strands in the soil, close to the trunk, is one of the signs that honey fungus may be responsible for the demise of a particular tree. There are other clues: tawny-coloured toadstools, up to 15cm (6in) high, with a somewhat scaly cap as much as 15cm (6in) in diameter and with a ring on the stem, may appear in the late summer and autumn close to the base of the trunk. There may also be sheets of white fungal growth, with more, but flattened, bootlace strands, beneath the loose bark.

If a tree or shrub appears to be dying or to have been killed by honey fungus attack, the entire stump should be uprooted and disposed of, preferably by burning, together with as much of the root system as possible. As large a hole as practicable must then be excavated, and the soil dumped in a part of the garden well away from other trees and shrubs.

Usually, the easiest way to do this is to dig a second hole in, say, the vegetable garden, and swap the soil between the two sites. The hole and surrounding area at the infested site may be drenched with a proprietary control solution, which may have some effect in killing the bootlace strands in the soil, although it is most unlikely to cure an already diseased tree. The affected site should not be replanted for at least one year and preferably two.

If honey fungus is known to be present in a neighbour's garden, the prospect of it marching under the fence to affect your plants can be extremely distressing. It is possible, in these cicumstances, to install a physical barrier to the bootlace strands. Dig a vertical slit trench, 1m (3¼ft) deep and as narrow as practical, close to the garden boundary, and in it bury vertically heavy-gauge plastic sheet. But be sure to use a continuous sheet and not to economise with old plastic bags. Allow a few centimetres of the plastic to protrude above the surface of the soil and be careful not to slice through it when hoeing or digging. A similar slit trench, dug in a circle around a stump known to be diseased, is sometimes effective in preventing further spread of honey fungus in a newly infested garden.

Once honey fungus is present, even if diseased stumps can be removed, any major new plantings should be with the more resistant tree and shrub species and never with those known to be highly susceptible.

Highly susceptible Apple, birch, cedar, cypress, lilac, pine, privet, walnut and willow.

Moderately resistant Ash, beech, box, clematis, Douglas fir, elaeagnus, hawthorn, holly, ivy, larch, laurel, lime, mahonia, robinia, silver fir, sumach, tamarisk, tree of heaven (*Ailanthus*) and yew.

Is it possible to move a mature shrub without harming it?

Yes, but with certain provisos. A mature large shrub will present more of a problem than a mature small one, while the ease with which any big plant is moved is influenced by the position in which it is growing, by the soil type and by the proximity of other plants (trees and shrubs especially). The species of plant is also of importance, for deep-rooted shrubs will present more difficulties than shallow-rooted ones, and evergreens more problems than deciduous types.

Certain general rules apply: perform the operation with the minimum of root disturbance; move the plant with as much soil as possible still adhering; prevent the roots from drying out; and move the plant at a time of year when it will suffer the least interruption to its growth. A deciduous plant may, therefore, be moved any time during its dormant, leafless period unless the ground is likely to be frozen — October or March are normally safe.

Evergreens present an additional complication because they retain their leaves throughout the winter and will thus continue to lose water through them at a time when the roots may be unable to replenish it. For this reason, I believe that moving evergreens in March or April, before the new season's growth has started, is the best plan.

Well in advance of the moving operation, water the plant and the surrounding soil thoroughly. The intention when digging up the plant will be to 'root-ball' it, and for this a supply of hessian sacking, plastic bags, or, if the shrub is a really large one, chicken wire, will be needed. Moving any other than fairly small shrubs is a two-person exercise and so an extra pair of helping hands should be ready.

Before making a start on the plant itself, ensure that the hole to receive it is well prepared, watered and liberally dosed with bonemeal. Then dig around, but well away from the plant; the distance will vary with the size of root system, but with a large shrub, a hole about 1 m (3¼ ft) in diameter must be planned for. The sacking, bags, or wire netting should gradually be eased underneath to form a large bag-like structure, tied at the top and holding soil and roots together.

Over a short distance, the shrub can be dragged, but for more than a few metres it must be lifted; but don't underestimate the weight! Even more pairs of hands may be needed at this stage. Once the plant is in position, any sacking or plastic bags should be cut away, although with a large root system encased in wire netting, the netting beneath may safely be left in place — new roots will grow through, and trying to remove it may well cause considerable damage.

If a stake is needed, it should be firmly driven in at this stage, while you can see exactly where it is going. Firm-in thoroughly, water thoroughly (and continue to do so until the plant is well established), and ensure that you have not left a hollow in the soil at the base of the stem where water might accumulate.

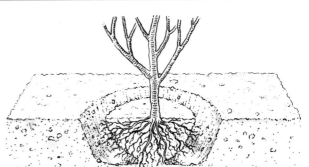

When moving a shrub, the objective is to leave a ball of soil around the roots. So, some time ahead, water the plant and the surrounding earth thoroughly. Dig well away from the plant; the size of the hole depends on the size of the shrub's root system.

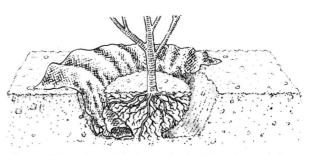

Ease sacking, a sheet of plastic or, with a large shrub, chicken wire into the hole and underneath the shrub. Keep the root-ball intact as far as you possibly can.

Gather up the sacking or plastic, tie it firmly around the stem of the shrub, and carefully lift it out of the hole. This is a job for two people if you are not to damage the plant.

Drag the root-balled shrub on a sheet of plastic to its new position if this is nearby. Otherwise lift the shrub or move it to its new hole on a wheelbarrow; cut away any sacking or plastic.

See also:
Pruning wistaria p 79
Transplanting trees pp 108, 109
Grapevines p 137

? When should I prune garden shrubs?

Books, big books, have been written on the subject of pruning, and they give detailed instructions for the whole range of common garden ornamentals. I do not intend to duplicate that advice, but I shall give some of the guiding principles behind pruning that should enable you to make judgements about particular species.

First, don't assume that a shrub must be pruned simply because it is there. Pruning is not an operation foisted on gardeners as some form of penance; it is carried out to improve the growth of certain types of plant, which it does in several ways. Pruning may remove dead or diseased wood and it may remove branches and shoots that have become so tangled together as to restrict the penetration of light and air into the plant. It may also remove dead flowering shoots, either to prevent them from becoming diseased or simply to improve the appearance of the plant. And it may, by removing some growth, stimulate the production of new leafy or flowering shoots to enhance the form or attractiveness of the plant as a whole.

So when should pruning be carried out? The best guide to the time of pruning is the time of flowering. Some shrubs flower on wood produced in the previous year and tend to bloom early in the season, before the current year's shoots have developed. These may be pruned as soon as the flowers fade. Shrubs that flower on wood of the current year may be pruned between late autumn and the end of February, the later the better. If you follow this rule of thumb, you are unlikely to do much harm and are unlikely to prune away all the next crop of flower buds.

Relatively few shrubs of the first type require a great deal of regular pruning, apart perhaps from the removal of old flower trusses and a little shaping. Some of the latter group require more severe and regular treatment to give of their best, but don't prune hard unless you have checked that this is appropriate. Amorpha, *Buddleia davidii* (not other buddleias), *Hypericum calycinum*, Indigofera, Lespedeza, and *Rhus typhina* (when grown solely for foliage) are among the few shrubs needing hard pruning to within a few buds of the base in February.

Comments on pruning certain other plants are made elsewhere, but a word should be added about clematis, for their treatment often causes confusion. Clematis can be divided into three groups on the basis of the pruning system to be adopted. The first group comprises the early-flowering species *alpina*, *macropetala* and their varieties, and *montana* and its varieties. Prune these immediately after flowering simply to remove dead shoots and to keep the plant within its allotted space.

The second group comprises the early, large-flowered varieties, such as 'Dr Ruppel', 'Nellie Moser', 'Elsa Spaeth', 'Étoile de Paris', 'Mrs Cholmondeley', 'Niobe' and 'The President', together with the Jackmanii group and the mid-season large-flowered varieties such as 'Beauty of Richmond', 'Duchess of Sutherland', 'Marie Boisselot' (also known as 'Madame le Coultre') and 'W.E. Gladstone'. These should have dead or feeble shoots cut out in February or March and other shoots cut back to a pair of strong buds.

The final group of clematis includes the *viticella* varieties and all the late-flowering species, such as *campaniflora*, *flammula*, *orientalis*, *rehderiana*, *tangutica*, and *texensis*. These should also be pruned in February or March, but much harder, with all the previous season's growth cut back to a strong pair of buds just above the base. Although this sounds complicated, it will be seen, in fact, to follow the guidelines relating pruning to flowering time, with the same proviso that some plants need a hard February pruning and some do not.

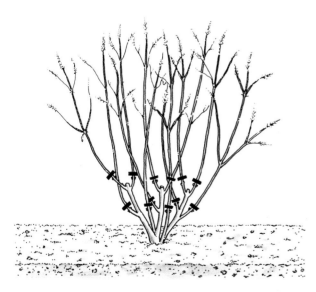

Deciduous shrubs, such as *Buddleia davidii*, that flower on the current year's wood must be pruned back almost to the base in February to ensure they bloom well. Prune shrubs that bloom on the previous year's growth as soon as the flowers fade.

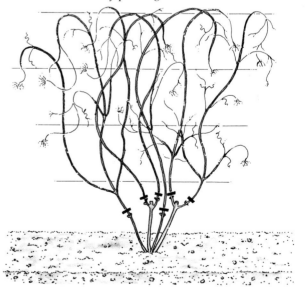

Prune late-flowering clematis to the lowest pair of strong buds on the previous season's growth in February, *above*. At the same time, merely cut out dead or feeble shoots on early and mid-season bloomers.

Why do some of the branches on my red rhododendron have purple flowers?

This situation is a common one, not only with rhododendrons that produce purple flowers but with other trees and shrubs also that bear flowers or even leaves different from those expected. Strangely, when this happens with roses, no one is surprised, for they realize that roses are budded or grafted on a rootstock of one of the wild rose species and that these basal suckers must be cut out.

Precisely the same phenomenon is responsible for the purple rhododendron flowers, for many varieties of rhododendron are grafted on rootstocks of the familiar, semi-wild species, *Rhododendron ponticum*, and from time to time a shoot of this will make its appearance on a variety. As with a rose sucker, this shoot should be taken out, although with rhododendrons it is better pulled away from the base than cut off. With other types of tree and shrub too, these suckers, or basal shoots, must be cut out.

The reason so many trees and shrubs are grafted is because the named variety (especially if it is a hybrid) may not grow as vigorously on its roots as a wild species does. Equally important from a commercial standpoint is that by grafting shoots of a variety on already rooted plants of a commonly available, fast-growing and inexpensive variety, a nurseryman can have a large number of plants more quickly than if he had to wait until they grew to comparable size on their own roots.

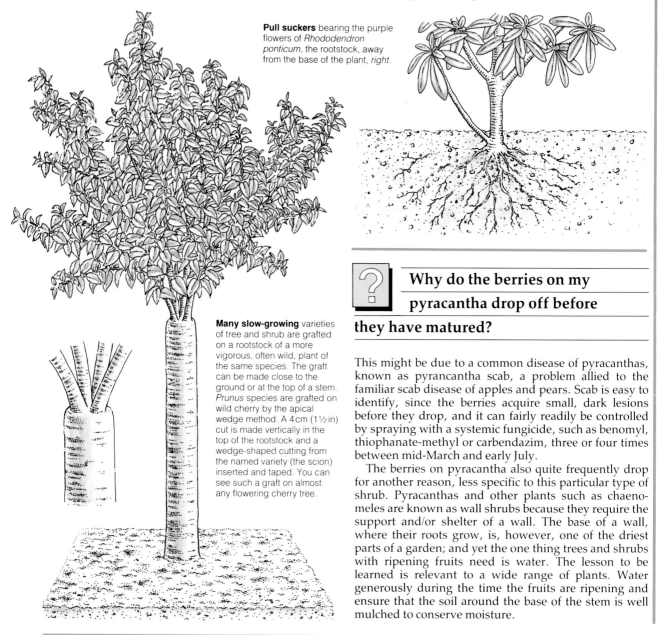

Pull suckers bearing the purple flowers of *Rhododendron ponticum*, the rootstock, away from the base of the plant, *right*.

Many slow-growing varieties of tree and shrub are grafted on a rootstock of a more vigorous, often wild, plant of the same species. The graft can be made close to the ground or at the top of a stem. *Prunus* species are grafted on wild cherry by the apical wedge method. A 4 cm (1½ in) cut is made vertically in the top of the rootstock and a wedge-shaped cutting from the named variety (the scion) inserted and taped. You can see such a graft on almost any flowering cherry tree.

Why do the berries on my pyracantha drop off before they have matured?

This might be due to a common disease of pyracanthas, known as pyracantha scab, a problem allied to the familiar scab disease of apples and pears. Scab is easy to identify, since the berries acquire small, dark lesions before they drop, and it can fairly readily be controlled by spraying with a systemic fungicide, such as benomyl, thiophanate-methyl or carbendazim, three or four times between mid-March and early July.

The berries on pyracantha also quite frequently drop for another reason, less specific to this particular type of shrub. Pyracanthas and other plants such as chaenomeles are known as wall shrubs because they require the support and/or shelter of a wall. The base of a wall, where their roots grow, is, however, one of the driest parts of a garden; and yet the one thing trees and shrubs with ripening fruits need is water. The lesson to be learned is relevant to a wide range of plants. Water generously during the time the fruits are ripening and ensure that the soil around the base of the stem is well mulched to conserve moisture.

See also:
Using heathers for groundcover
p 26
Pansy sickness p 52
Rose sickness p 91

Budding roses p 92
Suckers on roses p 94
Scab on apple trees p 134
Tomato wilt pp 146—47

Every time I plant clematis, they grow for a couple of years, then die. Why?

This is a distressing and all-too-common state of affairs. You have done everything correctly: the plants have been carefully planted in a fairly alkaline soil, they have had their roots shaded and have begun to establish satisfactorily when, without warning, the shoots die back. The problem is known as clematis wilt, and despite a good deal of study, no one is sure what causes it. It seems that some fungal infection may be partly responsible, but clearly this is not the whole story. What should be done, therefore?

You must certainly not uproot the plant and immediately put another in the same spot, for it is likely to suffer the same fate. My advice would be to give the existing plant a second chance. Cut it back to a good pair of buds or shoots close to ground level and drench the soil around thoroughly with a spray-strength mix of the fungicide thiophanate-methyl.

Give the plant a boost of nitrogen and phosphate (a generous dose of bonemeal raked into the soil will provide plenty of the latter and some of the former) and then wait and see. If the treatment has no effect, try with a new plant but dig a generous hole, about 60 cm (24 in) in both diameter and depth, and replace the soil with fresh earth from a part of the garden well away from any other clematis.

Can low-growing shrubs be used to suppress weed growth?

Weed control is a constant problem in gardens, and anything that can be done to make the task easier is to be encouraged. Mulching is both effective and fairly inexpensive, but in some situations plants themselves can be put to work. The basic requirements for an efficient weed-suppressing plant are that it should compete with the weeds for nutrients, moisture and light, especially light.

The groundcover plant need not, therefore, be prostrate, and many of the best, such as some of the spreading junipers, work more on the umbrella principle of casting shade than on smothering. Others in this category include several species of cotoneaster, some of the brooms, such as *Cytisus kewensis*, and the hypericums.

Of more smothering habit are the low-growing roses, such as *Rosa nitida*; the prostrate bramble, *Rubus tricolor*; heathers; *Pachysandra terminalis* and the extremely useful vincas. But be careful that plants used for weed smothering are not grown where they can themselves become a menace by invading beds and borders.

Weeds are suppressed by shading by *Juniperus horizontalis* 'Emerald Spreader', *right*, and by smothering by the creeping *Pachysandra terminalis, below*.

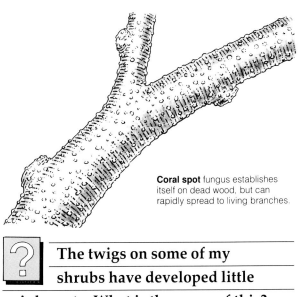

Coral spot fungus establishes itself on dead wood, but can rapidly spread to living branches.

The twigs on some of my shrubs have developed little pink spots. What is the cause of this?

The cause is one of the prettiest and one of the most underrated of garden diseases — coral spot. It affects many species of woody plant, although it is rare on conifers. One reason why coral spot is so commonly ignored is that gardeners normally see it growing on dead woody material (prunings and old pea sticks, for instance) and fail to realize it can attack living tissue also.

The coral spot fungus is of the type known technically as a weak parasite — it must first establish itself on dead wood but will spread from there to living parts of the same branch or twig. Thus, stubs of branches left after careless pruning are especially vulnerable as entry points for the infection of the remainder of the plant. The answer is to take great care when pruning and not to leave old woody material lying around.

Once the disease is present on a living tree or shrub, the affected parts must be cut out by pruning well back into the healthy tissue, and the plant sprayed with thiophanate-methyl, repeating the treatment after two weeks. Burn the diseased wood.

ROSES

Cultivating the garden favourites

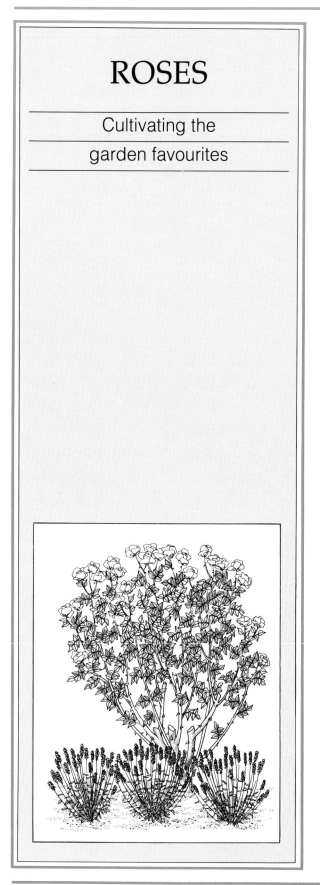

Rose terminology confuses me: can you please explain it?

The names used in rose catalogues can be confusing. There are so many different categories of rose, some of the category names have been changed recently, and, too, the names that describe the form of the plant can apply to more than one category. I shall first describe the various forms in which the rose plant exists or that it can be trained to take and then introduce the categories that will be encountered most frequently.

The origin of some of the Old Roses is obscure and they may be found in different categories in different catalogues. There are also several popular roses that do not fit into any of the main groupings, as well as many species roses that have altered little from the wild state.

FORMS OF ROSES

Shrubs A Shrub Rose can be of almost any size, but the name is generally used to describe a plant that retains its size and shape without extensive pruning.

Bush A Bush Rose when in flower may be of the same size and form as a shrub, but without annual pruning it will lose both its shape and its flowering efficiency. Most modern roses must be grown as bushes.

Standard This is a rose budded on the top of a bare stem, varying from 1.5m (5ft) to 75cm (30in) in length, so that the flowering head is raised. A weeping standard is usually a rambler variety budded on about 1.5m (5ft) of stem so that its flowers cascade down.

Miniature This could be called a very small shrub or a very small bush (the amount of pruning needed falls between the two). A Miniature is both a form and a type category, for only certain varieties may be grown this way; most derive from *Rosa roulettii*, probably the same as the old climbing China Rose 'Pompon de Paris'.

Climbers and Ramblers These roses produce long, pliable shoots requiring support to grow satisfactorily. In the wild, this is usually another plant, but in the garden, they are trained up trellises, walls or other frameworks.

TYPES OF ROSE

OLD ROSES (sometimes called 'Old-fashioned' Roses). These are the rose varieties that were grown extensively until early this century, when they gradually gave way to the Modern Roses. Most are of the Shrub Rose type, usually with a fairly short flowering season, but many of the categories include some climbing varieties.

Alba Roses These very old roses are early flowering, scented, disease resistant and extremely hardy. Recommended varieties: 'Alba Maxima', 'Félicité Parmentier' and 'Great Maiden's Blush'.

Bourbon Roses Nineteenth-century, repeat-flowering plants. Most are shrubs but there are a few excellent climbers. Recommended varieties: 'Commandant Beaurepaire', 'Honorine de Brabant', 'Mme Isaac Pereire' (shrub or climber), 'Souvenir de la Malmaison', and 'Zéphirine Drouhin' (climber).

Centifolia Roses These are very old, often extremely prickly, loose-growing shrubs, with large, scented and usually double flowers. Recommended varieties: 'Alfred Dalmas', 'Old Pink Moss' and 'William Lobb'.

See also:
Species tulips p 88
Distinction between Climbers and
Ramblers p 90

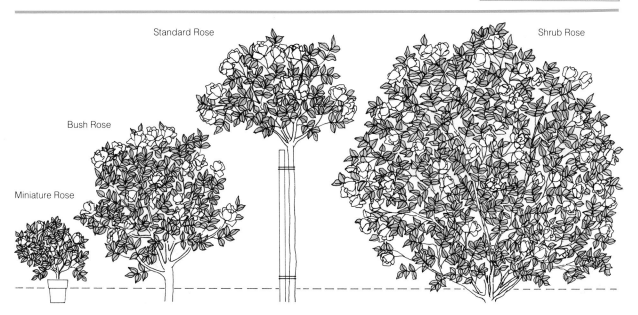

Standard Rose

Shrub Rose

Bush Rose

Miniature Rose

China Roses Mid-nineteenth-century roses with a long flowering season. Most are fairly small shrubs, but there are some good climbers. Recommended varieties: 'Cécile Brunner', 'Perle d'Or' and 'Pompon de Paris'.

Damask Roses These date from the sixteenth century, possibly earlier and are scented, summer- or repeat-flowering shrubs. Recommended varieties: 'Mme Hardy', 'The Portland Rose' and 'York and Lancaster'.

Gallica Roses Probably the oldest of all garden roses, these are often scented and often thornless shrubs. Recommended varieties: 'Belle de Crécy', 'Empress Joséphine' and 'Jenny Duval'.

Hybrid Musk Roses Disease-free, free-flowering, usually scented shrubs, with flowers in large clusters, they are rather reminiscent of Floribunda Roses; early twentieth century. The original musk was a vigorous climber, cultivated in the Middle Ages. Recommended varieties: 'Buff Beauty', 'Felicia' and 'Vanity'.

Hybrid Perpetual Roses These repeat-flowering shrubs are usually scented; they were popular in Victorian times. Recommended varieties: 'Ferdinand Pichard', 'Frau Karl Druschki' and 'Reine des Violettes'.

Moss Roses A sub-group of Centifolia Shrub Roses, with a highly individual, mossy appearance to the buds and stems. Moss Roses, too, were popular in Victorian times. Recommended varieties: 'Fantin Latour', 'Robert le Diable' and 'Petite de Hollande'.

Noisette Roses These are fairly vigorous climbers but usually not hardy. Recommended varieties: 'Gloire de Dijon', 'Jaune Desprez' and 'Mme Alfred Carrière'.

Polyantha Pompons A dwarf type of recurrent-flowering Shrub Rose that produces a mass of pompon flowers in clusters on short stems. The newer varieties are hardier than the old. Recommended varieties: 'Baby Albéric', 'Lady Ann Kidwell' and 'Mrs Joseph Hiess'.

Rugosa Roses Exceptionally thorny, disease-resistant, highly scented shrubs. Rugosa Roses have large flowers, large hips and good autumn foliage. Recommended varieties: 'Blanc Double de Coubert', 'Frau Dagmar Hastrup' and 'Roseraie de l'Häy'.

Spinosissima (Scotch) Roses Popular in Victorian times, they are usually extremely thorny and have ferny leaves; summer flowering. Recommended varieties: 'Burnet Double White' and 'William III'.

Sweet Briar Roses Vigorous shrubs with scented foliage. Recommended varieties: 'La Belle Distinguée' and 'Lord Penzance'.

Tea Roses Often slightly tender, these roses are similar to the China Roses, with (supposedly) a scent reminiscent of tea chests. Recommended varieties: 'Duchesse de Brabant', 'Homère' and 'Lady Plymouth'.

Wichuraiana Roses These are typical Rambler Roses, usually flowering once only, in early summer, and needing a great deal of pruning attention; they are often prone to mildew. Recommended varieties: 'Albéric Barbier', 'Albertine' and 'Dorothy Perkins'.

MODERN ROSES have been developed in this century. This is a loose term, but relates especially to those Shrub Roses bred in this century. Most are fairly tall growing and flower almost continuously. Recommended varieties: 'Aloha', 'Golden Wings' and 'Nymphenburg'. The Frühlings' series of hybrid Spinosissima Roses are summer-flowering modern shrubs.

Hybrid Tea Roses (now known as Large-flowered Roses). These originated late in the nineteenth century from crossing Hybrid Perpetuals with Tea Roses, and now number thousands of varieties. They are generally fairly small bushes rather than shrubs and require careful annual pruning. With so many, even a personal selection of dozens would be of little value, but there are three beautiful roses of Hybrid Tea type that should be more widely grown: 'Golden Melody', 'Mrs Herbert Stevens' (climber) and 'White Wings'.

Floribunda Roses (now known as Cluster-flowered Roses) These were derived early this century by crossing Hybrid Teas with a type known as Hybrid Polyanthas to produce a group bearing its flowers in clusters, with many blooms open at the same time and with a long flowering season. Like Hybrid Teas, they need careful pruning, but are neat and colourful all summer. Their biggest drawback is that many are almost scentless but three Floribundas do cling to their ancestral perfume: 'Arthur Bell', 'Orange Sensation' and 'Iceberg'.

What is the difference between a climbing and a rambling rose?

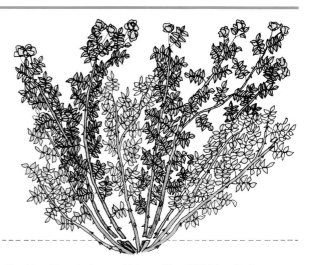

Despite what is popularly imagined (and, indeed, written in some gardening books), the distinction between climbing and rambling roses is not a rigid one. As its name suggests, the typical Rambler has long, pliable shoots and a vigour that enables it to grow in a spreading and almost smothering fashion. Most Ramblers derive these attributes from the Japanese species known as *Rosa wichuraiana*.

There is no such plant as a typical Climber, for the group includes roses ranging from the climbing sports of Hybrid Teas (Large-flowered Roses), such as 'Josephine Bruce' and 'Mme Caroline Testout', through old Bourbon Roses, such as 'Zéphirine Drouhin', to species or near-species, such as the incredibly vigorous *Rosa filipes* 'Kiftsgate'.

The most significant difference lies with the pruning, for almost all Ramblers, like their ancestor *Rosa wichuraiana*, flower only on the previous season's growth. Thus, once a shoot has borne flowers, it is of no further use and, like a raspberry cane after fruiting, should be removed. This is not true of most climbing roses and, although it is impossible to give hard and fast rules for such a diverse group, there are three factors to bear in mind. Old or diseased wood should be removed, overcrowded shoots thinned out and the bush cut back to maintain it in a manageable size and shape. For the really vigorous species and near-species Climbers that may be growing over an old building or through a tree, pruning of any sort is scarcely practicable or necessary.

Apart from the constant attention to pruning, a further factor precludes Ramblers, as a group, being as valuable in a garden as Climbers: most Ramblers have one flush of summer flowers and no more. While this is true of many Climbers also, especially the species roses, there are several recurrent-flowering and continuous-flowering Climbers that will give colour right through the season. The following is a small selection in a range of colours.

Ramblers bloom in June and July on long shoots produced the previous year. These shoots should be pruned back to about 30 cm (12 in) from the base soon after flowering, and the new shoots tied in horizontally.

'Albéric Barbier' (Rambler)

'Mermaid' (Old Climber)

CLIMBERS FOR ALL-SEASON COLOUR

Modern Climbers

'Bantry Bay'	deep salmon-pink
'Coral Dawn'	coral pink
'Danse du Feu'	vivid red
'Golden Showers'	yellow-cream
'Mrs Herbert Stevens'	white (scented)
'Pink Perpétue'	deep pink (scented)
'Schoolgirl'	copper-orange

Old Climbers

'Adam'	peach-pink (double; scented)
'Gloire de Dijon'	orange-buff (full; scented)
'Guinée'	very dark red (full; scented)
'Mermaid'	yellow (single)
'Paul's Perpetual White'	white (single; scented)
'Rêve d'Or'	yellow-buff (double; scented)
'Souvenir de la Malmaison'	white-pink (full; scented)

See also:
Pansy sickness p 52
Clematis wilt p 87
Apical dominance in roses p 96
Nutrients and crop rotation p 118–19

What roses can be used to make a hedge?

Although our native wild species of rose are almost entirely hedgerow plants, the idea of a planted rose hedge still strikes many gardeners as a peculiar notion. But some varieties do make excellent hedging subjects, requiring the minimum of attention. They grow to almost any height you choose, depending on the variety, and provide an almost impenetrable barrier to people and animals — with the bonus of attractive flowers.

Although a few modern varieties make good hedges, most of the better roses are old varieties or species; all are best planted about 1m (3¼ft) apart. The following are specially recommended:

'Blanc Double de Coubert'   'Meg Merilees'
'Nevada'   The 'Frühlings' series
'Lady Penzance'   'Great Maiden's Blush'
'Reine des Violettes'   *Rosa rubrifolia*
'Frau Dagmar Hastrup'

Is it true that new roses should not be planted in an old rose bed?

In general, yes. The reason is the likely presence in the soil of an organism that causes rose replant disease, or rose sickness. A comparable problem sometimes affects fruit trees and pansies. The symptom is a failure of the plants to establish themselves satisfactorily in the first season and gradually to decline in vigour thereafter. The reason is not fully understood, but it is certainly more complex than the exhaustion of nutrients that lies behind the general gardening practice of crop rotation.

It seems that some soil-inhabiting disease organism affects the roots of newly planted roses before they have had a chance to develop properly, while old roses, with new roots constantly being produced and able to tap fresh, uncontaminated parts of the soil, are perfectly satisfactory.

There are two ways around the problem. Either rest the bed from roses for two or three years to give the organisms time to die out (they seem to be specific to roses and will not survive on other plants), or replace some of the soil. For each new rose, dig a hole about 45cm (18in) deep and of a similar diameter and refill it with fresh soil from a part of the garden that has not previously grown roses.

Which roses can be particularly recommended for their perfume?

Although there seems to be little variation in people's ability to discern whether or not a rose is scented, some roses appear to develop a fuller perfume when grown in certain soils and possibly with certain fertilizer treatments. It is also true that some categories of rose are inherently more scented than others — many of the categories of Old Shrub Roses have a stronger, heavier and sweeter perfume than most modern varieties.

No two gardeners will agree on a short list of the best scented varieties and, from the thousands available, any short list can soon become a long one. I have, therefore, restricted my recommendations to five fairly easily obtained varieties in each of the main categories.

ROSES TO GROW FOR THEIR PERFUME

Old Shrub Roses

'James Mitchell'	bright carmine
'Koenigen von Dänemark'	pink
'Mme Isaac Pereire'	deep pink
'Odorata'	cream-white, flushed with pink
'Roseraie de l'Häy'	bright purple

Hybrid Teas (Large-flowered Roses)

'Ena Harkness'	bright crimson-scarlet
'Fragrant Cloud'	rich coral-red
'Golden Melody'	chamois yellow
'Josephine Bruce'	very dark red
'Prima Ballerina'	deep pink

Floribundas (Cluster-flowered Roses)

'Arthur Bell'	golden yellow
'Elizabeth of Glamis'	orange-pink
'Michelle'	salmon-pink
'Orange Sensation'	bright vermilion
'Pineapple Poll'	orange, flushed red

Ramblers

'Félicité et Perpétue'	white
'Goldfinch'	deep yellow bud, fading to cream
'Mme Alice Garnier'	light pink with a yellow centre
'Sander's White'	white
'Wedding Day'	pale creamy-yellow, turns white

Old Climbers

'Ard's Rover'	deep crimson
'Dr Van Fleet'	pale silvery pink
'Gloire de Dijon'	apricot and pink
'Kiftsgate'	white
'Lady Hillingdon'	deep yellow

Modern Climbers

'Bettina'	orange and pink
'Ena Harkness'	bright crimson-scarlet
'Josephine Bruce'	very dark red
'Pink Perpétue'	deep rose-pink
'Sterling Silver'	lilac

Is it possible to take cuttings from roses?

Yes — although this answer surprises many gardeners who expect roses to be budded on a rootstock. Rose varieties are grown on roots other than their own because the rootstock may be more vigorous and the plant will more rapidly reach flowering size. A further important consideration is that it is a bud, rather than a shoot (or, to give it its correct name, a scion), which is inserted into the tissues of the rootstock plant. There are a great many buds on a single rose plant, so a commercial grower can produce tens, if not hundreds, of new plants from one stock plant. Almost as many as if he were raising them from seed, which, with the hybrid varieties that do not set viable seed, he is unable to do.

Take rose cuttings during September from well-ripened wood of the current year. Select straight shoots 30 cm (12 in) long; make a slanting cut just above a bud at the top (to remind you which is the top) and a straight cut just below a bud at the bottom.

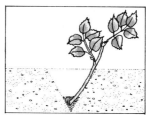

Trim off any lower leaves. Dig a narrow, V-shaped trench about 25 cm (10 in) deep and layer 2.5 cm (1 in) sand in the bottom. Dip the lower end of the cuttings in hormone rooting-powder and push them into the sand about 15 cm (6 in) apart so that they lean against the side of the trench.

Fill the trench with soil, leaving about 8 cm (3 in) of the cuttings exposed, and water well. The cuttings should form roots within 12 months, when they can be transplanted; they should flower within two years.

Roses are commonly budded on the rootstocks of wild roses. Cut a young stem that has just flowered from the variety to be grafted — the scion.

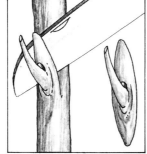

Strip the leaves from the stem and cut out a suitable bud, or eye, with a sharp knife. Shorten the leaf stalk to a stub and peel the bark away from the eye

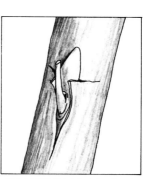

Just above the ground, make a T-shaped cut 2–3 cm (¾–1½ in) long in the bark of the stock. Slide the bud under the bark, right way up, and trim it level.

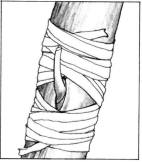

Bind the wound with tape or a special budding tie. The following spring, cut off the top of the rootstock before growth starts.

When is the best time of year to prune roses?

Few subjects in gardening are more likely to provoke controversy than this. The choice lies essentially between autumn (or, at least, before Christmas) and sometime in March. In the past, most gardeners probably opted for the latter, but increasingly, pre-Christmas pruning has become more popular.

First, you should be clear about the reasons for pruning. Although these differ slightly between types of rose, in general the operation is intended to remove old, worn out or diseased wood that will no longer contribute to the appearance and vigour of the plant. It is also done to maintain the plant in a size and shape appropriate to the position in which it is growing and to encourage new, flower-bearing shoots to develop. On a

wild rose, the flowers are often almost out of sight at the top of a gaunt, leggy plant that would be unacceptable in a garden.

There is nothing wrong with spring pruning, although there are many other gardening jobs to be done at this time. It is really more a case of autumn pruning having certain special attractions. If dead or useless wood is left on the plant during winter, there is always a risk of diseases becoming established at a time when the plant's resistance to attack is at its lowest. Moreover, the sheer bulk of the plant will be exposed to the full force of winter winds, and this will tend to loosen it in the ground (especially on a light soil), with consequent root disturbance. If this bulk is removed in the autumn, the plant will be better equipped to face the rigours of winter.

There are two other considerations. A certain amount of shoot death will inevitably be caused by winter frosts, so it may be necessary to follow autumn pruning by

See also:
Pruning Climbers and Ramblers
pp 90–1
Grafting trees and shrubs p 86
Staking trees p 109

Why do my roses always work loose in the ground?

There are several contributory factors to this common complaint. Not surprisingly, the most important factor is wind; a rose garden on a windy site will always give rise to problems of this nature. Nonetheless, the effects of the wind will be compounded if your roses are on a light, loose soil; if they are inadequately staked and if they have been inadequately pruned — especially if they have not had some superfluous top growth removed before winter sets in.

They will also be vulnerable if the plants have been inadequately fed and watered and have, therefore, not developed a deep and secure root system and if they were not planted deeply enough initially. Many of these features can fairly easily be put right, but it is most important to plant correctly, for many of the other problems will follow incorrect planting as surely as night follows day.

Most roses that you buy from a nursery or garden centre will have been grafted on a rootstock of a different variety. If you examine the base of the plant carefully, you will see the swelling where the graft union has formed. When planting, this union should be placed about 2.5 cm (1 in) below the surface of the soil. This advice applies, of course, to Bush or Shrub Roses.

It does not apply to Standards or Half-standards, where the graft union is at the top of a tall stem arising from the rootstock. Even so, I do know of instances where people have followed this advice to the letter and have buried their new Standard Roses more than a metre deep in the soil; and have then wondered why the results have not lived up to their expectations!

However, Standards and Bush Roses on their own roots should have a good 10 cm (4 in) of soil over the uppermost roots, and Standards require staking in the same way as trees.

further cutting back in the spring. It has also been claimed that autumn pruning stimulates the buds into growth earlier in the spring, when the new young shoots will themselves be prone to frost damage.

A compromise seems the best solution. Take off about half of the worn out or unwanted shoots in the autumn to lessen the likelihood of winter wind damage and complete the operation in March, when the frosts will have done their work. But always remember — prune according to variety. A vigorous grower, such as 'Queen Elizabeth' or 'Peace', should be pruned much more lightly than a weaker variety of rose, such as 'Duke of Windsor' or 'Tip Top'.

How important is dead-heading for keeping roses healthy and attractive?

Dead-heading is the removal of dead flowers, from roses or from any other garden plant. It is one of the more leisurely of gardening tasks and is an ideal accompaniment to a stroll around the garden on a summer afternoon, a good pair of secateurs in one hand and a trug in the other.

It has an obvious aesthetic effect, for dead flower heads are unsightly. It is, though, of rather more importance than this, for removing the dead flowering shoot will stimulate the production of new flower and leaf buds elsewhere on the plant, and it will also remove a potential point at which diseases can become established. Dead tissues of any sort, especially when they become wet, will attract the fungi of decay, which can easily spread to affect the open blossoms or even the shoots themselves. Thus, dead-heading is an important part of overall garden hygiene.

How much of the shoot must be cut away when the dead head is removed? There is no rule, but I always cut back to the first leaf that has five leaflets; this seems to be a good guide to cutting into strong wood with a strong bud. However, one cautionary note must be sounded with regard to the Old Rose varieties, for some of these should not be dead-headed at all. Many have only one burst of flowering, and removing the dead heads will not encourage more flowers to form.

More importantly, many old varieties produce extremely attractive hips in the autumn, which they cannot do if the dead head has been cut away. Indeed a few Old Rose varieties and rose species are well worth growing for their hips alone: 'Heather Muir', 'Lord Penzance', 'Mary Queen of Scots', *Rosa doncasterii, Rosa forrestiana, Rosa moyesii, Rosa rubrifolia, Rosa setipoda*; and many of the Rugosa Roses, especially *Rosa rugosa alba*, and 'Rose d'Orsay'.

Dead-head roses by cutting back to the first outward-facing leaf with five leaflets, so ensuring that you cut into strong wood with a strong bud.

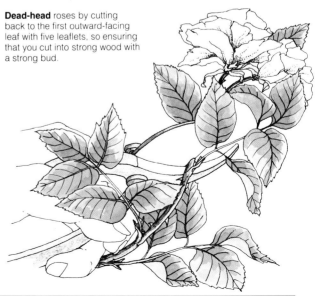

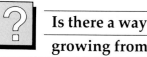

Is there a way to prevent suckers growing from the roots of roses?

The simplest way to prevent suckers from appearing is to grow your roses on their own roots so that every shoot appearing will be of the chosen variety. This is not practical as a general proposition, however, for any rose plants you buy will certainly be budded on a different rootstock and so will be prone to develop suckers. There is no short-cut to removing these physically, for they must be cut away cleanly, as close as possible to their point of origin below ground level. Although a sharp pair of secateurs is needed, I prefer not to use my best pair for this job, since the inevitable slicing into the soil blunts them quite quickly and may damage the blades.

Can selective weedkillers be used? Not really, for although some of the contact chemicals, such as paraquat, will kill off suckers, there is always the risk of spraying chemical on the bush itself, and you will still be left with a dead sucker to remove. Similarly, the systemic weedkiller glyphosate will kill suckers, but with this you stand a much greater chance of damaging the whole plant and, once again, there will still be a dead stem to cut away.

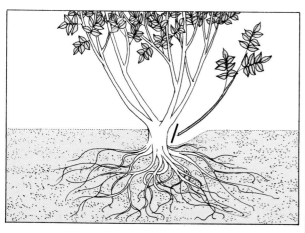

To remove a sucker from a Bush Rose, dig away the soil to find the junction with the rootstock, and cut off the sucker with secateurs.

Suckers sometimes form on the stem of a Standard Rose below the grafting point; they should be cut off, close to the stem.

Is it possible to control rose pests and diseases without using noxious chemicals?

This is an important and frequently asked question, so it is worth widening its scope to consider not only roses but garden plants in general, for the same criteria apply to all. How noxious is noxious, and what standard of control do you seek to achieve? The answers to these questions are critical if realistic guidance is to be given, for there are, in some instances, alternative strategies.

Those gardeners who eschew the use of modern pesticides may be willing to use more 'traditional' chemicals, such as sulphur, or more 'natural' products, such as pyrethrum or derris, feeling that these are less likely to contaminate either the environment or themselves. Even among the more modern, synthetic materials, there are varying degrees of toxicity to warm-blooded creatures and of the length of time they persist in the soil.

The extremely hazardous products, once so freely sold to gardeners, have been eliminated, and the United Kingdom, United States and other developed countries now have strict regulations and codes of practice to govern what may and may not be offered for sale. All chemicals available to gardeners must meet certain standards of safety when used in the ways and at the doses prescribed by the manufacturers. But it should be realized that all chemicals, used at certain doses, at certain times of the year, or in certain ways, can be noxious — the table salt that many people eat in large quantities at every mealtime is quite lethal to slugs if sprinkled over them.

Many gardeners achieve results with which they are well satisfied without any chemical, relying entirely on natural pest and disease regulation processes such as the many predator-prey interactions that occur among insects. One step back from this extreme is to use soapy water against mildew, a hose-pipe against aphids and sunken dishes containing beer to trap slugs. Gardening literature is full of such homespun remedies, as variable in their effectiveness as they are in their ingenuity.

It is not the purpose of this book to suggest to gardeners, who for moral, financial or other reasons do not wish to use some or, indeed, any chemicals, that they are wrong. But the level of pest and disease control that they achieve will, in almost every instance, be less than is theoretically possible. To rely on 'the balance of nature' to maintain adequate pest and disease control in the highly unnatural habitat of the rose garden, for example, is expecting rather a lot. Ultimately, this is a matter that each individual must decide for himself.

See also:
Suckers on rhododendrons p 86
Sumach suckers p 116
Predator-prey interactions in the
greenhouse p 149

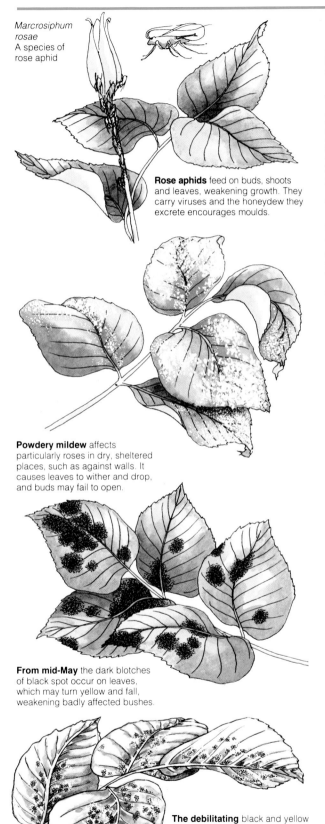

Marcrosiphum rosae
A species of rose aphid

Rose aphids feed on buds, shoots and leaves, weakening growth. They carry viruses and the honeydew they excrete encourages moulds.

Powdery mildew affects particularly roses in dry, sheltered places, such as against walls. It causes leaves to wither and drop, and buds may fail to open.

From mid-May the dark blotches of black spot occur on leaves, which may turn yellow and fall, weakening badly affected bushes.

The debilitating black and yellow pustules of rust fungus show on the undersides of leaves in summer. The spores survive the winter on fallen leaves.

Is there a single chemical that will control all the pests and diseases of roses?

I am all in favour of making the gardener's life as easy as possible, for gardening is only partly about doing; it is also about enjoying the results of what you have done. If you are a gardener who resorts to chemical controls for pests and diseases, you will be aware that spraying more than a modest number of rose bushes more than once in a season is time-consuming.

Your roses will, however, almost certainly suffer from several quite different problems, each requiring a distinct treatment. The insecticide that controls the aphids will have no effect on mildew, blackspot and rust; and even the fungicide that controls mildew and blackspot may have little impact on the rust that is caused by quite unrelated micro-fungi. Thus, to achieve perfect control of all, you would probably need to buy four different chemicals.

Even if you were prepared to go to such extremes, the question of chemical incompatibility could mean that each would have to be applied separately. Mixing two or more products is, on the face of it, an obvious labour-saving procedure, but chemical incompatibility means that some garden chemicals, when mixed together, form a brew that dimishes their effectiveness and may, at worst, actually harm your plants. The lesson to be learned from this is only to mix chemicals when the manufacturers' directions state specifically that it is safe to do so.

There are two other approaches you might consider. While conceding that an insecticide will be needed to protect your roses from aphid damage (and almost any of the garden insecticides will do the job satisfactorily), choose, in addition, a fungicide that will give reasonable control of the three common rose diseases, even if it falls short of perfection. Mildew and blackspot are the commonest of the three and are the easiest to control — benomyl, bupirimate + triforine, carbendazim, propiconazole and thiophanate-methyl are all fairly reliable used against them.

Rust is the least common disease and is reliably controlled only by propiconazole. This chemical should be your choice, therefore, if rust is a serious problem in your garden. The second approach is to use an insecticide and fungicide mixture prepared by the manufacturer. Unfortunately, the only such cocktail available contains a good insecticide, pirimicarb, together with the fungicides bupirimate and triforine; fine for blackspot and mildew, therefore, but of little value against rust.

How can I persuade a climbing rose to flower at the base as well as at the top?

Climbing roses with bare lower branches are surprisingly common, especially on a north or east wall. They are frustrating, too, for there is little satisfaction in having a plant whose blooms can be seen only from an upstairs window. Why does this happen?

The reasons are that the lower parts of the plant are shaded and suppressed, and, more importantly, that the plant is not being trained as it should be. It is expressing a phenomenon known as apical dominance, in which the tendency is for the buds at the tips of the shoots to grow, while the lower buds remain dormant.

Precisely the same effect will be seen on apple trees — leaves and fruit will form only at the tips of these shoots if the branch leaders and laterals are not cut back in winter. In the same way, the phenomenon can be remedied by shortening the long shoots of the rose, but if they are pruned too hard the lower buds will simply form more long shoots that will still leave the base bare.

A better plan is to force some of the buds lower down to break without drastic pruning, simply by putting them in a position where they are no longer subject to apical dominance. Untie the rose from the wall and pull down some of the long growths until their tips are at or just below the horizontal. Alternatively, where lateral space is limited, bend the long shoots at right angles, so they have a kink some way up, then retie them.

Why do some flower buds on my roses fail to open properly?

This is a common occurence in some seasons and on some varieties. It is known as balling, for the half-opened bloom becomes a rounded, rather wet, brown mass. The condition tends to be more frequent on those varieties with thin petals and normally occurs in rainy weather or, quite commonly, toward the end of the season, as the weather cools and early morning dews become commoner. Incorrect feeding predisposes blooms to balling, so use a balanced rose fertilizer twice each season, first after the spring pruning and then again in early summer after the first flush of flowers.

A severe infestation of aphids on young buds also appears able to cause sufficient damage to prevent the flowers from opening properly, enabling the grey mould, *Botrytis*, to establish itself and bring about the browning and decay. This can be lessened by routine fungicide spraying against mildew but, normally, once the young bloom has become really wet, little can be done to resuscitate it.

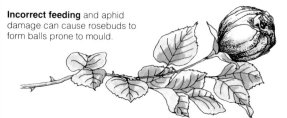

Incorrect feeding and aphid damage can cause rosebuds to form balls prone to mould.

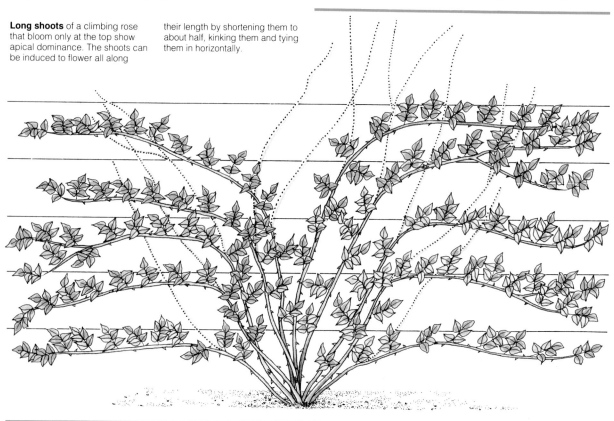

Long shoots of a climbing rose that bloom only at the top show apical dominance. The shoots can be induced to flower all along their length by shortening them to about half, kinking them and tying them in horizontally.

See also:
Groundcover plants pp 26, 59, 87
Mildew on michaelmas daisies p 65
Pruning Climbers and Ramblers
pp 90–1

What plants can I grow between roses to improve the appearance of the bed?

Generally I prefer to see a rose bed left to roses. It is true that during the winter a rose garden can have a bare and twiggy look, but in most years this bareness prevails for only about four months. If other plants are grown to relieve the bare earth, choose them carefully; almost any plant that flowers while the roses themselves are in bloom will detract from them and make a hotch-potch of the whole.

My suggestion would be to use small plants that flower when the roses are asleep and then disappear. Small bulbs are the obvious choice, but this is, I think, one instance when discrete clumps do not look right; and if you intend planting scillas, for example, be extravagant and carpet with them.

If you prefer a plant that will remain during the summer, I would suggest a choice of foliage plants with grey or silver leaves. Dwarf lavenders, such as *Lavandula nana atropurpurea* and *L. stoechas*, French lavender, can look most effective; both grow up to about 60 cm (24 in). The purple-blue flowers complement almost any colour of rose, and French lavender has purple bracts at the top of each flower stem that remain long after the flowers themselves have faded. Where bush roses are planted with plenty of space between them, and sunshine can penetrate, you might consider using a low-growing herb such as silver thyme.

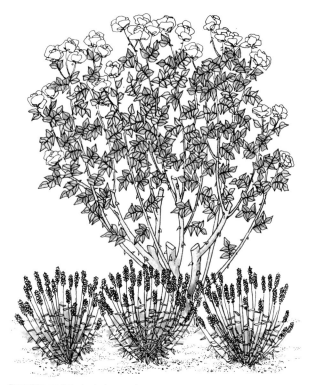

Dwarf lavender planted around the base of a large shrub rose, such as 'Mme Isaac Pereire', will mask the bare and sometimes leggy stem.

Why have my 'Super Star' roses, after many years, suddenly succumbed to mildew?

I have before me the 1961 edition of the *Rose Annual*, published in Britain by the Royal National Rose Society. It describes a new variety, introduced the previous year and illustrated on a coloured frontispiece. This variety won the President's International Trophy for the best new seedling rose of the year and a gold medal. It was awarded an astonishing 18 points out of 20 for freedom from disease, but only ten years later, in the Royal National Rose Society's 'Selected List of Varieties', it was suggested that it 'may need protection from mildew'. Yes, that variety was 'Super Star', rejected by many gardeners today who feel thay are fighting a losing battle against mildew. It is simply the best-known example of a common and widespread phenomenon: that plant varieties resistant to a particular pest or disease may not remain so in perpetuity.

Not unreasonably, gardeners want to know why. Without entering too deeply into the technicalities of the subject, it is really Darwinian evolution in action. Most probably, the genes of the mildew fungus have been 'challenged' by the genes in the rose that conferred resistance to the disease to mutate and so overcome the natural protection of the variety. There is nothing that you or I could have done about it — short of not growing 'Super Star' so extensively. There is, nonetheless, a lesson to be learned that is relevant to many other types of plant and many other diseases or pests.

Increasingly, in seed and nursery catalogues, you will see plants described as resistant to a particular problem. Should these varieties be chosen in preference to others? Or does the 'Super Star' experience mean that the tomatoes with virus resistance, for example, or the antirrhinums with rust resistance, are not really worth paying special attention to — that you may as well stick a pin into the catalogue? Not at all; but it does mean that, as with most commercial claims, it is folly to read too much into them.

Do not expect that a resistant plant will necessarily be equally resistant wherever it is grown; do not expect that its resistance will last for ever or that no chemical protection will be needed. You should certainly choose a resistant variety if you believe that the pest or disease concerned is likely to be troublesome, and if the particular variety also has other features (colour and habit, for example) that you are seeking. Resistance is a useful adjunct to other attributes, but it is rarely the sole justification for buying a particular variety.

LAWNS

Growing the perfect
patch of green

How can I prevent humps and hollows from appearing in a newly laid lawn?

The importance of site preparation so that you have a truly level surface on which to sow or lay a new lawn cannot be stressed too strongly. It is much easier to prevent bumps forming than to remove them later. Start your preparations six to eight weeks in advance of planting. In heavy soils, dig the area over to give large clods of earth time to break down. This has the advantage, too, of allowing weeds to grow up and be treated safely with weedkiller or by hoeing before seed is sown or turf planted.

Remove all stones. Rake the area carefully shortly before the lawn is sown or laid, working first in one direction and then at right angles, otherwise you will find that you are actually creating humps and hollows.

About one week before sowing seed, apply fine peat at the rate of about 4kg/sqm (5½lb/sqyd) — plus a dressing of coarse sand at twice this rate on heavy soils — and rake it into the top few centimetres of soil. If the area is fairly small, firm it by treading when the earth is dry, although this is clearly impossible for a really large lawn, or with the head of a rake. Resist the temptation to roll it, for, like careless raking, this will accentuate any irregularities. It can also produce future problems with drainage by compacting a heavy soil.

Finally, dress the surface with a phosphate-rich fertilizer to help the seedlings establish themselves. Ideally, this should be a fertilizer specially formulated for new lawns, but bonemeal at about 90g/sqm (2½oz/sqyd) will help. Allow 35 to 40g of seed per square metre (1½oz per square yard).

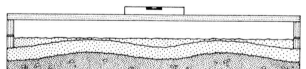

If the ground is very uneven, you will need to dig away some soil before making a lawn. At the level you want the lawn, hammer in a wooden peg, leaving 10cm (4in) of it showing.

Hammer in more pegs 2m (6½ft) apart in a grid, using a plank and spirit level to get the tops in the same plane; stretch string between the pegs at the desired lawn level.

Take off topsoil, fill in with soil to 10cm (4in) below lawn level and replace the topsoil so that the string lies on the surface. Firm the soil and check the level again before removing the pegs.

See also:
Weed grasses in lawns p 105
Non-grass lawns pp 106–7

Is it better to start a new lawn from seed or turf?

'Instant lawn; just add water', said the advertisement for turf. Misleading, I thought; for gardeners intending to buy turf should appreciate that almost as much soil preparation is needed for it as for sowing seed. Not quite instant, either; but undoubtedly speed of establishment is the biggest advantage turf has over seed, although the cost of producing a lawn from seed is less than it is from turf.

You may see cheap seed offered for sale, in bulk, from unbranded sacks. Avoid it, for you have no guarantee of its age or of how carefully it has been stored. Much more commonly, you will see turf offered at appealing prices; avoid this, too, for it is almost certain to contain a large weed population. The designation 'weed treated' or 'treated with weedkiller' in the advertisement means nothing; it is no guarantee that any weeds have actually been killed. Cheap turf will also, most probably, comprise a blend of grasses that may be satisfactory for grazing cattle but will be of little merit for a lawn.

With lawns, as with everything else in life, you get what you pay for, and since your lawn will be with you for a long time and be an important feature of your garden, always go to a reputable supplier and make sure you see the turf before you buy it. Similarly, buy seed only from an established seed company that is prepared to tell you the precise composition of the seed mixture.

What, then, should you look for when choosing turf? There are three main types: sea-washed turf, or Cumberland sea-washed turf, is the finest. Originally, it was dug from the Cumberland coast, but the term sea-washed now applies to any turf from coastal salt marshes. It contains a unique blend of grass species and is a difficult turf to manage correctly, for its base is a silt soil rich in sodium. It is the turf of bowling greens, but it is not a suitable choice for gardens.

Downland turf (or, at least, much of the best downland turf) originates on the South Downs, where a thin soil overlies chalk. The principal grasses it contains are sheep's fescue, bents and crested dog's tail, and there may be greater or lesser amounts of clovers and trefoils. Downland turf is the grass of cricket squares and high-quality lawns and should be chosen if turf is to be used for a respectable lawn.

The final type is the one you will see most commonly, meadow turf. Opinions as to what constitutes a meadow vary considerably, and meadow turf can be practically anything from the acceptable to the impossible. It should never be used for a fine lawn and even for rougher areas make sure you see it before purchase.

A week to 10 days before laying a new lawn, rake the area to clear away leaves, small stones and other debris. Then dress the surface with a phosphate-rich fertilizer and rake it in.

Stretch a string along one edge to give a straight line. Lay the first turves to this line, pressing them down firmly. Put a plank on these turves and, standing on it, butt the second row to the first and so on.

Stagger the turves as if you were laying bricks; fill the gaps between them with top dressing and work it in with the back of a rake or with a stiff twig broom.

Trim turves back neatly to the edge of the lawn with a turfing iron, making a sloping cut. Roll the lawn with a very light roller and brush again to raise the flattened grass.

Why does some lawn seed contain rye grass?

To many gardeners, grass is grass; it does not occur to them that there are different species, just as there are of other flowering plants. The grass family, however, is one of the largest, and in Britain alone there are well over one hundred different species. Many non-native species and hybrids, among them the group of species known collectively as rye grass, have been specially selected and bred for lawns and sports turf. They are coarse, hard-wearing grasses, suitable for a football pitch, but not for a fine lawn.

Some of the newer hybrids are, however, both lower growing and finer leaved than the traditional rye grasses, and mixtures containing a blend with other species are excellent for lawns that will suffer a fair amount of wear and tear. Rye grass is not a good choice for a fine lawn because it grows relatively fast and does not respond well to close mowing. One seed company describes seed mixtures containing rye grass as 'back lawn seed' and those without rye grass as 'front lawn seed'; this fairly well summarizes their relative uses in the garden.

For a fine lawn, choose mixtures containing a high proportion of fescues, **1**, and bent grasses, **2**.

Deeper-rooting rye grass, **3**, is much coarser and more hard wearing for a much-used lawn.

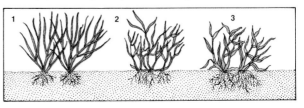

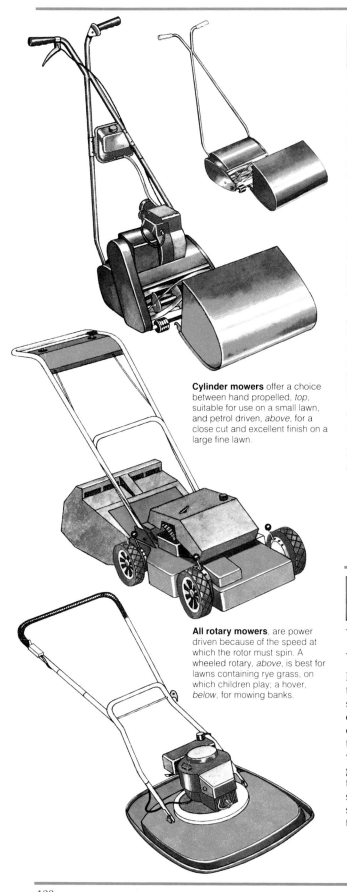

Cylinder mowers offer a choice between hand propelled, *top*, suitable for use on a small lawn, and petrol driven, *above*, for a close cut and excellent finish on a large fine lawn.

All rotary mowers, are power driven because of the speed at which the rotor must spin. A wheeled rotary, *above*, is best for lawns containing rye grass, on which children play; a hover, *below*, for mowing banks.

Which is the best type of lawnmower?

The type of lawnmower you choose depends on the type and size of your lawn, the time and effort you are prepared to expend on it and how much you can afford. A cylinder mower will give you the finest cut and the best finish on a fine lawn. There is, however, no merit in choosing a cylinder mower because of its finishing ability if your lawn contains rye grass and is a basic wear-and-tear lawn. If a cylinder mower must be set high to work effectively on your lawn, then a rotary mower would probably do the job better.

A lawn must be extremely good to be hand-mown satisfactorily and, unless you have time to spare, must also be fairly small. The rule of thumb for professional grass keepers used to be to use a powered machine on areas above 400 sq m (480 sq yds), but few gardeners would face up to hand-mowing a lawn of that size.

Given a large, fine lawn, therefore, choose the best cylinder petrol mower you can afford; and with a large lawn of moderate quality, choose the best petrol-driven rotary. Modern electric machines have many built-in safety features, but there is still some risk with cable draped over the lawn, so confine them to small areas; battery-powered machines are very heavy. If the lawn is flat, choose a wheeled rotary, but if there are banks and other tricky areas, such as between shrubs, a hover machine is probably a wiser choice.

The final decision relates to width of cut. At a speed of 3 m/h (5 km/h) and with an overlap of 5 cm (2 in), the approximate areas that can be cut in one hour are:

Width of cut	Area mown in 1 hour
30 cm/12 in	1,230 sq m/1,470 sq yds
40 cm/16 in	1,670 sq m/2,000 sq yds
50 cm/20 in	2,205 sq m/2,640 sq yds
60 cm/24 in	2,450 sq m/2,930 sq yds

How do the professionals obtain the spendid striped effect on their lawns?

It is surprising how often this question is asked, for there is no magic to the answer. The striping (always seen at its best in the pictures on lawn-seed packets) is caused by the blades of grass being pushed in opposite directions by the mower, or, rather, by the small roller at the rear of the mower. Consequently it is best achieved with a cylinder mower, although a wheeled rotary will give an indication of striping. Provided the mower is turned around at the end of each run, you will produce stripes; but ensure that you have a good eye for a straight line. If nothing looks better than stripes, few things look worse than drunken stripes.

See also:
Grass cuttings in compost p 10
Alternatives to grass under
    trees p 23

Role of earthworms in aerating
    lawns p 102
Grassing up to trees p 106

 ## Is spiking a lawn to aerate it worthwhile?

Unless you are an avowed masochist, you will need to be convinced that spiking is worth the effort before you embark on the exercise, for it is physically one of the most demanding of all garden tasks. So let me attempt to convince you.

Even the best-managed and most carefully used lawn will suffer some degree of surface compaction during the summer. Even if children never play on it and people never walk or sit on it (and what a dull lawn that would be), someone must mow it, and their feet and the mower's wheels — unless it hovers — will compress the surface. Indeed, even if no human ever went near the lawn, the effects of rain, worms and other 'natural' factors would ensure that the surface became compacted to some extent.

Once this has happened, water cannot drain freely into and through the turf, fertilizers cannot penetrate, and air (which most people forget is also needed by roots) will never reach below the surface. Make holes in the lawn, and all these problems will be alleviated to some degree. Any holes are better than none, but spiking with a garden fork or a hollow-tine fork is terribly irksome on any other than the smallest lawn.

Spiked shoes, rather like a rustic version of running shoes, can now be bought, but their spikes are fairly short, and a shoe with a really efficient length of spike would be quite likely to replace your horticultural problems with medical ones. It is also possible to buy or, more conveniently, to hire a powered spiking machine, and this is probably the best answer for most gardeners.

The ideal way to aerate a lawn is with a hollow-tine spiking machine that removes a small core of soil and does not simply compress it into the walls of the hole as normal methods do. Such machines, of necessity, have powerful engines and are extremely expensive to buy; they are also rarely offered for hire.

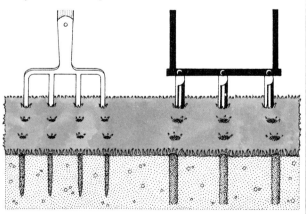

Small areas of compacted grass can be satisfactorily aerated with a garden fork. Drive the fork 10–15cm (4–6in) into the ground, then rock it back and forth to open the holes up. Space the sets of holes about 15cm (6in) apart.

A hollow-tine fork is more efficient, but very hard work. When driven into the ground, it removes small cores of earth which fall out as the fork is next driven in. Work backward to avoid walking on already aerated lawn.

 ## How important is it to keep the grass box on the mower?

The experts are not in great agreement on this, but I believe that, as with many other features of lawn care, the answer lies in how much time you have to spare. The argument in favour of keeping the grass box on is that the clippings will otherwise form a compacted mat on top of the turf, preventing air, water and fertilizer from penetrating to the roots. Clippings, also, so the argument goes, make good compost used in moderation and are collected most efficiently during mowing; raking them up afterwards is hard work.

The counter argument runs that if grass cuttings make such good compost and are thus a source of plant nutrient, why go to the trouble of carrying them across the garden to the compost heap? Left on the lawn, they could be feeding it and, more important, could be mulching the turf, preventing it from drying out.

Allowing mowings to accumulate on the lawn during early spring and late autumn probably does no good and may do harm. But personal experience has demonstrated the benefits of removing the grass box in May and leaving it off for the summer, *provided* you are able to mow the lawn at least twice a week so that the amount of grass taken off at each cut is relatively small. Provided also that you are prepared to give the lawn a thorough raking in the autumn to prevent a thick, impenetrable 'thatch' remaining throughout the winter.

 ## Is it possible to persuade grass to grow beneath trees?

Take a walk into your nearest woodland. Look down at the natural vegetation. How much grass is there? Not much; and if the woodland is coniferous, probably almost none. Do not, therefore, expect grass in your garden to behave very differently, for shade is generally not to the liking of grasses and certainly not to the liking of those grasses that respond well to mowing and so make decent lawns.

Some lawn grass species grow better in partial shade than others but, in deep shade, anything resembling a proper lawn is impossible. Most seed companies offer 'shade mixtures', which usually contain a high proportion of fescues. But if your shaded area is small, and if you are sowing your main lawn with a blend that already contains fescues, it is probably safe to sow the same mixture in the shaded area also. Do not, however, expect the results to be as good.

Should earthworms in a lawn be controlled?

Apart from moving the earth and breaking down organic matter elsewhere in the garden, worms play a specific role in the life of a lawn. The most obvious sign of their activity is the casts they produce: small piles of soil expelled on the surface. But even this is a generalization, for most worms are unable to form casts and never make their presence known in this way.

Many people dislike casts, since they make the lawn surface slippery and unsightly when it is wet; they can be the means by which weed seeds are brought to the surface, and they can also form the starting point for some of the diseases of turf grasses. Perhaps most annoying on fine, closely mown lawns is that the grit contained in the casts will blunt the blades of cylinder mowers. Do these features mean then that worms in lawns should be controlled? I think not and welcome their aerating and draining activities, which more than compensate for the problems caused by their casts.

If, however, you wish to eradicate worms in the cause of maintaining your billiard-table turf, use a worm expellent and not a worm killer. The best expellent is probably potassium permanganate, which can be bought from a chemist's shop, rather than a garden shop. Make up a solution containing 38 g/9½ litres (1¼ oz/2 gallons) and apply this at the rate of 1 litre/sq m (1½ pt/sq yd) in warm, moist weather in early summer — in cold, or hot, dry weather the worms will be much deeper in the soil. As potassium permanganate is not harmful to fish, it may be safely applied even on lawns close to garden pools. The worms will come to the surface after treatment and can then be swept up and deposited elsewhere in the garden.

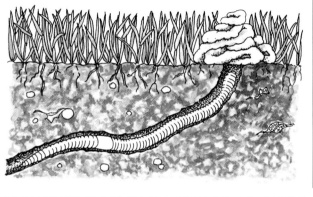

Why does my lawn have bare patches?

The lawn that does not develop bare patches at some time has not yet been laid. There are four probable reasons for this, and a measure of common sense will be needed to determine which applies in which particular instance. The most usual causes of bare patches on turf are detailed below:

☐ Something noxious has been spilled on the grass: petrol slopped out carelessly when filling a lawnmower, a household chemical or even boiling water tipped on the turf; it has been injudiciously overdosed with lawn fertilizer; or a dog or, more seriously, a bitch, has urinated on the lawn (urine is a powerful grass killer). Although a mild dose with any of these substances may only scorch the foliage, a persisting bare patch indicates root death, and the affected areas will have to be relaid or resown. The simplest plan is to dig out the dead turf and so eliminate any chemical that may remain in the soil. Then use one of the modern 'lawn repair kits' that contains treated grass seed in an organic growing medium with added fertilizer.

☐ The grass has suffered locally during a period of drought. If the soil is shallow or compacted, prolonged dryness will cause the turf to die, either above ground only, in which event it will regenerate, or, more exceptionally, below ground too, when the roots die. Even if the entire patch of turf is not killed, it may by so weakened that lawn weeds can establish

Bare patches form in grass for a number of reasons, ranging from an overdose of fertilizer to drought. The grass yellows and dies back and the earth shows through.

Dig out the dead grass and soil from the affected patch with a trowel and then loosen the surface of the soil with a fork.

See also:
Aerating lawns p 102
End of summer treatment of
   lawns p 106
Garden damage from drought p 108

? How can toadstools be eradicated from a lawn?

The short answer is that you cannot eradicate them and, in my view, it does not matter that you cannot. Toadstools are the reproductive structures of certain types of fungi; they are the means of producing and dispersing the spores, which play a similar role in fungi to seeds in flowering plants. But, and a most important but, they represent a small fraction of the whole organism, for beneath the lawn surface is a vast number of microscopic threads, weaving their way through the soil. You can pull up, mow off or even dig out toadstools to your heart's content, but you will make no impact on the subterranean fungal growth, which will simply produce more toadstools again next year.

Only by a lengthy and difficult operation, involving the excavation of large areas of turf and drenching the soil with noxious chemicals, is there any likelihood of killing the fungus below ground. And, in the end, is it worth it? Virtually no harm to your lawn, to your soil or to any other garden plants will result from the presence of toadstools. There may be some localized areas of poor turf with the concentrated growth of toadstools such as

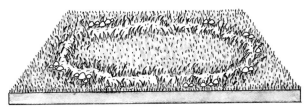

Fairy rings, caused by fungi in the soil, show as bands of dark green grass around a patch of discoloured grass or bare earth. In late summer or autumn in damp weather, a ring of toadstools appears in the grass.

occurs in fairy rings, but even here it seems hardly worth the effort to try to eradicate them.

Finally, a cautionary note: the toadstools that grow on your lawn may or may not be edible and they may or may not be poisonous, so do not be tempted to experiment with them unless you have had them authoritatively identified. It is most improbable that domestic pets will come to harm through eating toadstools on lawns, but if you are concerned about this, routine mowing or raking will remove the toadstools; even if it does not eliminate them at source.

themselves on the area before the grass has a chance to grow again. These areas may be treated in the same way as described earlier, but see also the comments regarding end-of-summer operations on the lawn.

☐ Leather jackets (the larvae of crane flies) have been feeding on the roots and stems. The effects of this — irregular yellow patches in the grass — are seen most commonly early in the season on new lawns, and they become worse if a dry spell places the grass under further stress. Regular watering helps to minimize the problem. The simplest way to control the pests is to lay plastic sheeting over the well-soaked bare patches late in the evening. Any larvae in the soil will work their way up to the surface during the night, and they can be swept up in the morning and disposed of.

☐ One of several different types of soil fungi is causing the roots and stem bases of the grass to rot and die in patches. Sometimes the mould growth may be seen even on the grass leaves. Drenching the affected areas with a spray-strength mixture of benomyl, carbendazim or thiophanate-methyl fungicide immediately after mowing will often cure the problem, but if the soil is compacted it should be spiked. Lawn feeds containing a high level of nitrogen (usually called spring and summer feeds), should be stopped after the end of August and an autumn and winter feed used instead, for the high dose of nitrogen promotes disease-prone lush growth during the cold winter weather.

Fill the hole with turves or by using a 'lawn repair kit', *above*, containing treated grass seed in an organic growing medium to which fertilizer has been added.

Level off the replaced turf and fill the gaps with top dressing. If using a kit, firm the mixture down and, with a plank, make sure it is level with the existing lawn.

What can be done to remove moss from a lawn and to improve the turf?

The eradication of moss from a lawn is not too difficult, but unless the underlying factors are corrected as well it will return.

To remove moss, a combination of chemical and physical methods should be used in the spring or autumn, when cool, damp conditions encourage it to grow vigorously. First apply a proprietary moss killer, either one of the modern products containing chloroxuron or dichlorophen (which are commonly sold in combination with a fertilizer), or one of the more traditional lawn-sand types, based on ferrous sulphate.

Lawn sand can be made quite cheaply, using the following formula:

3 parts by weight	ammonium sulphate
1 part by weight	ferrous sulphate
7 parts by weight	fine sand

Apply the mixture at the rate of 135g/sqm (4oz/sqyd) during fine weather and, if it does not rain within 48 hours, water the lawn well. Once the moss has been killed and blackened by the chemical treatment, rake it up thoroughly with a spring-tine rake or, much less laboriously, with one of the modern wheeled or powered devices.

Then it is time to put right the factors that predispose the lawn to moss infestation. Spike a poorly drained or compacted soil to improve drainage and aeration; treat an underfed lawn with spring and autumn fertilizer, and lighten a heavily shaded lawn by removing as many overhanging branches as possible without spoiling the shape of the trees. Above all, set the mower so that it does not shave the grass — not less than 1.25cm (½in) for an average lawn and 2 to 2.5cm (¾ to 1in) is better.

Weedkillers do not have much effect on my lawn; are they a waste of money?

There is a common tendency to think of garden chemicals as a unified group of substances with similar properties. This is not only wrong, it is also misleading, especially with regard to weedkillers, fungicides and insecticides. Generally speaking, as long as the manufacturer's directions are followed, a fungicide or insecticide is effective regardless of the weather conditions when it is applied and is fairly consistent in its action from year to year.

This cannot be said of many weedkillers. Some of them have well-defined weather requirements to enable them to act effectively; glyphosate, for example, requires six hours without rain after its application to foliage in order to be absorbed by the plant. Many more will be affected by such factors as variation in temperature and in soil moisture. Thus, a chemical that worked well last year, or even last week, may produce less satisfactory results following a repeat application. This is true especially of many of the weedkillers that are taken up by plants from the soil rather than through the foliage. Some lawn weedkillers come into this category and, in hot, dry seasons or cold, wet ones, they may give results that fall below expectation.

Lawn weedkillers are, therefore, not a waste of money, but they must be applied under optimum conditions. Almost more than with any other garden chemical, follow to the letter the advice given by the manufacturer regarding time of application for weed-killers; and don't be tempted to push your luck if conditions are only marginally correct.

There are blobs of slime on the lawn; what are they?

A 'blob of slime' conjures up a fairly precise image of the problem, although there is slime and slime; the potential harmfulness of the growth depends upon its form.

The commonest slimy growth is the green, jellylike masses found in wet weather on shaded lawns especially, and on those on shallow soils or those that are poorly drained. These conditions are similar to those in which moss flourishes; the slime is not moss, however, but a form of alga, related to the algae that grow in garden pools and can make pathways slippery. Although proprietary algicides are available and are fairly effective on paths, they are of limited value on lawns where, as with moss. the underlying conditions must be corrected first.

Sometimes, rather more colourful blobs of slime will be found — ranging from red, through yellow to white. These are the growths of organisms called slime moulds, which are unrelated to true moulds and are harmless in the sense that they are not parasitic. I prefer to leave them alone to pursue their fascinating, amoeba-like existence — they will wander away in due course.

Occasionally their presence may cause slight damage through the smothering of the grass; or you may simply find the idea of accidentally treading or sitting on them repellent. In such instances, they are best disposed of with a hose-pipe.

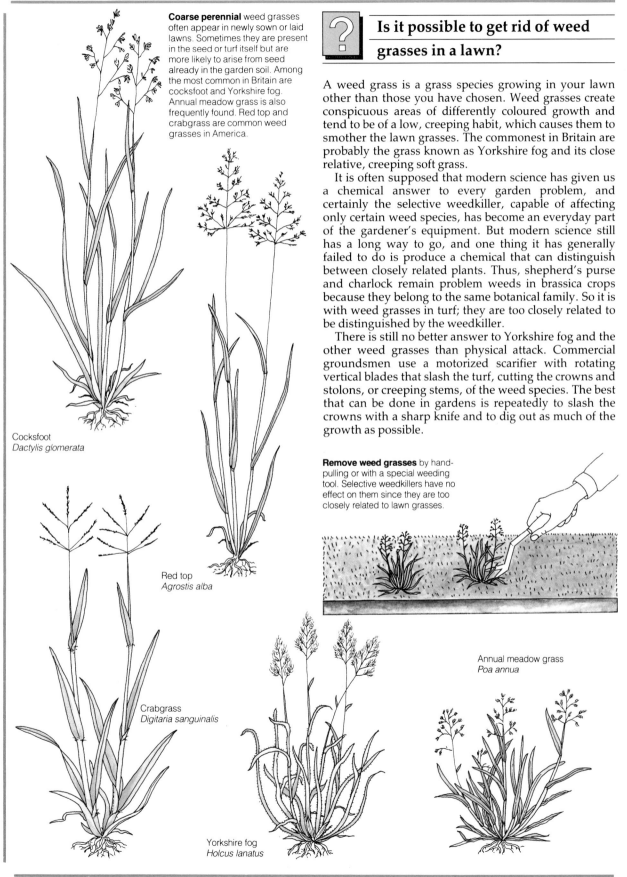

See also:
Fertilizer and weedkiller mixtures
   for grass p 18
Algae in garden pools p 38

Coarse perennial weed grasses often appear in newly sown or laid lawns. Sometimes they are present in the seed or turf itself but are more likely to arise from seed already in the garden soil. Among the most common in Britain are cocksfoot and Yorkshire fog. Annual meadow grass is also frequently found. Red top and crabgrass are common weed grasses in America.

Is it possible to get rid of weed grasses in a lawn?

A weed grass is a grass species growing in your lawn other than those you have chosen. Weed grasses create conspicuous areas of differently coloured growth and tend to be of a low, creeping habit, which causes them to smother the lawn grasses. The commonest in Britain are probably the grass known as Yorkshire fog and its close relative, creeping soft grass.

It is often supposed that modern science has given us a chemical answer to every garden problem, and certainly the selective weedkiller, capable of affecting only certain weed species, has become an everyday part of the gardener's equipment. But modern science still has a long way to go, and one thing it has generally failed to do is produce a chemical that can distinguish between closely related plants. Thus, shepherd's purse and charlock remain problem weeds in brassica crops because they belong to the same botanical family. So it is with weed grasses in turf; they are too closely related to be distinguished by the weedkiller.

There is still no better answer to Yorkshire fog and the other weed grasses than physical attack. Commercial groundsmen use a motorized scarifier with rotating vertical blades that slash the turf, cutting the crowns and stolons, or creeping stems, of the weed species. The best that can be done in gardens is repeatedly to slash the crowns with a sharp knife and to dig out as much of the growth as possible.

Remove weed grasses by hand-pulling or with a special weeding tool. Selective weedkillers have no effect on them since they are too closely related to lawn grasses.

Cocksfoot
Dactylis glomerata

Red top
Agrostis alba

Crabgrass
Digitaria sanguinalis

Yorkshire fog
Holcus lanatus

Annual meadow grass
Poa annua

What can be done to revive a lawn at the end of summer?

This is almost everyone's question at the end of a period in which most lawns take a battering from cricket, barbecues and even walking to and fro with the lawn mower. Indeed, after a really hot, dry summer, lawns often look as if they could never turn green and lush again. But they have astonishing powers of recovery from natural catastrophies; it is only when you do something unnatural, such as spilling petrol on a lawn, that it will show signs of long-term damage.

The tasks necessary at the end of summer may be summarized as follows:

Raking Even if the grass box has been kept on the mower all summer and moss-killing chemicals have been applied assiduously, there will be a 'thatch' of dead plant material to be removed so that it does not prevent winter rain from draining away. Leaves also obstruct the drainage of water and must be raked up regularly.

Spiking This, too, assists with drainage and facilitates aeration of the turf and penetration of fertilizer.

Feeding It may seem strange to apply fertilizer to a lawn at a time when it is not growing actively. Logic suggests that the nutrient will be washed away long before it has a chance to act. But it is important for grass to have nutrients available in the soil so that it may start to grow early in the spring. A specially formulated autumn fertilizer, low in nitrogen, should be used. Spring and summer feeds containing a high level of nitrogen are of no value later in the year and can cause damage.

Should grass be allowed to grow right up to the trunks of trees and shrubs?

Opinions vary more widely on this subject at the present time than they used to, for there is now evidence from carefully conducted trials that some of the old ideas may not be correct. Nevertheless, I believe that, in the formative years, grass growing close to the base of a tree or shrub will provide fairly serious competition for water and nutrients.

Until the shrub or tree is well established, therefore, (about five years with apples), an area of turf of about 1m (3¼ft) in diameter should be removed around the base. No harm is likely to result from growing relatively undemanding plants, such as small bulbs, within this circle. Once a tree is well established, grass may safely be allowed to grow up to the base of the trunk and, indeed, if a tree is growing unacceptably vigorously, grassing up to its base will frequently achieve the objective of slowing down its overall growth.

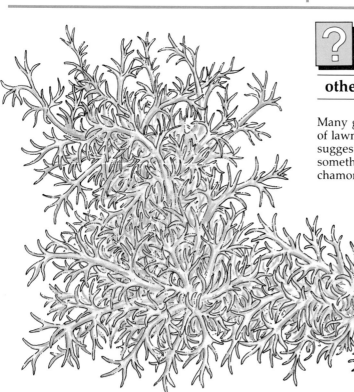

How good are lawns made from low-growing plants other than grass?

Many gardeners live their entire lives happily thinking of lawns as areas of close-mown grass. Others hear the suggestions put forward from time to time to 'try something different' and may even read that there is a chamomile lawn at Buckingham Palace. What, they

Common chamomile is a low-growing plant that forms a mat of finely cut dark green leaves. It is highly aromatic and will stand being walked or sat on, provided it is not too roughly used. The non-flowering form *Anthemis nobilis* 'Treneague' is most suitable for use as a lawn, since it is a vigorous grower which can even be lightly mown.

See also:
Fertilizers and weedkiller mixtures
    for grass p 18
Naturalizing bulbs in grass
    pp 26, 68
Grass species p 99

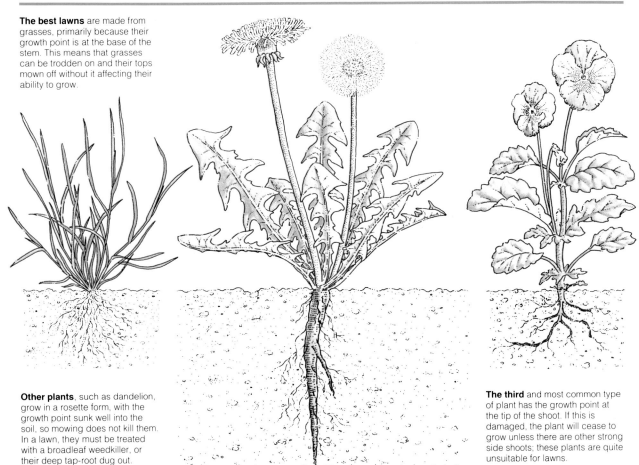

The best lawns are made from grasses, primarily because their growth point is at the base of the stem. This means that grasses can be trodden on and their tops mown off without it affecting their ability to grow.

Other plants, such as dandelion, grow in a rosette form, with the growth point sunk well into the soil, so mowing does not kill them. In a lawn, they must be treated with a broadleaf weedkiller, or their deep tap-root dug out.

The third and most common type of plant has the growth point at the tip of the shoot. If this is damaged, the plant will cease to grow unless there are other strong side shoots; these plants are quite unsuitable for lawns.

wonder, is a chamomile lawn and will it be easier than grass to look after; not need mowing (hurray!); and cause comment and envy among the neighbours? I have great sympathy with those who live in blissful ignorance of chamomile lawns and their kind, for I believe that, other than for curiosity value, grass is the stuff of which lawns should be made.

If a plant is to create a conventional lawn, it must tolerate being mown and walked on, which it does by having a basal meristem. This may conjure up visions of plants enjoying the low life, but, in fact, a meristem is composed of a group of cells that continually divide to produce new cells — it is, in everyday terms, the growth point. If the growth point is at the tip of the shoot, as it is in most plants, then one mowing will remove it and the plant will grow no more unless a bud lower down takes over the function.

Grasses, however, have the growth point, the meristem, at the base; they grow from the bottom upward, thus mowing does them no harm. An alternative to a basal meristem is a meristem that is sunk out of harm's way, and this is a feature of plants that grow in a rosette form. Many of the most successful lawn weeds, such as daisies and dandelions, have this habit, but a lawn composed of dandelions might take some managing.

The third option is to choose a plant that is naturally low growing and of compact, branching habit, such as

chamomile, a member of the daisy family. It has attractive, feathery foliage and a most appealing aroma; it is widely used as a herb. To a limited extent it will tolerate being walked on and can even be mown if the mower is set high. The variety to choose for a lawn is the non-flowering form 'Treneague', which is propagated by cuttings. It should be planted in March on a site prepared as for a normal lawn, and the cuttings spaced about 20 cm (8 in) apart.

It must not be imagined, though, that a chamomile lawn is in any way a substitute for a grass lawn. It will tolerate nothing like the amount of wear and tear; it will look decidedly miserable and brown during the winter; it is highly intolerant of any shade and of wet, cold soil and, above all, it will create enormous problems of weed control. While you can readily use a selective weedkiller on grass to kill broadleaved weeds, there is nothing you can do about them in a broadleaved lawn except get down on your hands and knees and pull them out.

TREES AND HEDGES

The garden's living backdrop

This question is usually, and unfortunately, not asked until the tree is half-grown and the owner believes it may be posing a threat to his house. Such threats take several forms: the roots may grow into and block drains; they may grow into and damage the foundations or may damage foundations indirectly by causing expansion of the surrounding soil. And as the tree grows, the branches and foliage may obstruct light from the windows. Lesser, but still significant, considerations are that fallen leaves may block gutters and drains, sticky honeydew from leaves may drip on paths or paintwork, and that flowers and shrubs will not flourish beneath a large, spreading tree.

The problems from root growth will be worst in peaty or clay soils and in extremely dry seasons; a drought year always brings a large number of insurance claims in its wake. Moreover, the roots of certain types of tree are much more prone than others to invade drains — willows are especially notorious.

With so many variables, it is difficult to give specific planting distances but, as a rough guide, find out the likely ultimate height of the tree (don't rely on the dimensions given by the nurseryman who is attempting to sell it to you) and plant at least one and a half times this distance away from the building.

How large a tree can be transplanted with a good chance of its surviving?

Extremely large, up to 4 m (13 ft) and more — but not by the average gardener. There have long been nurserymen who specialize in moving and replanting large trees; old gardening books often show photographs of strange and ingenious contraptions being used for this purpose. In more recent times, the need of industrial and new town developers, of builders of top-of-the-market housing estates, and of landscape gardeners, for the 'instant' landscape with built-in maturity has given an incentive for the safe moving of large trees to be perfected.

But before you plan to create mature woodland in this way overnight, consider these factors. It is a job for the expert with specialized knowledge and specialized equipment and is, in consequence, extremely expensive. Additionally, the trees to be used in this way are usually grown expressly for the purpose so that they may be dug up with the minimum of disturbance to the roots.

If you truly need one large specimen and cannot wait for nature to produce it for you, call in an expert and be prepared for the bill. Don't imagine that by hiring a Land-Rover and winch you can transplant a huge tree from a friend's woodland over the weekend.

See also:
Alternatives to grass under a large tree p 23
Relative heights of trees p 24
Herbaceous perennials for shade p 56

Shrubs for shade p 79
Transplanting shrubs p 84
Grassing up to trees p 106

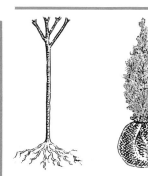

Trees may be bought from a nursery bare rooted, or they may come with a ball of soil around the roots which is wrapped in sacking or plastic. Increasingly, however, trees are grown in disposable containers from which they can be easily removed, with the least possible damage to the roots.

What are the basic rules for planting trees; can they be planted year-round?

Thinking to enhance the environment, many people enthusiastically buy trees, which then fail to survive because the three fundamental rules of planting have been forgotten. First, trees cannot necessarily be planted at any and every time of the year; second, planting a tree requires both planning and care; and third, the actual planting is not the end of the exercise if the tree is to stand a reasonable chance of reaching maturity.

At one time, purchasing a tree from a nursery for planting (or, strictly, replanting) meant that the nurseryman had to lift the growing tree from the ground. If the tree was large, the potential for root damage was significant, and it was necessary to wrap the soil around the root-ball with care. The delay between lifting and replanting had to be kept to a minimum; and because of the inevitable root disturbance and risk of frost damage to exposed roots, the operation could not be carried out in the coldest months of the year.

Two other factors were also important. A tree in leaf continually loses water through the foliage, and while its roots are out of the soil it is unable to take up water into its tissues. Thus, deciduous trees were almost always moved when the leaves had dropped; given the constraints of frost damage, this confined moving and planting to autumn and spring. Evergreens were even more of a problem, for they are permanently in leaf, so special care was needed, since they were always likely to suffer through water loss.

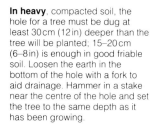

In heavy, compacted soil, the hole for a tree must be dug at least 30 cm (12 in) deeper than the tree will be planted; 15–20 cm (6–8 in) is enough in good friable soil. Loosen the earth in the bottom of the hole with a fork to aid drainage. Hammer in a stake near the centre of the hole and set the tree to the same depth as it has been growing.

Nowadays, gardeners and nurserymen have a much easier life, for even fairly large trees can be bought in containers. This has the merit that the plant can be removed and planted into the garden with almost no disturbance to the roots. Even so, handle the soil-ball carefully; keep intact but gently tease out at the edges any roots that have begun to spiral around the inside of the container. Remember that even this movement will cause some shock to the plant. All newly planted trees must be watered assiduously, and evergreens planted in winter will benefit from some protective screening to minimize the drying effects of cold wind.

Fork in about 15 cm (6 in) of manure or leaf-mould, then begin to fill in with topsoil. When the hole is about half full, firm the soil around the roots by treading it, holding the tree upright while you do so. Work in a couple of handfuls of bonemeal, some general fertilizer and a bucket or two of peat. Finish filling the hole and again firm the soil to the old planting level of the tree.

Don't buy on impulse; decide what shape of tree will satisfy your needs and suit the chosen site, and ensure that this is well prepared at least six months in advance. If you are planting in a lawn or an uncultivated part of the garden, a roughly circular area at least 1 m (3¼ ft) in diameter must be cleared and all weeds removed.

Even a fairly small tree will need staking for at least two years until its roots are established, and since most people plant relatively few trees, the additional investment in a purpose-cut stake with belt-style tree ties is worth the money.

Finally, the aftercare. A young tree will suffer during dry spells, so water it regularly and mulch around the base to help retain moisture in the soil. And don't force young trees to compete with other vegetation; keep the area around the base of the trunk free from weeds.

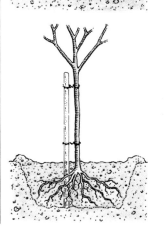

All young trees need staking. Use a stake about 5 cm (2 in) in diameter and equal in height to the tree, plus 45 cm (18 in) for driving into the ground. Tie the tree to the stake with belt-style tree ties made of rubber or heavy webbing. Use one tie every 1.5 m (5 ft) and tighten it against the stake, not the stem of the tree. Water copiously and mulch around the base of the tree.

Is it worth propagating trees from cuttings or seeds?

I hesitate to suggest that any aspect of gardening is not worthwhile, for there is satisfaction and enjoyment to be gained from all. Every task performed, whether it succeeds or not, teaches you something about the way plants behave and grow. However, most people have only a limited amount of time to devote to their gardens, and usually their horticultural education must take second place to the family's vegetable needs, the importance of bringing colour to the beds and borders and the routine seasonal tasks that even a small plot imposes.

The propagation of trees illustrates this point well, for although many can be raised from seeds or cuttings, the procedures are not always straightforward, and few gardeners will be fortunate enough to see the results of their endeavours approach maturity. My feeling, therefore, is that you should embark on the raising of young trees solely for interest; and then only if you can spare the time.

Although all wild trees propagate themselves through seed, many of the trees grown in gardens are natural or artificial hybrids, which do not set viable seed or, in fact,

set seed at all. So before attempting to germinate seed, it is wise to check in an authoritative reference book whether the plant is a hybrid and whether the seed is likely to be viable. Having determined that the seed does have the potential to produce another tree, the fun really begins, but you may have to be prepared to wait one or two years before anything springs into life.

Although the seeds of some trees will germinate fresh, many require a period of some weeks or months before they will do so, and they often need some exposure to cold. It is impossible to list the conditions necessary for each and every species (and, in fact, the optimum conditions are not known for many), so I suggest that you hedge your bets. Use a soil-based seedling compost and sow some seeds in a cold frame and some in a greenhouse as soon as you obtain them. Soak the remainder in water, seal them in a plastic bag, place them in a fridge and sow half after one month and half after two months. Then be prepared to wait.

With cuttings, too, it is impossible to generalize, but experiment with any and every type of tree that takes your fancy. Try striking semi-hardwood cuttings in late summer in sharp sand in a propagator; and remember the golden rule with cuttings of any sort: keep them in a moist atmosphere, but don't allow the whole to become waterlogged.

Some trees root easily from semi-hard cuttings taken from firm shoots of the current year's growth in late summer. Choose a well-grown 20-cm (8-in) shoot with leaves and cut it close to the stem.

Take out the tip of the shoot, trim off the lower leaves and cut the stem through just below the bottom leaf node. The cutting should now be about 10 cm (4 in) long.

Dip the end of the cutting in hormone rooting-powder and push it into a pot containing a mixture of peat and sand. A 7.5 cm (3 in) pot will hold up to five cuttings. Press the compost down and water thoroughly by spraying.

To keep the atmosphere around the cuttings moist, make a framework with flexible canes or wire and cover it with a plastic bag held in place by a rubber band. Keep the cuttings in a warm place until they root: 2–3 weeks.

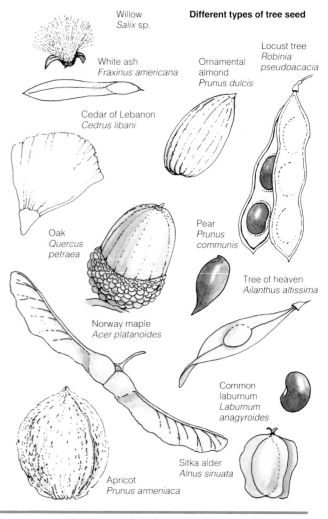

Different types of tree seed

Willow
Salix sp.

White ash
Fraxinus americana

Ornamental almond
Prunus dulcis

Locust tree
Robinia pseudoacacia

Cedar of Lebanon
Cedrus libani

Oak
Quercus petraea

Pear
Prunus communis

Tree of heaven
Ailanthus altissima

Norway maple
Acer platanoides

Common laburnum
Laburnum anagyroides

Sitka alder
Alnus sinuata

Apricot
Prunus armeniaca

See also:
Germination of seeds p 44
Cold frames pp 44, 45
Shrubs for autumn colour p 78

Flowering trees for a small garden
pp 111–12
Propagators p 142

What are the best trees to give attractive autumn colour?

Maples are popularly believed to be the beginning and end of autumn coloration, and undoubtedly some maples are indispensable on any gardener's list, as those who have visited such gardens as Westonbirt in Gloucestershire will testify. But it is also true that anyone who has seen the scarcely believable displays of autumn colour of the maples in the United States or Canada will be disappointed if they select the same species for their own gardens. Several of the most vivid North American maples, such as *Acer saccharum*, are often something of a let-down in Britain.

The selection of maples among the trees given here is deliberately limited, but it includes those most reliable and most appealing during the remainder of the year as well. It is all too easy to choose a tree that looks spectacular for two weeks and to forget that you have to live with it for the remaining fifty. Most of the plants should be obtainable at a good garden centre, but if they are not you may find closely related species or varieties with similar colouring. But be careful, relatedness is not necessarily a guarantee of a good colour. The heights are those likely on good soils after ten and twenty years.

TREES FOR AUTUMN COLOUR

Acer capillipes	7–13m (23–42½ ft)
Acer griseum	3–5m (10–16½ ft)
Acer palmatum 'Ozakazuki'	2–5m (6½–16½ ft)
Acer platanoides 'Schwedleri'	8–13m (26–42½ ft)
Acer rubrum	8–12m (26–39½ ft)
Amelanchier lamarckii	6–9m (19½–29½ ft)
Betula costata	8–12m (26–39½ ft)
Betula jacquemontii	8–12m (26–39½ ft)
Crataegus prunifolia	3–5m (10–16½ ft)
Liquidambar styraciflua	5–12m (16½–39½ ft)
Liriodendron tulipifera	8–16m (26–52½ ft)
Malus florentina	6–9m (19½–29½ ft)
Parrotia persica	4–7m (13–23 ft)
Prunus sargentii	5–9m (16½–29½ ft)
Quercus rubra	10–15m (33–49 ft)
Sorbus commixta	6–9m (19½–29½ ft)
Sorbus 'Joseph Rock'	6–12m (19½–39½ ft)
Stewartia pseudocamellia	5–9m (16½–29½ ft)

In addition to fine leaf colour in autumn, many trees suitable for a small garden have attractive flowers and extremely ornamental fruits. Some of these are described on the next two pages.

Is it true that some trees poison the ground?

This question clearly stems from the observation that some plants do not grow well when planted close to certain others. The truth of the observation is not in doubt, but there are few authenticated instances of one species of plant producing a poison that has an adverse effect on other plants growing close by.

The best-known example is that of the walnut tree, which manufactures a chemical, juglone, in the leaves. When washed into the soil, this can have the effect of retarding plant growth and may offer an explanation of the poor condition of other plants in the vicinity. But this is an exception; the explanation is usually the more straightforward one of competition for nutrients and water in the soil.

Look closely at the soil beneath a privet hedge, for example, and you should be able to see one reason why privet is so often blamed for the poor performance of plants near by. The ground, even in wet winter weather, is dry; in summer, it is really parched and dusty. Some plants simply have a root system that so thoroughly exhausts the soil as to make them appear to be resorting to Borgia-like ploys to stifle the opposition.

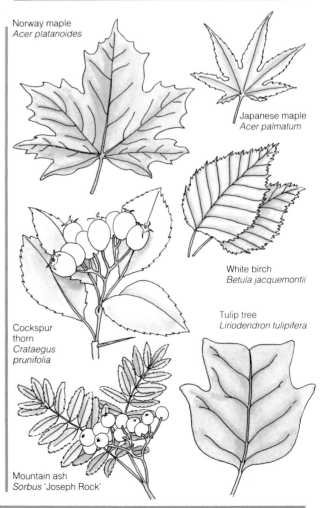

Norway maple
Acer platanoides

Japanese maple
Acer palmatum

White birch
Betula jacquemontii

Tulip tree
Liriodendron tulipifera

Cockspur thorn
Crataegus prunifolia

Mountain ash
Sorbus 'Joseph Rock'

111

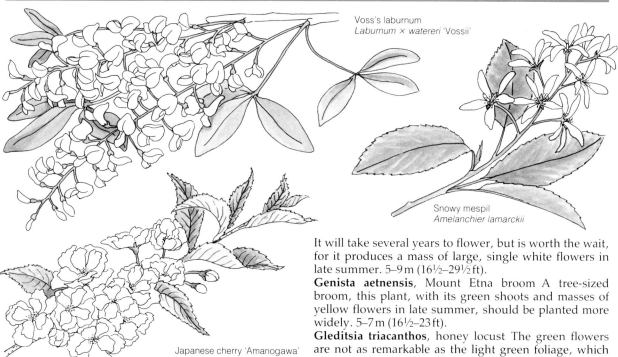

Voss's laburnum
Laburnum × watereri 'Vossii'

Snowy mespil
Amelanchier lamarckii

Japanese cherry 'Amanogawa'

? What flowering trees are suitable for a small garden?

The small trees suggested here are especially appealing for their blossoms, although it is always important, and doubly so in a fairly small garden, to choose plants that have other attractions. I have, therefore, indicated where a blossom tree has features such as good autumn colouring or ornamental fruits as well. Almost inevitably, there is a majority of *Prunus* species, although often people ask for a list of blossom trees, specifically excluding cherries. This is understandable, for some flowering cherries are downright dismal once their brief days of spring glory are over.

The heights given are those to be expected on good soils after 10 and 20 years' growth:

Amelanchier lamarckii, snowy mespil One of the most perfect small garden trees, with a delicate tracery of winter twigs, delightful small white flowers in spring, soft green foliage in summer and rich autumn leaf colours and fruit. Ensure that you obtain the true *lamarckii*. 4–6 m (13–19½ ft).

Arbutus unedo, strawberry tree This small, evergreen tree with shaggy, reddish bark bears white and pink flowers in panicles from October to December, at the same time that scarlet berries, or 'strawberries', from the previous year's flowers ripen. 4–6 m (13–19½ ft).

Cercis siliquastrum, Judas tree A rounded or drooping tree, with bright pink, broom-like flowers in late spring. 3–5 m (10–16½ ft).

Eucryphia nymansensis 'Nymansay' This could be described as a large, many-stemmed shrub, but it is a glorious evergreen plant, given shelter from cold wind.

It will take several years to flower, but is worth the wait, for it produces a mass of large, single white flowers in late summer. 5–9 m (16½–29½ ft).

Genista aetnensis, Mount Etna broom A tree-sized broom, this plant, with its green shoots and masses of yellow flowers in late summer, should be planted more widely. 5–7 m (16½–23 ft).

Gleditsia triacanthos, honey locust The green flowers are not as remarkable as the light green foliage, which turns a clear, pale yellow in autumn, but they are followed by long, twisted, brown seedpods that turn in the wind all through the winter. 6–9 m (19½–29½ ft).

Laburnum × watereri 'Vossii', Voss's laburnum By far the best laburnum, with masses of long, pendulous flower heads. (7–8 m (23–26 ft).

Magnolia soulangiana The best widely available magnolia, this spreading tree has large, tulip-shaped flowers, which are white with varying amounts of purple, depending on the variety. 2–3 m (6½–10 ft).

Malus spp., flowering crab apples The main drawback to the crabs is that, like apples, they suffer from scab, canker and mildew, which can be disfiguring. When in flower in spring or in fruit in autumn, they are extremely beautiful. Among the best for blossom are 'John Downie', 5–8 m (16½–26 ft), with large, single white flowers in May, which is arguably the best for crab-apple jelly, and 'Profusion', 3–5 m (10–16½ ft), which has deep red flowers and coppery-red leaves. 'Golden Hornet', 4–6 m (13–19½ ft), has smaller white flowers, but produces a bounteous crop of shiny yellow apples that remain on the tree well into the winter.

Prunus spp. This selection is planned to give a range of flowering times, and a concerted effort by a small neighbourhood, in which each gardener chose one variety, could give an extended blossom period for the benefit of all. The flowering times will vary slightly from season to season, but the order will be fairly constant.

Prunus subhirtella 'Autumnalis', winter-flowering cherry This tree is rather large and spreading for a small garden but is invaluable for its flowering period — from October to April. There is a flush of blossom after the leaves fall and again before the leaf buds break in spring, with irregular flowering throughout the winter. Twigs cut at any time during the winter can be relied on to produce flowers in the house. 3–5 m (10–16½ ft).

See also:
Relative height of trees p 24
Feature shrubs for a small garden
p 80

Rose hedges p 91
Hedging plants for a seaside
garden p 114

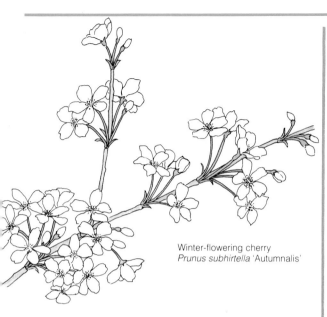

Winter-flowering cherry
Prunus subhirtella 'Autumnalis'

Prunus sargentii Deep pink, single flowers appear in late March; autumn colour is excellent and the bark is a rich brown. 5–9 m (16½–29½ ft).

Prunus hillieri 'Spire' Single pink flowers bloom in a cloud in late March on a compact, upright tree; the leaves often turn a deep red in autumn. 6–7 m (19½–23 ft).

Japanese cherry 'Shirotae' The single or semi-double, pure white flowers appear in early April on spreading or drooping branches, to be followed by leaves that are bronze when young. 4–5 m (13–16½ ft).

Japanese cherry 'Kiku-shidare Sakura' (often erroneously called Cheal's Weeping) Deep pink, double flowers are borne on upward arching and then weeping branches in early April. 2–3 m (6½–10 ft).

Japanese cherry 'Hokusai' This tree is fast growing in its early years; it has pale pink, semi-double flowers in mid-April and good autumn colour. It is earlier and smaller than 'Kanzan'. 5–6 m (16½–19½ ft).

Japanese cherry 'Amanogawa' A markedly upright tree, specially good for small gardens, with pale pink, semi-double flowers in late April. 5–7 m (16½–23 ft).

Japanese cherry 'Pink Perfection' The deep pink, double flowers, produced in early May on a compact, fairly upright tree, fade almost to white, and are followed by leaves that are copper-red when young. 5–6 m (16½–19½ ft).

Japanese cherry 'Shirofugen' This fairly upright, moderately large tree is valuable for its large, white double flowers in mid-May. 5–8 m (16½–26 ft).

Sorbus spp. These easily grown trees and shrubs are good for town gardens, since many species can withstand atmospheric pollution and will grow in the shade.

Sorbus 'Joseph Rock' Clusters of creamy flowers in May followed by golden berries and brilliant orange-red leaves in early autumn. 4–6 m (13–19½ ft).

Sorbus vilmorinii The white flowers, produced in loose clusters in June, are followed in September by bunches of round, rosy fruits that ripen white with a pink blush. 2.5–4 m (8–13 ft).

What is the best plant to produce a quick-growing and fairly tall screen?

There are several requirements for a plant to be used for screening. It must give cover all year round; it must grow quickly but not unacceptably tall; and must not require a great deal of attention. It must not adversely affect other parts of the garden and so not spread too widely beyond its allotted line. Finally, it must be reasonably attractive. No plant known to me fulfills all these criteria and, inevitably, there must be a compromise.

Beech Beautiful and with appealing colour variation, the dead brown leaves in winter contrast with the soft pale green in spring and darker green in summer. It is not fast growing and is better used for low hedges.

Hawthorn This is sometimes sold as quickthorn, emphasizing its fairly rapid growth; although dense, it seldom forms a satisfactory tall garden hedge.

Holly Fairly slow growing, impenetrable, holly is good for a low hedge, but the wait for a tall screen is too long.

Laurel Fairly slow growing and, with its large leaves, a nightmare to clip if it is not to appear unsightly.

Lawson cypress There is a wide range of varieties, some much better as hedging plants than others. They are generally fast growing, dense, and some are extremely attractive, especially the golden forms.

Leyland cypress This, too, is fast growing, but not as dense as Lawson and hence not as attractive. If speed of growth is not the overriding consideration, try the slightly slower, golden form, 'Castelwellan Gold', in preference to the dull, common variety.

Privet Low, slow and dull! Not suitable for a hedge; the golden form is not to be scorned as a specimen shrub.

Rhododendron ponticum Only suitable for acid soils and a with loose, spreading habit, this species is useful for deep shade.

Yew Not as slow growing as many people imagine, but, as with holly, yew is still too slow for use as a screen.

Underrated by comparison with cypresses, *Thuja plicata* is dense and fast growing, with pleasantly scented foliage.

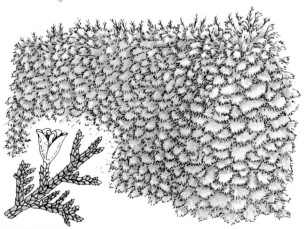

Is there a suitable hedging plant for a seaside garden?

Seaside gardening is not easy because many of the familiar garden plants grown inland cannot tolerate the combination of exposure and salt. With so much more limited a choice of plants in general, it is small wonder that the range of those suitable for hedging is correspondingly restricted. There are some compensations, however, for many coastal localities have a milder or, at least, a more equable climate.

In a truly mild coastal area, there is no more splendid sight than a fuchsia hedge in full flower; but only gardeners in the extreme south and west of Britain will be able to grow this successfully. The most generally satisfactory coastal hedging plants are escallonias, especially *E. macrantha*, followed by olearias such as *O. haastii*. Among others worth trying are *Euonymus japonicus*, pittosporum, and, for a rough boundary rather than a hedge, tamarisk.

Quite commonly, cypresses are recommended for seaside gardens, but they brown too readily to be effective as hedges. For a large windbreak, a maritime pine, such as *Pinus nigra* or, in milder areas, *P. pinaster* or *P. radiata* makes a good choice.

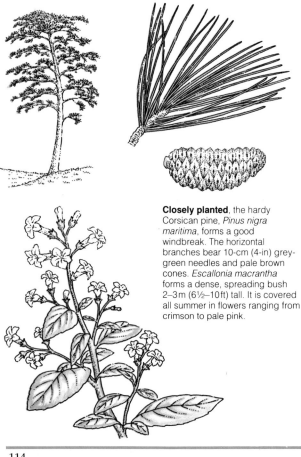

Closely planted, the hardy Corsican pine, *Pinus nigra maritima*, forms a good windbreak. The horizontal branches bear 10-cm (4-in) grey-green needles and pale brown cones. *Escallonia macrantha* forms a dense, spreading bush 2–3 m (6½–10 ft) tall. It is covered all summer in flowers ranging from crimson to pale pink.

How can I dispose of a tree stump easily and safely?

From time to time, firms offering apparently effective, not to say magic, substances for the removal of tree stumps advertise in the columns of the gardening Press. Most of these firms are considerably more short lived than the tree stumps they claim to eradicate, for none of the chemical treatments on offer has stood up to careful scientific scrutiny. But when these miracle cures have been discounted, what is left?

Nature, left to her own devices, will in time make a tree stump easier to remove by physical means. A stump up to about 25 cm (10 in) in diameter of most types of tree (oak being the most conspicuous exception) will become unstable after a couple of years as its roots decay. It can then be levered from the ground without too much difficulty.

If you do not want to wait, you have two options: either brace yourself and a small army of friends for a massive excavation with spades, crowbars and levers, or call in a contractor. He will approach the problem in one of two ways. Provided you have left a decent length of trunk (a metre, say) it should be possible to winch out the stump if a vehicle can approach closely enough. Alternatively, the contractor may suggest grinding the stump with a device rather like an enormous mincing machine. This, too, requires access for a large machine

Does the greenish powdery growth that appears on tree bark do any harm?

This green growth is a combination of a form of green alga and a type of lichen (a curious dual organism, comprising both an alga and a fungus). Algae and lichen will colonize bark and other rough surfaces free from regular disturbance, wherever moisture collects. Boy Scouts and Girl Guides are taught that the simplest way to find a compass direction in a wood is to note on which side of tree trunks the green growth occurs, for it always colonizes the damp, north face. It does no harm to the trees on which it grows.

This is also generally true of the larger, tufted growths of lichen that sometimes clothe the branches and twigs of trees in really wet areas. When extensive, these growths can have a smothering effect and are best removed. On deciduous trees, a tar-oil winter wash applied during December or January, while they are dormant, will kill lichen; but on evergreens, there is no alternative to brushing them off.

See also:
Removing leaf-mould from woods
p 14
Water rights p 40
Burning pampas grass p 61

Dwarf conifers p 82
Honey fungus p 83
Rose hedges p 91
Quick-growing screens p 113

and would be extremely expensive for a single stump, although worth the cost if a small area of woodland has been clear-felled.

One technique you should not attempt is burning. A tree stump, once ignited, can smoulder for a long time, the fire spreading into dead, dry roots. On peaty soils in summer, it is possible with this procedure to set the soil alight underneath the surface with potentially serious consequences.

If all else fails or you are not able to afford the expense, try turning a stump to good purpose by growing groundcover and climbing plants over it. Low-growing roses such as 'Nathalie Nypels', the variegated bramble, *Rubus tricolor*, or some of the more vigorous clematis look excellent when allowed to scramble freely in this way.

Turn necessity to virtue when a large tree stump cannot easily be removed by using it as a support for a climbing plant. The free-flowering Old Rose 'Nathalie Nypels' will rapidly grow over a stump and produce sweet-scented, clear pink semi-double flowers throughout the summer.

 ## What causes the large growths like birds' nests in some trees?

Such large growths are seen most frequently on birches. They are known as witches' brooms and, if seen at close quarters, do sometimes bear a resemblance to the besoms that witches bestride to journey around the countryside. Although witches' brooms are caused by parasitic organisms (fungi, bacteria or viruses may all be responsible), they apparently have little deleterious effect on the trees.

It is clear that the brooms arise when the tree's growth-regulating chemicals, or hormones, have been disturbed in some way, with the result that masses of short, twiggy growths are produced. If they are severely disfiguring, witches' brooms should be cut out and burned although, interestingly, several varieties of dwarf conifer originated as brooms cut from the parent tree and deliberately propagated by cuttings and grafts.

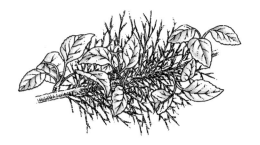

Must I obtain permission before I can cut down a tree in my garden?

Yes, and no; it depends where you live, how large the tree is, what type of tree it is, and if it is dead. Generally speaking, you may cut down a dead, dying or dangerous tree without asking anyone. If the tree is alive and well, it may have one of two types of legal protection.

A fine, specimen tree may be protected by a Tree Preservation Order, taken out by a local authority whose permission will be needed before the tree may be pruned, let alone felled. You may be unaware of an existing preservation order on one of your trees, so it is wise to check. If an authority proposes to take out a new preservation order, they will inform you of this.

Even if a tree is not protected individually, it will automatically acquire protection if you live in a designated Conservation Area and if it has a trunk diameter of more than 7.5cm (3in) at a height of 1.5m (5ft) above ground level. In such circumstances, you are obliged to inform the local authority of your intentions and obtain their permission; and even if they agree to your actions, they may still require you to replace any tree that enjoys legal protection.

What can be done about a sumach tree that produces suckers on the lawn?

This feature of *Rhus typhina* is a good reason for not planting it in a small garden, when there are so many other, better trees that do not have this annoying and troublesome habit. So, don't grow sumachs.

If you are unfortunate enough to inherit a sumach from a previous garden owner, you will find it difficult to divest yourself of the bequest. Merely cutting down the tree is of little help, for this will stimulate the production of more suckers from the rootstock unless it, too, is removed completely. Mowing off the suckers as they are produced will gradually eliminate them, and the process can be hastened by carefully painting them with the systemic weedkiller glyphosate.

The suckers must be in a well-leafed state for the chemical to be effective, and there must be no rain for six hours after its application. Glyphosate is a total, although non-residual, weedkiller, so care must be taken not to splash any on the lawn or on other plants. Finally, you will need to be patient, for the suckers will take several weeks to show the effects of the treatment.

The brilliant autumn foliage colours of the stag's horn sumach, *Rhus typhina*, is not really sufficient compensation for its habit of sending up countless suckers from the roots. The best way to get rid of them is to paint the leaves with a systemic weedkiller such as glyphosate.

What makes the best dwarf hedge, of the type formerly used around herb gardens?

The dwarf hedge makes an attractive garden feature and was the backbone of the old English knot gardens, in which beds were laid out in complex and intricate patterns, with the hedge marking the boundaries of each. The essential features of such a hedge are that it should be small leaved, slow growing and either naturally low growing or highly responsive to being maintained in miniature form.

Around a herb garden, what more natural than to use a herb or an aromatic plant itself? Rosemary can, with care, be kept as a low-growing hedge, but perhaps best of all is lavender. Choose one of the forms known as *nana*, for these are inherently lower growing. Cut back the dead flower shoots after flowering and gently perform any necessary shaping at the same time.

Another good choice is that adaptable plant, box, of which there are many dwarf forms, such as *Buxus sempervirens* 'Suffruticosa'. Other suitable plants are lavender cotton (*Santolina incana* = *chamaecyparissus* 'Nana'), *Cotoneaster microphyllus*, *Hebe cupressoides*, *Berberis buxifolia nana*, and many dwarf ericas and callunas.

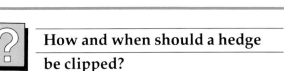

How and when should a hedge be clipped?

This depends to some extent on the type of hedge and, more essentially, on the amount of time you have. The guidelines given here relate specifically to more or less formal hedges, which are retained in a defined shape. Informal hedges need only occasional pruning in accordance with the principles relating pruning time to flowering in shrubs.

In general, hedges should not be clipped before late May or after mid-October. If you have a long hedge and little time, one annual clipping may be all that can be managed, but this should not be done until the season's growth is complete. Many hedging plants, and privet in particular, quickly become straggly and untidy if they are clipped only once a year. One of the drawbacks to privet for hedging is that it requires clipping almost more often than any other if it is to look attractive.

Most other garden hedges will thrive and retain their attractiveness with two annual clippings, one in July and one in October. The flowering hedges such as roses, berberis, olearia or fuchsia are best pruned fairly hard once a year after the flowers have faded. Newly planted hedges generally benefit from slight shortening of the longer shoots to encourage bushiness.

Although I have described hedge-cutting as clipping, implying that shears should be used, some hedges look unsightly treated in this way and should be cut with

See also:
Dwarf conifers p 82
Pruning shrubs p 85
Rhododendron suckers p 86

Flowering trees for a small garden
pp 112–13
Rose suckers p 116

1 2 3 4 5

Lavender makes perhaps the most attractive dwarf hedge. The variety *Lavandula nana atropurpurea*, **1**, grows up to 60cm (24in) tall and bears spikes of deep bluish-purple flowers throughout the summer. *Santolina incana*, lavender cotton, **2**, forms a dense bush about 45cm (18in)

high. The finely cut leaves are woolly-looking and silvery; the flowers in July a bright, sharp yellow. Dwarf box, *Buxus sempervirens* 'Suffruticosa', **3**, was commonly used in Elizabethan times for the neat hedges that formed the threads in knot gardens. Its bright green, shiny

leaves give it an immaculate appearance, and it responds well to clipping. The scent of box is strong and pleasant. Hardy *Hebe cupressoides*, **4**, has pale blue flowers among its tiny grey-green leaves in June. It grows to 1.5m (5ft) and must be clipped if it is to make a low hedge. Frequently

used for groundcover, *Cotoneaster microphyllus*, **5**, reaches a height of up to 60cm (24in) or so. It has dark green, glossy leaves with grey undersides, and the tiny white flowers are followed by crowds of red berries.

secateurs. This applies especially to the large-leaved evergreens, such as laurel, and many common hedging conifers. But anyone faced with 50m (165ft) of hedge to cut with secateurs will rightly consider this advice academic.

When a hedge has become overgrown through neglect, it should be cut back hard into the old wood early in the season — the beginning of April is ideal. Growth will then start almost immediately. At the same time, any weeds, ivy or brambles should be cleared out from the bottom of the hedge and a mulch of well-rotted farmyard manure applied.

Sometimes an old farm hedge of hawthorn or a mixture of other native species has been left to form a garden boundary, and, commonly such old hedges become bare at the base and entwined with weeds. They can be completely rejuvenated by layering, an operation

that was once a routine feature of the English countryside but which has largely given way to tractor-driven slashers (the 'circular saw on a stick' devices) that merely mutilate and compound existing branch death.

Although layering is a skilled and thorny operation, there is no reason why a gardener with time and energy to spare should not attempt it. First clear out the weeds and other debris from the hedge bottom and cut away dead branches. Then, starting at one end, lay the main branches at a steep angle and secure them to stout stakes driven into the ground. New growth will be stimulated by the layering, and a hedge treated in this way in winter will improve beyond recognition by the end of the following summer.

The country craft of layering helps to make a hedge thick and to stop it from becoming leggy. Starting at one end of the hedge, lay the main branches almost horizontal and secure them to strong stakes driven into the ground at intervals. Cut any thick branches partially through with long, sloping cuts and bend them into place. As the layering progresses, cut back the side branches and reduce the top to a uniform height.

VEGETABLES

A profusion of crops
for the kitchen

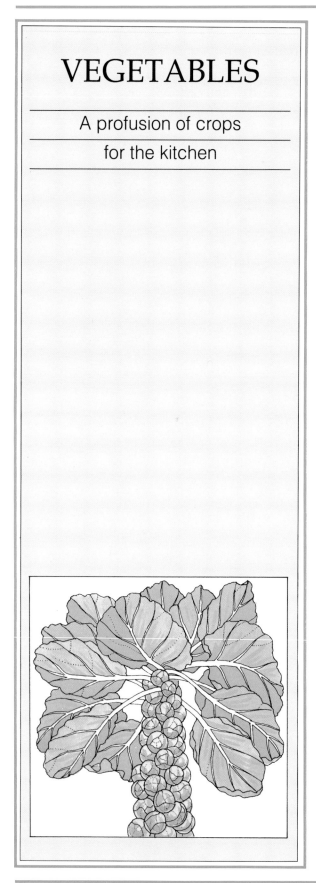

How important is it to rotate vegetable crops?

A change is as good as a rest, we are told. Apply the maxim to the vegetable garden, and you have the underlying motive behind the practice of crop rotation, whereby individual types of vegetable are grown on a different part of the garden each year so that like never follows like. There are two main reasons why this change, or rest, is good for the garden.

The first is that different species of plant utilize different amounts of nutrient from the soil, although most require more or less the same types of nutrient. Thus, brassicas need large amounts of nitrogen to promote the vigorous leafy growth that is the object of their cultivation. While peas and beans require little nitrogen, for they are able to 'manufacture' it through the activities of bacteria that live on their roots.

Similarly, fruiting crops such as tomatoes have a much higher demand for potash than root crops like carrots. By ensuring that the same type of crop occupies a particular area for only one season, the available nutrient resources in the soil are tapped to the full.

The second reason for rotating vegetable crops is to help keep them free from pests and diseases. Many of the pests and even more of the diseases that live in the soil are fairly specific in the types of plant they will attack. In the absence of these plants, they die away. Thus, if the length of time they can persist in the soil is less than the number of years before the plants are grown on the same site again, the potential problem should be kept at bay. Or so goes the theory.

This logic works fairly well in commerical cropping because the size of the crops and the land on which they are grown is relatively large; the distance on a farm from one brassica field to another may be a couple of kilometres or more. Thus, there is little likelihood that a soil-inhabiting disease or even a pest with an adult flying phase will be readily transferred from one field to another. These arguments scarcely apply in gardens, where the distance from this year's brassicas to the plot where they were grown in previous years is only a few metres.

Could you please explain what an F_1 hybrid is?

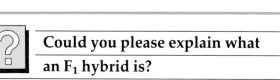

The designation F_1 hybrid is seen increasingly in seed catalogues, not only in relation to vegetables but to other garden plants as well. Many of these varieties have obviously Dutch or Japanese names, indicating where most modern vegetable varieties originate. The most immediately apparent difference between an F_1 hybrid variety and an 'ordinary' one is that the hybrid seed is much more expensive. Understandably gardeners question whether the extra cost is worth it, especially when they read that the seed from an F_1 hybrid plant cannot be used the following season.

A hybrid is a cross between parents of different types,

See also:
Compost p 10
Organic v artificial fertilizers p 12
Fertilizers for different types of plant p 17

Liquid and solid fertilizers p 18
Hiding a vegetable plot p 29
Vegetables used ornamentally pp 28, 49, 121

It seems improbable, therefore, that the rotation of vegetable crops in a garden will have any impact on pest and disease incidence, although it clearly confers benefits in plant nutrition. There is also the incidental but significant advantage that the soil becomes more uniformly cultivated overall. The rotation of crops that require deep cultivation and manuring before planting will ensure that in time the whole vegetable garden receives this treatment.

But there are still a few crops for which the benefits of rotation are outweighed by other considerations. Runner beans are the best example among the crops grown as annuals, for in many gardens a robust system of supports is used that would be difficult to move. Sweet corn and celery can be grown on the same area each season, while the perennial vegetables, such as asparagus, rhubarb and some of the less common crops, are necessarily grown in the same place year after year. Where the soil conditions are not suitable for any particular type of vegetable, it is sometimes advantageous to develop a semi-permanent bed for them: a specially lightened area on a heavy clay for carrots, for instance.

In designing a rotation plan, these basic horticultural rules should be remembered. Root crops (carrots, parsnips, beetroot) will not grow well on land that has been freshly manured. Brassicas (cabbages, cauliflowers, Brussels sprouts, broccoli, turnips, swedes) and other leafy vegetables such as spinach require a high level of nitrogen, and brassicas often also benefit from liming. Peas and beans need a low level of nitrogen but benefit from manuring; and some crops (radishes and lettuces for instance) grow and mature quickly and can be fitted in among slower-growing crops. You will, in addition, need to adapt the plan to suit your family's likes and requirements.

In a 3-year rotation plan, the area is divided into four parts: a standing bed and three beds 1.25 × 6m (4 × 20ft) in which crops are rotated. Bed A has manure or compost dug in to feed the tomatoes, marrows, cucumbers and legumes that require a rich soil but little nitrogen. Bed B has fertilizer and lime applied and contains leaf crops that need nitrogen, such as spinach, and brassicas that also need lime.

Bed C is for root crops, which grow mis-shapen if given manure, get enough lime from that left after brassicas have been grown, and need only general fertilizer. The second season, the crops in Bed A are grown in Bed C; the crops in Bed B in Bed A; and those in Bed C in Bed B. Crops follow each other in the same order for year 3. In this way, fertilizers are economically used and crops enjoy the conditions they require.

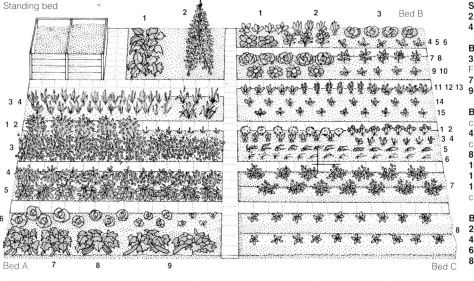

Standing bed

Bed B

Bed A   7   8   9   Bed C

Standing bed: 1 Rhubarb; **2** Runner beans; **3** Asparagus; **4** Salsify.

Bed A: 1 Tomatoes; **2** Leeks; **3** Peas; **4** Broad beans; **5** Dwarf French beans; **6** Lettuces; **7** Courgettes; **8** Marrow; **9** Cucumbers.

Bed B: 1 Spinach beet; **2** Swiss chard; **3** Summer cabbages; **4** Calabrese; **5** Broccoli; **6** Winter cabbages; **7** Spring cabbages; **8** Kale; **9** Mini-cauliflowers; **10** Autumn cauliflowers; **11** Swedes; **12** Turnips; **13** Kohl-rabi; **14** Winter cauliflowers; **15** Brussels sprouts.

Bed C: 1 Early carrots; **2** Parsnips; **3** Beetroot; **4** Maincrop carrots; **5** Onions; **6** Shallots; **7** New potatoes; **8** Maincrop potatoes.

be they species, natural varieties or artificially created varieties (cultivars). An F_1 hybrid comprises the first generation of progeny from such a cross, although not from a cross made at random. The process of hybridization has become technically complicated but, at its simplest, two parent plants with desirable attributes (large flowers, good fruit quality and so forth) are each artificially fertilized with their own pollen.

After eliminating those that fall short of the desired quality, carefully selected progeny plants from this fertilization are also self-fertilized. The process is repeated many times until the desired characteristics predominate in most individuals; the resultant plants are known as an inbred line. Although these plants now have the chosen, highly appealing feature, their general vigour will be low because of the repeated inbreeding.

When two inbred lines are crossed, however, the vigour returns in the hybrid, together with the selected features in 'concentrated' form. Hence the appeal of an F_1 hybrid: it will have larger, better flowers or fruit and, above all, greater uniformity. The artificial pollination needed each year to produce the seeds accounts for their high cost, but seed from an F_1 hybrid will be a genetic hotch-potch and is thus, in itself, useless.

If you seek bigger flowers and higher-yielding vegetables, then an F_1 hybrid variety is probably worth the extra cost. Remember, though, that they were produced originally for the commercial market, where uniformity of produce and of time taken to mature is important. You may well not want all your sprouts to ripen at the same time and should think carefully before rejecting older, less uniform varieties.

The **deep bed** system of growing vegetables makes more economical use of the garden space than single-row cultivation.

Mark out as many beds about 1.25m (4ft) wide as you can accommodate, leaving narrow paths between them.

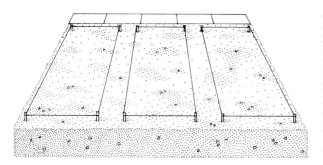

Then set about digging the earth in each bed to two spade-depths, removing weeds and stones and breaking up any clods. Add plenty of well-rotted farmyard manure or compost. You will not need to dig the beds so deeply again for four or five years, but you should top them up with manure and compost every autumn.

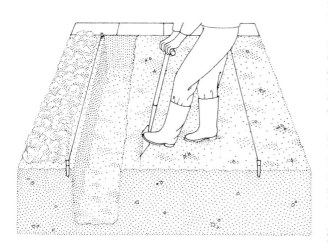

If a wide bed poses problems when you are sowing seed or planting out seedlings, set a broad plank across it. Prop the plank up firmly on bricks at each end, so that it is a few inches above the surface of the soil, and work from it.

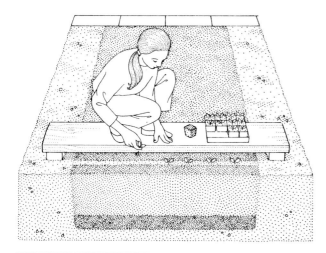

What is the 'deep bed' system of vegetable growing?

There are two parts to this answer. First, why bed? Many years ago, farmers sowed their seed by broadcasting it. They walked across the field and threw, or cast, handfuls of seed in a broad sweep as they went. In many parts of the world, this system is still used, but it is wasteful of seed and also inefficient, for some seeds fall close together and the seedlings compete with each other, while others fall sparsely and the potential of the ground is not fully utilized.

Later, the advent of the horse-drawn corn drill meant that cereals came to be grown in rows; and later still, the same system was adopted with commercial vegetable growing. It has carried through to the present-day garden, where the traditional way for vegetables to be grown is still in rows. But have you ever queried the logic of having plants close together within the rows, while between them there are wide, open spaces, intended for a horse to walk down but now serving merely as a no man's land for weeds?

The pendulum has begun to swing back again as many people realize that their garden space is more efficiently utilized by growing vegetables in beds, although with the plants uniformly spaced and not by broadcasting seed. The ideal width for garden beds is about 1.25m (4ft), for this enables the soil to be worked easily from either side.

The significance of working from either side is that the soil where the vegetables grow is not trodden on. Walking on soil compresses and compacts the surface, hindering the free penetration of water, air and fertilizer, all necessary for good plant growth. And if the soil is not compacted, there is no need to dig it; hence less time and effort each year.

It is no use, however, earmarking a random patch of garden, bringing a halt to annual digging and calling it a vegetable bed. It must first be rendered 'deep' by digging to two spade-depths, and plenty of well-rotted farmyard manure or other organic matter must be incorporated. Thereafter the site can be topped up with compost and manure each autumn, and it should not be necessary to dig it again for at least four or five years. If the 1.25m (4ft) width presents something of a stretch (which it may do when sowing seeds), place a couple of bricks on each side of the bed, lay a plank across, bridge-fashion, and work from this.

See also:
Organic v artificial fertilizers p 12
Fertilizers for different types of plant p 17

Liquid and solid fertilizers p 18
Garden planning pp 28–9
Unusual vegetables pp 122–3

Concentrate on those crops that are best enjoyed fresh when you have only a tiny vegetable plot. Among the most rewarding are French beans, summer lettuce, spring onions, cut-and-come-again Swiss chard, early carrots, radishes and cucumbers.

Which are the best vegetables to grow in limited space?

There are several ways of approaching this problem; you can restrict yourself to those vegetables that are the most satisfying, challenging or rewarding to grow; those that occupy the least space per plant or per crop; or those that are the most expensive to buy. In some instances, adopting a well-planned and efficient cropping system will help to ensure that the space is used to the full.

Any answer to this question inevitably leaves out someone's favourite vegetable; so I shall simply outline my own solution to the problem, detailing which plants I discard as space becomes increasingly limited. Maincrop potatoes are, for me, almost the least rewarding of all plants, let alone vegetables. They have none of the appeal of the new potato, occupy a vast amount of space, offer little of a challenge and are never prohibitively expensive to buy.

Next to go are swedes, which are never successful as garden plants unless you grow them, as farmers do, in large blocks. Turnips, cabbages, Brussels sprouts, winter cauliflowers, leeks, maincrop beetroot, parsnips, maincrop carrots and maincrop peas follow. I have now brought you down from the self-sufficient vegetable garden to a modest, but still rewarding, plot.

The next step is to eliminate those vegetables that occupy a disproportionate amount of space, even if they are satisfying and delicious. So out go bush tomatoes, second early peas, dwarf beans, marrows, broccolis, celeriac, summer and autumn cauliflower, new potatoes, the rest of the beetroot, bulb onions, sweet corn and celery.

Allowing for differences in growing seasons, this still leaves a most appealing small vegetable and salad garden, including overwintered broad beans, winter radish, possibly winter lettuce, continuous summer lettuce, radish, spring onions, early carrots, Swiss chard (the best form of spinach), staked tomatoes (which could even be grown in growing bags off the plot altogether), herbs, early peas, runner beans, and ridge cucumbers.

This selection includes almost all those crops that taste better absolutely fresh. The one I have excluded, and to which this also applies, is sweet corn, since it takes up so much space in relation to its yield. But why not try treating sweet corn as an ornamental grass and making a feature of a clump in a mixed border?

Can I use one fertilizer for all my vegetable crops?

The extent to which gardeners can minimize the number of different types of fertilizer they need has been discussed elsewhere in this book; I am all for simplicity where it does not too adversely affect results. Vegetable crops are a good case in point, for perfectly acceptable results can be achieved using a single, balanced fertilizer such as Growmore. The most important ingredient of this fertilizer is nitrogen. And if a dose supplying sufficient of this element is selected for each type of plant, there should be adequate amounts of phosphorus and potassium, too.

HOW MUCH FERTILIZER TO USE

Vegetable crop	Total amount of fertilizer	
	g/sq m	(oz/sq yd)
Peas	0	0
Radish; carrot	17	½
Broad bean; parsnip; swede	51	1½
Lettuce; onion	68	2
Runner bean; broccoli; turnip	83	2½
Leek; potato	102	3
Beetroot; spinach; cauliflower	136	4
Brussels sprouts; cabbage	170	5

The best results will be achieved if roughly half the required amount of fertilizer is applied about a week before planting or sowing and the remainder when the crop is half grown.

⃞? How can I achieve successful lettuce crops all year round?

To be truly self-sufficient in lettuce all through the year, you need both a cold frame and a greenhouse. Much easier is self-sufficiency during the summer, when a little planning will ensure that you do not have a glut one month and a shortage the next. The planning is not solely a matter of sowing seed at regular intervals through the season, for early in the year the seeds germinate and the plants grow and mature more slowly than they do later on.

The scheme set out here should give a constant supply of lettuce, but you can adapt it to suit yourself.

A PLAN FOR LETTUCE YEAR-ROUND	
Harvest during	**Plant or sow**
Early May	Sow in a frame or under cloches in October and transplant outside under cloches in late February or early March
April to late May	Sow outside in late August in mild areas
Late May to early June	Sow in a cold frame in late February; transplant outside under cloches in early April
June to early October	Sow outdoors from late March to early August; sow a new batch of seeds as the previous batch emerges
October to December	Sow outside in late August, protecting with cloches from late September
December to early March	Sow under glass in late September; plant out in a greenhouse heated to a minimum of 8°C (46°F)

It is important to choose appropriate varieties. For normal summer cropping, the common butterhead or crisp varieties are suitable, but plants overwintering outdoors, such as 'Valdor' or 'Winter Density', must be hardy; the glasshouse lettuce 'Kloek' is best for the mid-winter crop.

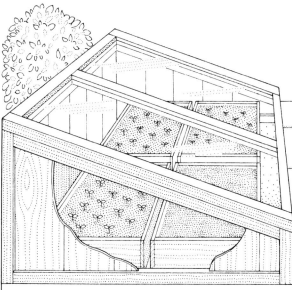
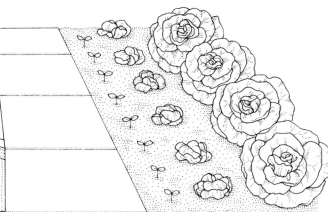

⃞? Which of the less commonly grown vegetables are really worth trying?

There are fads in gardening, as there are in most other pursuits, and 'unusual' vegetables constitute one of those current at present. This is partly because, in recent years, supermarkets have discovered a few vegetables new to the British palate that have achieved wide popularity. The best known are calabrese and Chinese cabbage, or Chinese leaves.

Understandably, gardeners wish to try growing these in their own gardens, but they have, in addition, been tempted by seed companies with several other less worthy candidates. Some of these are exotic crops, and others are resurrections of the winter vegetables that were grown before modern transport and storage facilities provided the year-round choice there is today.

Crops such as okra are probably better left to climates where they can be grown decently, amaranthus and basella to those who know properly what to do with them, and Good King Henry, cardoons and scorzonera consigned to the annals of history. Lest you think me too conservative, however, there follows a short list of the less common vegetables that really can be said to repay experimentation.

Celeriac Perhaps the most familiar of the 'uncommon' vegetables, celeriac is well described as turnip-rooted celery, for it has the flavour of the latter and something of the appearance of the former, except for a hairy covering of fibrous roots. Sow in pots in March; transplant into a sunny, well-manured site in late May on a 25 cm (10 in) square spacing, water well and gradually pull away the lower leaves as the crown swells. Harvest in autumn; scrub the surface thoroughly and either grate raw or boil.

Dandelion The thought of cultivating as a crop what most people spend their gardening lives trying to eradicate strikes many as a wholly perverse notion. It is

See also:
Liquid and solid fertilizers p 18
Cold frames pp 44, 45
Heating greenhouses p 141
Propagators p 142

Florence fennel

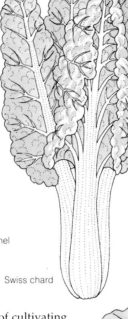

Swiss chard

Celeriac

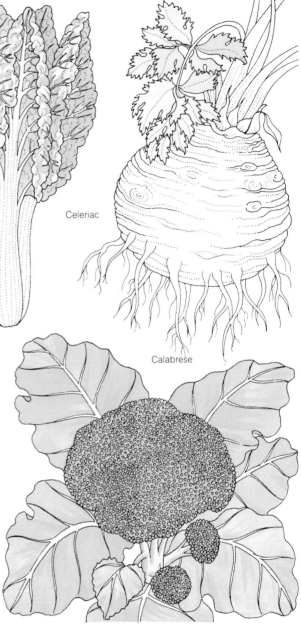

Calabrese

the French who first recognized the value of cultivating dandelion leaves as a salad green, and, although you can use the wild dandelion, it is better to grow the selected French varieties, of which 'Ameliore Géant' is most frequently seen. Sow seed in blocks in April and thin to a 30 × 30cm (12 × 12in) spacing. Although dandelions are sometimes bitter, the young leaves are agreeable, and when established plants are blanched by being covered with a light-tight cover for a couple of weeks, the flavour is milder still.

Florence fennel There are two common types of fennel, the herb, grown for its seeds and its attractive feathery foliage, and Florence fennel or *finocchio, F.v.dulce*, which is raised for the bulbous stem base. It is not a plant for limited space, for you need several large stem bases for a meal for a family. It requires a warm, well-drained site but plenty of water. Sow in April and gradually earth up the stem base as it swells. Cut in late summer, boil and serve with butter or raw in salad. The taste is strongly that of aniseed.

Sugar pea Also known as *mange-tout*, these are the peas harvested when the seeds are tiny and the complete pod eaten. They are grown in exactly the same way as garden peas but are, if anything, easier and less prone to problems. Sow in April or May, harvest in late summer. The best variety for a small garden is 'Oregon Sugar Pod'. 'Sugar Snap' is a much taller-growing type that can be used as *mange-tout* or, after the pods have filled, as a conventional garden variety.

Swiss chard Far and away the best and easiest form of spinach. Half a dozen plants will keep a family of four well supplied, for you can pull and pull again as the leaves keep coming. Sow in April in well-manured soil; a single row of plants about 25cm (10in) apart will suffice. The leaves are ready for pulling by mid-summer and, with cloche protection, can continue right through the winter. Separate the mid-rib from the rest of the leaf; treat the latter as spinach and boil and serve the ribs

separately with a white sauce or, like asparagus, with butter or a dressing.

Welsh onion If you have limited space but enjoy onions, this is the plant for you. It is a hardy, perennial, leafy form of onion and will provide you with fresh onion flavouring all year round. Divide established plants every three or four years. If you prefer a conventional onion bulb, rather than just the leaves, try the Egyptian, or tree, onion. This is another perennial, but one that produces its bulbs at the top, instead of at the bottom of the stem in place of flowers.

What is the secret of obtaining good tomato crops outdoors?

In three words, feed, water and sunshine; the right blend of the first, plenty, but not too much of the second, and a great deal of the last. There are two main types of outdoor tomato, bush and staked, and they require somewhat different treatment and management. Most gardeners still grow staked, or, as they are sometimes called, cordon varieties, although I feel that open ground is wasted on them and that they are much better raised in growing bags against house walls and on path and patio edges.

For both bush and staked crops, the first requirement is good plants. To raise your own, you will need a greenhouse or kitchen window-ledge to germinate the seeds and then a cold frame to grow on and harden off the plants. Depending on the part of the country in which you live, you will be able to plant out from the third week of May onward, and you should allow nine weeks from sowing to planting. Late March or early April are, therefore, the times to sow.

The seeds may be sown in seed trays and pricked on into pots, but if you plan to grow only a few plants, they are better sown directly into 7.5-cm (3-in) pots. Sow two seeds per pot into a peat-based compost, then remove the weaker of the two seedlings. After about a month's growth, the young plants should be hardened off in a cold frame. Adequate hardening-off is essential if the plants are to crop well.

If you intend to buy plants, ensure that they have not been brought straight from a heated greenhouse into the open. And choose those that have good, dark leaves and stout stems and are about 20 cm (8 in) tall.

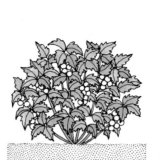

Bush tomato varieties are usually robust plants and they need no staking or pruning.

Staked plants must be loosely tied in to canes every 25 cm (10 in) or so, or twined about taut strings as they grow.

If you are planting directly into the open ground, the site should be one that has not carried a tomato or a potato crop for at least three years (because of the danger of there being virus or wilt present in the soil), and it should have been manured the previous autumn. Plant about 45 cm (18 in) apart and water thoroughly. The best crops will be obtained if the seedlings are planted through slits made in black plastic sheeting spread on the soil surface. This will retain moisture and warmth and suppress weeds.

If you prefer to grow your staked tomatoes in growing bags, use two plants for each standard-sized bag. The main difficulty with growing bags is in finding somewhere to put the stakes or canes. Proprietary devices are now available that are anchored beneath the bag, but if the plants are grown against a wall, the best system is that shown in the illustration opposite.

The plants will need feeding, those in open ground

How should I set about growing asparagus?

Read any of the old gardening books and the instructions you will see for growing asparagus will be very different from those followed by asparagus growers today. Formerly asparagus was almost always grown on raised beds, but, recently, extensive trials have revealed that the crop is better grown on the flat, in beds 1 m (3¼ ft) wide, with 30 cm (12 in) spacing between the plants.

Asparagus is tolerant of a fairly wide range of soil types, although the crowns are prone to rotting if the site has a tendency to become waterlogged. When preparing the bed, remember that the crop will be in the same position for many years; it is essential, therefore, that any perennial weeds (couch especially) are eradicated. Trying to remove them from among growing plants is a nightmarish task. Planting should take place in spring, and the soil should be prepared by thorough manuring in the previous autumn. It is worth preparing the bed with care; it could be productive for 20 years.

Although it is possible to raise asparagus from seed, it

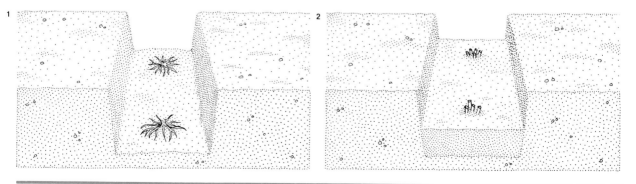

See also:
Liquid fertilizers p 18
Hardening off seedlings p 44
Deep bed system of growing
   vegetables p 120
Greenhouse tomatoes pp 144–47

less so than those in growing bags, for they soon exhaust the nutrients initially present in the compost. Several excellent proprietary tomato feeds are now available, and these are better than the more general liquid feeds, for they are high in essential potash. Follow the manufacturer's directions carefully with regard to amount and timing of feeding.

The natural inclination of all tomato plants is to adopt a branched habit, and, although bush plants should not be staked or 'pruned' in any way, the varieties grown as staked plants must be side-shooted and stopped if they are to crop efficiently. Young side shoots should be pinched out as they form. Finger and thumb remain the best tools for this purpose, since scissors or knives will easily damage the main stem.

Once the plants have four or, in extremely favourable areas, five fruit trusses, the tip of the main stem must also be pinched out, since the plant's energies are best directed into producing a few good trusses rather than many feeble ones. Remember to tie in the main stem to the support regularly, using soft, loose twine.

Almost inevitably, the end of the summer will come and a fair proportion of the fruits will still be green. Don't discard them, or convert them all to chutney. It is warmth, not sunlight, that causes tomatoes to ripen, and if the green fruits are placed in an airing cupboard, they will continue to redden. Indeed, if green fruits are stored in a refrigerator and then taken to the warm cupboard to ripen in small batches over a period of weeks, the fresh tomato season can be continued almost until the end of December.

Any side shoots that form on a staked tomato plant must be pinched out. The tip of the main stem must also be removed when four or five trusses have formed to ensure a sturdy plant.

Staked tomatoes are easy to raise in growing bags against a wall or fence. Plant out good, robust 20-cm (8-in) plants when flowers are just beginning to form on the first truss. Insert short canes into the bag at an angle to the wall supports and lightly tie in the young plants. Tomatoes grown in bags need regular watering and liquid feeding, but be careful they do not become waterlogged or the roots will rot.

---

is far better to buy crowns, which will establish and crop much more quickly. Even so, you should be selective and choose one-year-old, rather than two- or three-year-old crowns. Try also to buy frame-raised rather than field-raised crowns and, if you can find them, buy the French selections, such as 'Lorella' or 'Minerve', which are higher yielding than the more familiar 'Connover's Colossal'.

It is essential to allow the crowns to build up and the shoots, or spears, appealing as they may look, must not be cut until the second year after planting. Then use a long, preferably curved and serrated knife and ensure

that the cut is made below soil level. Begin cutting in late April and continue until mid-June. Thereafter, the shoots must be allowed to elongate and form the feathery growth that is essential for the crowns to build up their reserves again for the following season. Cut the shoots back in the autumn, when they yellow.

A top dressing with a general fertilizer should be applied to the bed early in the season, and liquid feeding will be found beneficial once the feathery shoots begin to lengthen.

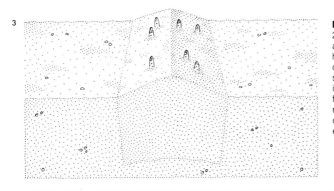

Dig the trench for asparagus 20 cm (8 in) deep, and then build a ridge of soil about 10 cm (4 in) high in the bottom. Place the crowns on this mound, carefully spread the roots on each side of it, **1**, and cover the crowns with a few centimetres of soil, **2**, but do not fill the trench. This should be done gradually as the shoots extend during the summer so that

by autumn the soil in the trench is level with the surface, **3**. When the plants are three years old, cut from late April to mid-June, then allow ferns to form to nourish the plant and build up food reserves to produce the next season's crop. Cut ferns back in autumn and feed the crowns with a balanced fertilizer.

How do seed potatoes differ from those used for cooking?

Botanically there is no difference between a 'seed' potato and a potato on its way to be boiled or baked. Indeed, you can plant potatoes from the supermarket and they will grow perfectly well. Why, then, bother to buy special tubers for planting? The first reason is that they will be uniformly smaller: two or three shoots only per tuber are needed to avoid overcrowding of the stems. Large tubers will produce more shoots than this, and it is wasteful simply to rub them out (since potatoes are bought by weight) and inefficient to cut up the tubers because, weight for weight, there will be more shoots on small tubers than on large ones.

A second important reason for buying specially grown seed tubers is to ensure freedom from virus contamination, which diminishes plant vigour and results in poor yields. Seed tubers are normally raised in northern areas (Scotland and Northern Ireland especially), where there are relatively few of the aphids that are responsible for introducing viruses into the crop. As a consequence, it is unwise to save tubers from your own potato crop for planting the following season.

The name 'seed' is applied traditionally to tubers used for planting, although botanically they are not seeds but dormant plants. In recent seasons, however, so-called true potato seed has appeared on the market. This is, indeed, the seed of the potato plant and is produced in the small, green, tomato-like fruits borne by some potato varieties that are, incidentally, poisonous. The results from these true seeds will almost certainly fall short of those from tubers; were it not so, commercial growers would have given up tubers long ago, for they are

Buy seed potatoes certified as virus free or your plants may develop leaf roll disease. The leaves will curl under and pucker and the enfeebled plants produce a poor crop or none at all.

expensive to raise, store and transport. Additionally, true potato seed is not easy to germinate, and the resulting plants are often difficult to establish and grow on to maturity.

What is commonly known as a potato 'variety' is in technical terms a clone: it is propagated vegetatively without cross fertilization, and the off-spring are genetically like the parent plant. Thus you know exactly what sort of plant will be produced by a 'King Edward' or a 'Desirée' tuber, while you have no such certainty with true seed and will be taking part in a lottery if you plant it in preference to tubers.

Why do my carrots never develop long, smooth, straight roots like those on the seed packet?

Carrots and parsnips are not easy vegetables to grow well, which is why carrots in particular carry high points ratings at horticultural shows. The secret of success lies with the soil, which must be light and free draining. It must not contain stones, lumps or clods, for these impede the free growth of the main tap-root, which consequently forks and kinks. Indeed, a heavy, lumpy soil is the commonest of all reasons why the roots develop this phenomenon, known as fanging.

A second, common reason for the distortion is that fresh farmyard manure has been applied to the soil too soon before planting. Never apply manure of any sort closer to sowing time than in advance of the previous crop; this is the reason for the positioning of root crops in a rotation.

Quite commonly, however, in tones of disbelief, gardeners tell me that they have followed the guidance about manuring to the letter and that their soil is light, free draining and with no lump or stone in sight. And

yet their carrots still look like distorted tuning forks. The answer is usually that the soil, being so light and free-draining, has not been dug deeply for several years. As a consequence, a pan has developed 25 to 30 cm (10 to 12 in) below the surface.

A pan is simply a fairly impervious layer of mineral matter which has been leached, or washed, from the upper layers of soil, carried downward and redeposited. It forms a barrier, effectively impeding the growth of carrot or parsnip roots, and the remedy is regularly to dig deep and thoroughly in order to break it up.

The long tap-roots of carrots may become distorted when they are in contact with fresh manure or their growth is impeded by stones, clods or a pan of mineral matter in the soil.

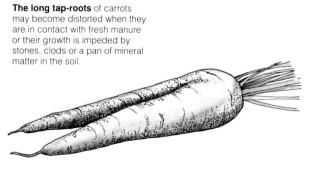

See also:
Clubroot on brassicas p 14
Disinfection of contaminated soil
    p 14
Striped petals on wallflowers p 48
Crop rotation pp 118–19

How can I control clubroot on my brassicas?

Just as honey fungus strikes fear into the tree and shrub grower, so the thought of clubroot causes gloom among those who grow vegetables. Justifiably, for this disease has a number of features that make it specially difficult to deal with. It affects all members of the cabbage family, which accounts for a greater proportion of common vegetables than any other. It includes cabbages, cauliflowers, broccolis, Brussels sprouts, turnips, swedes, Chinese cabbage, kale, and kohl-rabi, as well as several types of garden flower such as wallflowers and stocks. The family also includes radishes, horseradish and watercress although, fortunately, clubroot is rarely a problem on these.

The effects of clubroot will be familiar to any experienced vegetable grower; the plants wilt during hot weather, produce poor, stunted growth, and their roots become grotesquely swollen and malformed. Eventually, these swollen roots decay in a particularly revolting and foul-smelling manner. The cause of clubroot is a soil-inhabiting fungus and, once contaminated, garden soil is likely to remain so, for the organism can survive for 20 years or more in the absence of brassicas and cannot be eradicated by treament with chemical fungicides.

If your garden is free from clubroot, spare no efforts to ensure that it remains so. Always raise your own plants from seed, for the disease is usually undetectable at transplanting age, and bought plants may have been grown in contaminated soil. You should never borrow garden tools from friends whose gardens may contain clubroot unless the implements are thoroughly scrubbed in hot, soapy water. Nor should you walk from an affected vegetable plot on to your own without similarly scrubbing your boots

If your soil is contaminated, don't despair, however; there are measures you can take to enable you to grow some brassicas. Clubroot is always worst in an acid, poorly drained soil and you should do everything possible to improve these conditions. On a really wet site, the chances are that plants are suffering in other ways too, and it might be rewarding to install a proper drainage system. Liming will help correct acidity, but for clubroot suppression you will need to add half as much again as is indicated on the graph on page 8.

Where clubroot contamination is severe, it is worth revising your plan for vegetable rotation, going against the rules and establishing one, heavily limed plot specifically for brassicas. If brassicas are transplanted (as they usually are with all except swedes and turnips), their roots can be given some protection by dipping them in a thick paste of fungicide before planting; the systemic fungicide thiophanate-methyl is available in a special formulation for this purpose.

There are no vegetable brassicas that are reliably resistant to clubroot, although the swede 'Marian' will fare better than most varieties.

You can still grow brassicas with some success if your soil is contaminated by the clubroot virus by establishing the young plants in sterilized compost in 12-cm (5-in) pots.

When the plants are sturdy and well grown, with strong root systems, plant them out into a well-limed bed, specially for brassicas, taking care to keep the root-ball intact.

Plant all brassicas firmly, then water them in thoroughly. The ball of sterile compost will ensure that only those roots that extend beyond it will be prone to develop clubroot; so you stand a good chance of reaping a fair crop.

My onions are always soft and mouldy; what is going wrong?

There are two main reasons why onions turn soft and mouldy. The differences lie in the time that the mould appears and, to some extent, on the type of onions affected. If spring onion foliage turns yellow while the plants are still growing, and, when pulled up, the base of the bulb is soft, with a cottony mould growth, then you have onion white rot to contend with.

This is a fungal disease and is one of those problems that, like clubroot on brassicas, must be lived with rather than eliminated. If you find a few plants affected for the first time, it may still be possible to prevent contamination from spreading to the rest of your vegetable plot. Dig out a large spadeful of the soil around the affected plants, taking great care not to spill any as you do so, place it in a large plastic bag and transport it to the nearest municipal dump.

As with the clubroot fungus, the organism causing white rot can persist in the soil for a long time and, again like clubroot, it is practically impossible to eradicate. Protection of the plants is the best that you can hope for and, although total success cannot be guaranteed, thoroughly dusting the seed drill with either benomyl, thiophanate-methyl or carbendazim fungicides before sowing will help.

Once the disease becomes severe, there is little alternative but to abandon growing onions apart, perhaps, from some spring onions in large pots of potting compost. All members of the onion family can be affected, including leeks and ornamental alliums, although white rot is almost always most severe on salad onions.

If bulb onions appear perfectly sound at the time you pull them from the garden, but subsequently decay during storage and develop a greyish mould around the neck, just below the point at which the leaves emerge, the problem is onion neck rot. This is much easier than white rot to contend with but, because of the rather curious biology of the causal fungus, control measures are not taken at the time you might imagine. Treating onions with fungicide just before they are stored has no effect whatever.

The fungus originates on the onion seed, grows slowly into the tissues of the plant while it is in the garden, and only when it has been put into store does the mould become evident. It can be eliminated by routinely dusting onion seed before sowing with benomyl or thiophanate-methyl fungicide. Similarly, onion sets can be protected by soaking them before planting in a suspension of the same fungicides, exactly as described for ornamental bulbs.

As an added precaution, and to eliminate any possibility of contamination originating on old plants, always remove the remains of last year's crop and dispose of them by burying or properly composting. Don't leave piles of rotting onions in the garden.

Why are my Brussels sprouts always loose and poorly formed?

One thing the supermarket vegetable trade has established is that Brussels sprouts must be round and firm; Brussels sprouts used to range in consistency from small green bullets to growths with the texture of miniature cabbages. The reason for this change has been largely the shift from old varieties such as the 'Cambridge' strains 'Rous Lench' and 'Bedfordshire Fill-basket' to modern, uniformly cropping F₁ hybrids. So you must expect some variation in texture if you still grow old varieties. There is more to the phenomenon of loose, or 'blown', sprouts than this, however.

Although all brassicas are great consumers of nitrogen, over-dosing with nitrogen-containing fertilizers can sometimes be responsible for loose 'buttons', as the sprouts are known technically. Follow the guidelines

Plant Brussels sprouts firmly and bank up soil around the roots to enable them to withstand windy conditions. Some taller-growing varieties may even need staking in light soil. Use a square-sectioned stake and tie the plant in just below the top.

See also:
Disinfection of contaminated soil
p 14
Germination of seedlings p 44

Hardening off seedlings p 44
Soaking ornamental bulbs before
planting p 71
Firm planting of roses p 93

Bulb onions commonly suffer
from neck rot, a disease carried
in the seeds. The white fungal
growth of onion white rot is a more
serious problem, affecting spring
onions especially.

Why do my vegetable seedlings shrivel and die?

The problem of seedlings dying as, or shortly after, the seeds germinate, takes several forms, known collectively as damping-off. Most forms of damping-off are caused by microscopic fungi in the soil, although a few (of less importance with modern standards of seed production) may be carried on the seeds themselves. Commonly, damping-off appears as a small, but enlarging, patch of dead seedlings in an otherwise healthy box, although sometimes the young plants continue to grow in a stunted and feeble manner.

On brassicas especially, the form of damping-off known as wirestem is common: the stem of the young seedlings develops a pinched appearance close to soil level and, in time, becomes wiry in texture. Once damping-off is found among seedlings, the entire boxful should be disposed of, for even apparently healthy plants will carry the fungus on their roots and die in due course.

Damping-off should be combatted by prevention rather than by attempted treatment. Always use fresh compost for sowing seeds; always scrub and disinfect seed boxes and pots thoroughly after use; and always ensure that the young plants are not placed under unnecessary stress through overwatering, inadequate warmth or too little light.

given on page 121 for calculating the amount of a general fertilizer, such as Growmore, to apply; and remember that, since Growmore contains 7 per cent nitrogen, you can easily calculate the appropriate dose, in grams per square metre or ounces per square yard, of any other nitrogen-containing fertilizer from the following formula:

g/sq m (oz/sq yd) of Growmore ÷ nitrogen % of alternative fertilizer.

Water, too, is important for a leafy crop such as Brussels sprouts and can sometimes add to the looseness of the sprouts. Water thoroughly at transplanting time, and, if you are growing the plants closely spaced, water throughout the life of the crop. Sprouts grown at spacings wider than about 45 cm (18 in) need additional water after they have been transplanted only in very dry years.

But perhaps the commonest reason for Brussels sprouts to form loose buttons is that they are not planted sufficiently firmly. It used to be said that the way to plant Brussels sprouts was to hammer the ground hard and then form a hole with a crow-bar. This is an extreme approach, but it does make the point that they must be planted very firmly; on a windy, exposed site and on a light soil especially, they should also be staked. Incorporate large amounts of organic matter on a light soil, too, to help improve its body, and grow the shorter varieties, such as 'Peer Gynt' or 'Achilles', rather than taller types, which are inherently more prone to becoming top heavy

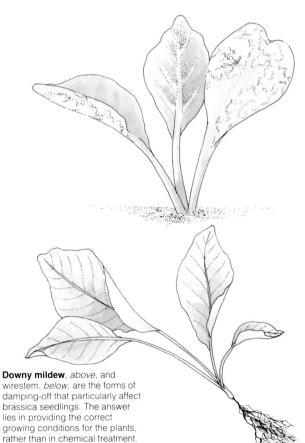

Downy mildew, *above*, and
wirestem, *below*, are the forms of
damping-off that particularly affect
brassica seedlings. The answer
lies in providing the correct
growing conditions for the plants,
rather than in chemical treatment.

FRUIT

Succulent specimens
for every taste

How much does the average gardener need to know about the rootstocks of fruit trees?

Enough not to make a serious and long-term mistake when buying new fruit trees for the garden. Most modern fruit trees comprise two separate individuals grafted together to produce a single tree. One individual comprises the fruiting variety, shoots of which are grafted on to roots of a totally different variety.

In years gone by, apple, plum and pear varieties were always grown on their own roots, but, curiously, some varieties produce rather poor fruit when grown in this way. Although the plants were originally selected for their fruiting efficiency, they may have been so chosen that root vigour has been inadvertently selected *against*. The result is a plant that can never yield to its full potential becuase the root system cannot give the top of the tree the physical or nutritional support it needs.

Fruit growers gradually came to appreciate this and to graft fruiting varieties on more vigorous root systems, often of wild apples, pears and plums. Eventually, it was realized that the rootstock exercised considerable influence over the final size and form the tree took. So tree breeders embarked on programmes for breeding plants with particular types of rootstock quite separately from those to improve fruiting varieties.

The breeding of rootstocks has been more adventurous and more successful with apples than with other tree fruits. In Britain, much of the early work was carried on at the Merton and East Malling research institutes, the rootstocks they bred being prefixed by the initial letters MM (Malling-Merton) or M (Malling). These letters are followed by numbers; those most commonly offered to gardeners are M.9, M.26, M.27 and MM.106.

The type of rootstock can influence the form of the resulting tree most significantly in relation to its size. Thus, a variety grafted on MM.106 will produce a tree about 3m (10ft) tall, whereas those on M.26 and M.9 will produce trees only 2.5m (8ft) and 2m (6½ft) tall respectively. The rootstock M.27, a very dwarfing stock, produces apple trees less than 2m (6½ft) tall.

The implications are obvious; a more dwarfing rootstock, giving rise to a smaller tree, will produce a smaller crop, but it will be much more manageable with regard to pruning and picking and can be grown in a limited space. But the more dwarfing the rootstock, the better the soil must be for the tree to crop well.

Other fruit trees too are available on a range of rootstocks, but the choice is more limited. Pears are almost always grafted on selected varieties of the related quince. Most widely available are Quince C, the best for poorer soils, and the more dwarfing Quince A. Plums, gages, peaches, nectarines and apricots used to be available principally on a rootstock St Julien A, but now a dwarfing stock has been introduced called Pixy, which restricts trees to about 3m (10ft). Damsons are usually grown on their own roots, as were sweet cherries, which grew far too large for most gardens. Now, with a dwarfing rootstock called Colt, the height can easily be restricted by pruning to about 3m (10ft).

See also:
Grafting trees p 86
Budding roses p 92
'Family' apple trees p 132
Effect on a grape-vine of too
    much nitrogenous fertilizer p 137

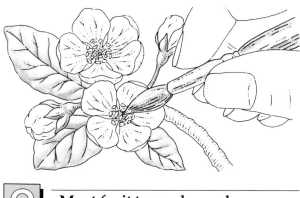

Must fruit trees always be planted in twos to obtain satisfactory pollination?

No, but rather strict rules must be adhered to regarding which varieties will crop well when planted alone, and which varieties must be planted in combination in order to obtain optimum pollination and fruit crop. Those of us who routinely give gardening advice dread more than any other questions concerning the correct combinations to choose of fruit tree varieties, especially of the less common ones. Retaining in one's head the inumerable permutations requires considerable mental gymnastics.

The basis of the matter is that fruit tree varieties display varying degrees of self-sterility; that is, to a greater or lesser extent, they cannot fertilize their flowers with their own pollen. The situation is further complicated because, even if one variety is capable of satisfactorily pollinating another, both need to flower at the same time for this to become possible in practice. There are, moreover, some varieties that are incapable of pollinating certain other varieties (they are said to be incompatible). Yet others, for reasons of their genetic constitution, require not one, but two further varieties to effect pollination; so three trees are required.

In an attempt to simplify matters, I have listed the commonest varieties of the major types of fruit tree and indicated recommended varieties to grow with them; but these are not the only possible combinations. And if you wish to grow a more unusual type, you must seek guidance from the nursery where you buy the tree regarding a suitable pollinator variety.

People with small gardens, with room for, perhaps, only one tree, have two options. Either they must choose from the rather short list of self-fertile varieties or check on varieties already present nearby in neighbours' gardens and choose one to match. A neighbouring tree should be as close as possible to your own, up-wind and preferably not screened by a high boundary.

Hand pollination is occasionally the best way to ensure that some fruit trees will produce crops. Wait until the pollen is ripe and the fine yellow grains are being shed by the stamens, **2**. Choose a warm, dry day with little wind, and using a large soft paintbrush, or cotton wool on a small stick, transfer the pollen to the stigma, **1**. From here the pollen tube grows down to the ovule, **3**, where fertilization occurs.

Fruits of medlar and quince, *far left*.

VARIETIES FOR CROSS-POLLINATION

Variety	Recommended pollinator varieties
Dessert Apples	
'Crispin'	'Cox's Orange Pippin' or 'Discovery'
'Cox's Orange Pippin'	'Discovery', 'Greensleeves' or 'James Grieve'
'Discovery'	'Cox's Orange Pippin' or 'Greensleeves'
'Fortune'	'Greensleeves', 'Discovery' or 'James Grieve'
'Greensleeves'	'Discovery' or 'Grenadier'
'Idared'	'Cox's Orange Pippin' or 'Discovery'
'James Grieve'	'Cox's Orange Pippin' or 'Discovery'
'Jupiter'	'Discovery', 'Spartan' or 'Sunset'
'Kent'	'Cox's Orange Pippin' or 'James Grieve'
'Laxton Superb'	'Cox's Orange Pippin' or 'Greensleeves'
'Spartan'	'Greensleeves' or 'Discovery'
'Sunset'	'Cox's Orange Pippin' or 'James Grieve'
'Tydeman's Late Orange'	'Greensleeves' or 'Spartan'
'Worcester Permain'	'Cox's Orange Pippin' or 'Greensleeves'
Cooking Apples	
'Bramley's Seedling'	'Spartan' plus 'Discovery'
'Grenadier'	'Discovery' or 'Greensleeves'
'Lord Derby'	'Spartan' or 'Tydeman's Late Orange'
'Rev.W. Wilks'	'Idared'
Pears	
'Conference'	'Onward' or 'Lousie Bonne de Jersey' ('Conference' will set some fruit on its own but is always better with a pollinator).
'Doyenne du Comice'	'Conference' or 'Onward'
'Louise Bonne de Jersey'	'Conference'
'Onward'	'Conference' or 'Williams' Bon Chrétien'
'Williams' Bon Chrétien'	'Conference' or 'Onward'
Plums	
'Cambridge Gage'	'Czar' or 'Marjorie's Seedling'
'Czar'	Self-fertile
Damson varieties	Self-fertile
'Marjorie's Seedling'	Self-fertile
'Rivers Early Prolific'	'Czar' or 'Victoria'
'Victoria'	Self-fertile
Cherries	
'Morello' (cooking)	Self-fertile
'Stella' (sweet)	Self-fertile
Peaches	
'Peregrine'	Self-fertile but use a paint brush to aid set
Nectarines	
'Lord Napier'	Self-fertile but use a paint brush to aid set
Apricots	
'Moorpark'	Self-fertile but use a paint brush to aid set
Quince	
'Vranja'	Self-fertile
Medlars	
'Nottingham'	Self-fertile

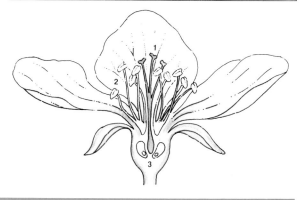

Is it possible to grow a fruit tree in a container?

Yes, although at one time the containers used were relatively enormous, the advent of the modern dwarfing rootstocks has meant that quite modest containers can be used, and fruiting trees grown even on patios. The best fruit trees to grow are apples on the particularly dwarfing M.27 rootstock — most of the popular varieties can now be obtained in this way. Bearing in mind the need for pollinator varieties, it may seem that more than one tree will be needed and that, on a small patio, the project will become impracticable.

Not so, for it is possible to buy a so-called family apple tree, which comprises two or three varieties grafted on the same rootstock. Thus, you have both a built-in pollination mechanism and a range of apples. Although the family tree is thought of as a recent phenomenon, I have a tree at least 80 years old that is 'Blenheim Orange' at the bottom and 'Wyken Pippen' at the top. Although few nurseries have family trees available now on the recent M.27 rootstock, they can be expected to become increasingly widespread.

The best container to use for a fruit tree is a wooden half-barrel, for its shape gives adequate but not over-extensive root spread. Drill drainage holes in the bottom of the barrel before you fill it, and don't economise on compost. Your tree will be in the container for a long time and it is essential to use a good-quality John Innes No 3 compost. Remember, too, that a tree in a container needs copious watering during the summer and that a surface mulch will help the soil to retain moisture in hot, dry weather.

What do the terms espalier and cordon mean?

Neither espalier nor cordon is an English word, indicating that these two methods of training fruit trees came originally from the continent of Europe. The names have been variously applied over the years, but, in modern usage, an espalier is what a well-known novelist, Aldous Huxley, has vividly described as

How can I persuade an apple tree to crop well every season?

The phenomenon of biennial bearing is one of the most annoying things in all gardening; yet it is common, and little can be done about it. It is a feature of certain apple varieties, 'Bramley's Seedling' and 'Newton Wonder' perhaps most notoriously; although other varieties sometimes adopt a biennial cropping habit after a season of particular stress — an abnormally heavy crop or a severe drought, for instance. Often there seems little reason for a tree to choose a particular year in which to crop. And if you have more than one tree of a variety, you will be unlucky if both crop on and off in unison.

Careful pruning can sometimes help to bring a tree out of biennial bearing, or at least minimize its effects. The pruning system to adopt is renewal pruning, in which shoots are left unpruned until they have borne fruit, which on most varieties will occur in the third year of growth. This system is different from spur pruning, and the technique should be studied carefully before commencing. Fruit tree pruning cannot, however, be explained in only a few lines; so if you have a problem with biennial bearing, refer to the Bibliography for the titles of good books on the subject.

See also:
Apical dominance in roses p 96
Planting trees p 109
Pruning a grape-vine p 136
Storing apples p 135

crucified fruits. On either side of a central stem, opposite pairs of branches are trained outward at right angles.

Usually, although not invariably, espalier trees are trained against a wall or other support. Done well, a mature espalier-trained tree looks magnificent, and the method need not be restricted to fruit trees. One of the most splendid sights I know of is a large, old pineapple broom, *Cytisus battandieri*, espalier-trained against an ancient, mellow stone wall.

A cordon is a much simpler training system, useful for a small garden or where a large number of varieties is to be grown. The essential features of the cordon are that the growth of side branches is restricted and that the fruit-bearing spur shoots are induced to form along the length of an upright main stem which is trained either vertically or at an angle of 45 degrees. In double and triple cordons, two or three such stems are made to branch from the base of the tree and are then trained upward, parallel to each other.

In the cordon method of training fruit trees, *left*, the fruiting variety is usually grafted on a dwarfing rootstock and planted at an angle of 45°. Prune laterals in summer to stimulate the growth of fruiting spurs; cut back the leader in spring only when the tree reaches the desired height.

An espaliered tree, *right*, has a central stem from which branches are trained horizontally in pairs about 45 cm (18 in) apart. Any vertical shoots that grow from the branches must be cut back in summer to form fruiting spurs. Espaliers take up more space than cordons, so are less suitable for a really small garden.

How do cooking and eating apples differ; can any varieties be used for both?

This seems such an obvious question, that many people hesitate to ask it for fear of appearing ignorant. But it raises an important matter, for gardeners with limited space may well find a dual-purpose apple particularly useful. The family apple tree is one way out of this dilemma, but there are also some varieties that can be used for both purposes.

There is a more blurred line between cooking and eating, or dessert, varieties of apple than many gardeners are prepared to admit, and it is generally tradition and conservatism that prevents people cooking with certain varieties. One highly respected authority, H.V. Taylor, author of *The Apples of England*, used to say simply that an apple pleasing to the palate is a dessert apple; this tends to be most true of those apples low in sugar, acid or tannin.

Conversely, an apple makes a good cooker if it forms a soft, juicy pulp, which tends to be true of the acidic and moderately acidic types. Highly acidic varieties include the cider apples, as well as some of those traditionally thought of as cookers, but few dessert varieties. Even within the broad categories, there are variations, and some apples are more suited than others to certain purposes. Some types of cooking apple ('Emneth Early' and 'Rev. W. Wilks', for example) are called coddlings because they become soft and frothy when coddled, or parboiled. Dumpling apples are generally large, and among modern varieties 'Bramley's Seedling' is most often used. In former times, a group of cooking apple varieties suitable for drying was also popular, but these are now seldom seen.

The dessert apples best for cooking are, therefore, the more acidic varieties and 'James Grieve' and 'Cox's Orange Pippin' can be used successfully. Good dessert apples among traditional cooking varieties are rarer; my personal favourite is an old, early apple, 'Stirling Castle', unfortunately seldom seen today.

Why do my apples always have black blotches on them and little maggots inside?

Black blotches and little maggots fairly well sums up the appearance of many apples in many gardens every summer, for these are the symptoms of two of the commonest of all apple problems. The black blotches are the effects of scab disease, and the little maggots are the caterpillars of the codling moth. They are quite distinct problems, therefore, requiring quite different treatments. But working on the assumption that to know your enemy is at least half the battle in defeating him, it is instructive to understand how scab and codling moth set about their wicked work.

Scab is caused by a fungus that spends the winter months dormant, mainly on fallen leaves beneath the tree, although some fungal growth is also present in cankerous lesions on the twigs. Spores are produced on the leaves and in twig lesions in spring and are carried by rain splash and wind to the young foliage, which they infect to produce dark brown blotches.

More spores are formed there, and these, in turn, infect more leaves and also the young fruits, which develop the characteristic crusty, or scabby, patches that make them so unattractive to eat. The disease always tends to be worse when there is cool, wet weather around blossom time. Nothing can be done to cure the problem, but scab can to some extent be prevented.

The procedure usually recommended is to spray with a fungicide, as commercial growers do, in order to eradicate the fungus before it can infect the young leaves and fruit. The best chemicals for this purpose are benomyl, thiophanate-methyl or carbendazim, applied fortnightly from the time of bud burst until the petals fall from the blossom. This certainly works well on small, young trees, but the advice is largely academic for the many gardeners who have big, old trees that are quite impossible to spray effectively.

Although scab is probably the most important disease in commercial apple crops, and is treated by spraying, the reason for doing so is largely cosmetic in that consumers do not relish apples with black blotches on supermarket shelves. But the expenditure of time and effort on fungicides for gardeners to produce blemish-free apples seems neither correct nor justifiable. Take preventative measures by all means: collect up and burn or otherwise destroy (but do not compost) leaves from beneath affected trees, and cut out and burn scabby twigs in the winter. And if you have a young tree, spray it with fungicide to protect it from persistent and severe attacks of scab that could weaken it, but don't bother with a large, old tree.

Why have the leaves on my peach tree curled up and turned red?

The cause is peach leaf curl, a disease that is responsible also for the disfigurement of the leaves on most ornamental almond trees — which makes them relatively unsuccessful garden features. It is always most severe in a season following a cold, wet spring, for this provides just the right conditions for the leaf curl fungus to thrive. It survives the winter within cracks in the bark and on the leaf buds, from where it emerges to infect the young leaves as they unfold.

This infection causes the characteristic puckering, and later, as the fungus grows within the leaf tissues, a white powdery bloom forms and a reddening develops. This powder is a mass of fungus spores, which are subsequently blown to the twigs, where they germinate in preparation for the winter once more. Spraying the leaves with fungicide is of no value, for by the time they have unfolded the fungus will be too well entrenched. Much better is to spray the shoots just as the leaves are opening in March and again just after they have dropped in autumn.

None of the modern fungicidal chemicals has much impact on peach leaf curl disease and the best treatment is to use a copper-containing product such as liquid copper or Bordeaux mixture. It is possible to eradicate the problem from a fairly seriously diseased tree within three seasons if the spraying is done assiduously.

The blistered and distorted leaves on many peach and almond trees are the result of infection by peach leaf curl fungus. Leaves develop a white powdery bloom, then redden, before falling, and the growth of the trees, deprived of nourishment, is retarded.

See also:
Scab on pyracantha p 86
Cooking and eating apples p 133

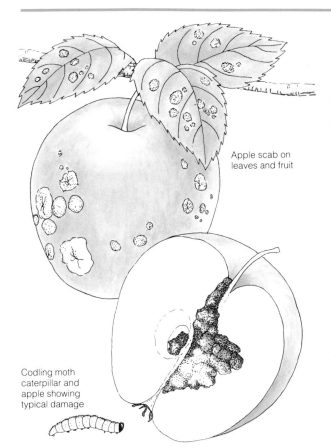

Apple scab on
leaves and fruit

Codling moth
caterpillar and
apple showing
typical damage

What then of the codling moth caterpillars? These insects pass the winter in a pupal state in crevices in the tree's bark. In late spring, the adult moths emerge and the small, dingy females lay their eggs on leaves and young fruit. The resulting caterpillars burrow into the fruit, usually entering by the eye or close to the stalk so that the entry hole is undetectable. After dining on the inner parts of your apples for a few weeks, the caterpillars re-emerge, crawl down to the bark and pupate until the following season.

How can you stop them? A modern chemical treatment can be resorted to, but, once again, this is affected by the difficulties of spraying large trees. The problem is compounded by the need to time the spraying sufficiently precisely to catch the caterpillars after they have hatched, but before they have actually entered the fruit. If you wish to try this approach, use a modern contact insecticide, such as permethrin, and spray first in mid-June and again about three weeks later. This is really only worthwhile on small trees however.

One of the traditional remedies for codling moth was to tie sacking around the tree trunks in early summer in the hope that the caterpillars would pupate within it and could be destroyed when it was removed. This is of doubtful value, however, as the damage for the season will already have been done, and next year moths can easily fly in from neighbouring trees. Indeed, other than on small trees, it seems hardly worth the effort to try to control codling moth. A large proportion of the affected apples will drop prematurely, and a mature tree, well pruned and cared for, should produce more than enough healthy fruit for average domestic needs.

Why do the leaves on my plum tree have a silvery shine?

Possibly because it has a disease called silver leaf, although not inevitably so. If there are obvious signs of branch death, you will be able to determine the cause more precisely. Saw off any dead branches and look carefully at the wood inside. If there is no obvious discolouration, then the problem may simply be a condition known as false silver leaf; an indication that the tree is short of water and/or fertilizer.

Dark staining of the wood, however, means you have genuine silver leaf to contend with, and the causal fungus may make its presence apparent later in the year, when dark purple, bracket-shaped or crusty bodies appear on the bark. There is no chemical answer to silver leaf, and the best policy is simply to wait and see what happens after any dead branches have been cut off and destroyed. Affected trees often recover naturally.

But if the symptoms spread, and especially if the silvery effect appears on any suckers, the portents are ominous, for this signifies that the entire root system is diseased. In these circumstances, fell the tree and dig up and burn as much of the root system as you can.

What is the secret of storing apples successfully?

If there is one rule that must be followed above all others, it is that any fruit intended for storage must be of the very best, blemish-free, unbruised, undropped, and altogether of pristine quality. Friends sometimes think my views on this rather extreme, but experience has shown that you cannot handle fruit too carefully if you expect it to stand a better than average chance of surviving in store for more than a couple of weeks.

Never pull the stalk from fruit intended for storage and ruthlessly reject any with the merest hint of pest and disease activity. Admittedly, some things are beyond your control; it is not often appreciated, for instance, that apple scab may occur in a latent state, with no external symptoms while the fruit is on the tree, and then manifest itself later.

It is important that fruit stores should be kept cool, and a small, ventilated shed dedicated to the purpose is ideal. Store apples individually, unwrapped and not touching on slatted racks; or place ten or so in a clean, dry plastic bag with the top half-closed.

What varieties and quantities of soft fruit are needed for an average family?

In gardening terms, there is no such thing as an average family, for everyone's tastes and needs are different. However, my own family of two adults and two children is probably representative of many and so is an appropriate example of what is needed.

I am assuming that all the main types of common soft fruit are to be grown but that if any are less popular than others it is likely to be gooseberries; that reasonable continuity of fruit is required through the summer and that, in addition to the commonest fruits, a little adventure with less common ones would not come amiss. I am assuming also that space is not unlimited, but that a fruit cage or garden of about 7 × 7 m (23 × 23 ft) can be accommodated.

In such an area, by pinching a little on plant spacing and by training some of the fruits carefully, I grow the following range:

Raspberry Two rows, comprising five each of the early and later mid-season varieties 'Glen Clova' and 'Malling Joy', and five canes of an autumn-fruiting variety. You could choose 'Zeva' or 'September', but to bring a little fun into the proceedings I have the North American yellow-fruited variety 'Fallgold'.

Blackcurrant Two bushes each of the early and later-fruiting varieties 'Ben More' and 'Malling Jet'; both are late flowering and so escape much of the frost damage to which blackcurrant blossom is so prone.

Red currant Two plants of 'Stanza'; planted 1 m (3¼ ft) apart and trained as double cordons.

White currant One double cordon of the prolific early cropper 'White Versailles'.

Gooseberry Two plants each of the new, mildew-resistant variety 'Invicta', trained as single cordons planted 45 cm (18 in) apart.

Berry Fruits These are all trained on the inside of the north and east sides of the fruit cage, which prevents them taking the sun from other plants. The selection includes the best of the modern hybrid berries and one most attractive and less commonly seen fruit.

Blackberry One plant of 'Merton Thornless', a compact, easy-to-pick variety.

Loganberry One plant of 'LY 654', a compact and thornless variety.

Tayberry One plant of what is far and away the best of the blackberry-raspberry hybrids.

Japanese wineberry One plant of that attractive species, *Rubus phoenicolasius*, which has reddish stems and prickles and most palatable reddish-orange, grape-flavoured fruit.

This scheme could, of course, be amended with respect either to varieties or numbers of plants. Strawberries are excluded from this listing but they are considered in detail on pages 128–9.

A greenhouse vine should be planted in a pit outside, with the stem trained in through a gap in the wall. In the first year, train one shoot under the greenhouse roof. Stop this by taking out the tip before it becomes too weak, and similarly train the lateral shoots and stop them as they reach about 50 cm (20 in). Try to develop a system of trained laterals about 45 cm (18 in) apart and remove any intermediate ones; stop shoots growing from the laterals after the first leaf.

At the end of the first year, in December, cut the main stem back to half its length and prune back the laterals to one or two buds. In the second year, halve the most recent growth on the main stem and again select and train laterals; continue this process each year until the vine has filled its allotted space.

Thereafter, treat the main stem in the same way as a lateral; prune back to basal buds each winter and stop laterals at about 50 cm (20 in) and sub-laterals after the first leaf each summer. In a large greenhouse, two main stems may be trained instead of one.

See also:
Garden planning pp 22–3
Windbreaks, hedges, walls and
    fences p 25
Container-grown fruit trees p 132

Espalier and cordon fruit trees
    pp 132–3
Container-grown strawberries
    p·138

Site a fruit cage in a warm, sunny position. Some fruit will tolerate partial shade if the soil is kept damp and water does not drip from overhanging branches. Provide a windbreak if the site is an exposed one.

Make the cage from 13–19mm (½–¾ in) mesh wire netting, attached to uprights 2–2.25m (6½–7 ft) high. Cover the top with 19-mm (¾-in) lightweight plastic netting, which can be removed if snowfalls are heavy.

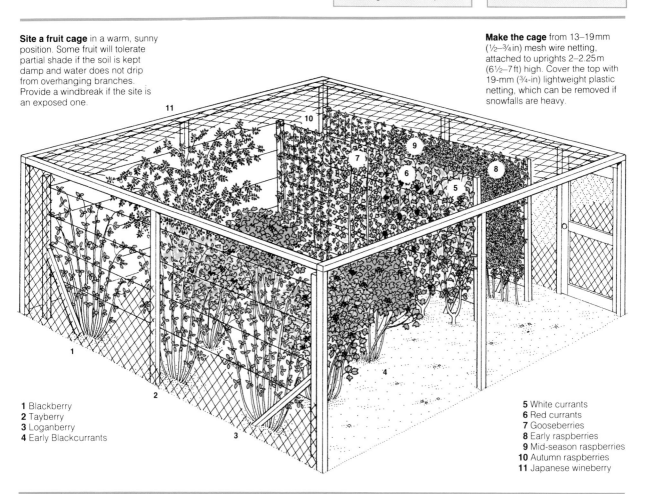

1 Blackberry
2 Tayberry
3 Loganberry
4 Early Blackcurrants

5 White currants
6 Red currants
7 Gooseberries
8 Early raspberries
9 Mid-season raspberries
10 Autumn raspberries
11 Japanese wineberry

My grape-vine produces all leaves and no fruit; where am I going wrong?

This common complaint is an example of what results when gardening experts give the correct advice for performing certain tasks but with no indication of what will happen if the advice is not taken. Plants generally produce flowers and fruit as a means of ensuring the survival of the species and are more likely to do so if there is evidence that this survival is threatened.

A grape-vine producing masses of foliage is a classic instance of a plant under no threat at all. It plainly has abundant soil in which to develop an extensive root system, it has ample water and, above all, abundant nitrogenous fertilizer. The correct way to grow a grape-vine is to channel its energies in a slightly different direction from that which it takes naturally, so as to ensure good fruit production.

Start at the bottom; with a grape-vine, this means with confining the roots. If you are planting a new vine, therefore, dig a pit about 1m (3¼ ft) cubed and line the sides with concrete slabs. Do not waste money refilling the hole with specially formulated potting compost but use your normal garden soil and add well-rotted manure to it at a ratio of about one part manure to four parts soil, by volume. I have used this system for outdoor, wall-trained vines as well as for greenhouse vines.

The second important feature to consider is pruning. The essence of the system is to build up a framework of 'rods' on which fruiting spurs will form. Assuming that you have planted a one-year old rod in winter, cut this back to within several buds of the base. In the first year, train one shoot under the greenhouse roof or along the outside wall, as shown in the illustration. Aim for the form of plant shown there by following the pruning instructions detailed in the caption. Wall-trained vines should be treated in exactly the same manner.

This system of training and root confining should be coupled with a feed with potash, either bonfire ash or sulphate of potash, at about 34g/sqm (1oz/sqyd) in early spring and copious watering during the summer. This should give you a good crop of flowers and fruit, but don't be greedy. If you expect too much of the plant, it will produce masses of small grapes. The individual bunches should be thinned, therefore, with a pair of scissors with rounded blades, taking out every second fruit as soon as all the young grapes have set.

How much space do I need to grow strawberries?

Judging by the relative quantities of different soft fruits bought annually, strawberries must be far and away the most popular. Accordingly, they might be expected to be the most widely grown in gardens, but my experience suggests that raspberries outnumber them. The reason is probably that the yield of raspberries per unit area of garden is much higher and, indeed, if you want strawberries for jam-making, you will need a pretty large strawberry bed to satisfy all your needs.

There are several aspects to consider before starting with garden strawberries. First, do you want fruit solely for eating fresh, or for jam-making or freezing? This will dictate not only the space required but also, to some extent, the choice of varieties. Second, if fresh fruit is a major requirement, are you prepared to sacrifice quantity for flavour? Third, do you want to eat strawberries at the same time as everyone else, or does the idea of extending the season well into the autumn appeal to you?

Option one is to have a fairly conventional strawberry bed in the open garden. I stress open garden because, even if you have available a fruit cage, the relatively short cropping life of strawberry plants means that they are better considered as long-rotation vegetables than as soft-fruit bushes. Protection from birds can be provided by wire netting cloche-type covers.

As with any other garden crop, prepare the land in advance of planting by incorporating well rotted compost or manure. If the compost is truly well rotted, this need not be done in autumn, for I believe in planting strawberries in summer rather than spring. The basic preparation should, however, be completed by the end of May. About two weeks before planting, rake in a 6:1 mixture of bonemeal and sulphate of potash at the rate of about 135g/sqm (4oz/sqyd). It is sometimes suggested that a fertilizer with a higher rate of nitrogen should be used, but it tends to produce soft, disease-prone foliage.

But the nub of the question remains: how big should the bed be? Calculate how much fruit you need and then plan on the basis of about 1kg (2¼lb) of fruit per plant after the second season; (there will, of course, be much less in the first year). The rows should be about 75cm (30in) apart, with a space of about 45cm (18in) between individual plants.

Summer planting gives the plants a much better chance to become well established before the first winter. For the same reason, buy the biggest container-raised plants on offer rather than bare-rooted plants, since they establish themselves much better, especially in my preferred planting time of July. Many nurseries sell so-called economy plants in small, netting-wrapped peat 'pots'; they will not do as well as plants in larger, more conventional pots and, despite the higher cost, these are definitely my preference. Be sure to buy from a reputable supplier and to obtain plants raised from virus-free stock.

Once established, strawberries are not demanding plants: they will benefit from an early season dressing with potash and should be watered once the fruit has set. A mulch of straw, which always has much more appeal than black plastic, will help keep the fruit clear of the soil. The main disease problem is *Botrytis* grey mould, which can be devasting in a wet summer. A spray with benomyl, thiophanate-methyl or carbendazim, when the flowers open and repeated at 10-day intervals until the fruit reaches the stage of turning white, will help keep it in check.

Strawberries are accommodating plants, which will produce an abundant crop in compost-filled pots and planters, or even when planted into a wooden barrel through holes cut in the sides.

See also:
Formulae for John Innes potting
   compost p 11
Planting and training sweet peas
   pp 52–3
Fruit cages p 136

Sweet and juicy wild, or alpine, strawberries bear little red fruits well into the autumn.

Cultivated strawberries come in many sizes and shapes, with a variety to suit every taste.

For those with neither space nor inclination to embark on a conventional garden strawberry bed, there is an alternative. Strawberries can be grown successfully in containers, and many firms now market 'strawberry tubs' — either plastic or terracotta structures, with holes in the sides through which the plants are inserted into compost. They work fairly well, but tend to be expensive, to which must be added the cost of good-quality compost: John Innes No 2 is suitable. Remember that plants in tubs need watering frequently and that they should be replaced every three years.

Perhaps the biggest drawbacks with a strawberry tub are its enormous weight (once you have decided on a place for it, it will be there for years) and the difficulty of protecting it against birds. Although some manufacturers sell netting covers for their tubs, they tend to look unsightly — especially if your tub is on a patio. The third option is to grow strawberries in John Innes No 2 compost in 20 to 25cm (8 to 20in) plastic plant pots in the fruit cage. With this system, you gain the advantage of protection from birds that the fruit cage affords without the problems of growing plants with two different cropping lives close together.

And so to the choice of varieties. It is possible to buy plants that yield prodigious quantities of fruit, but they are often rather tasteless and my personal selection to give fruit over several months is:

'Royal Sovereign' In my opinion, no strawberry has a better flavour than this old, early-mid season variety; the taste is ample reward for its low yields.

'Tantallon' A high-yielding and acceptably flavoured early-mid season variety.

'Harvester' A high-yielding variety, particularly good for jam-making.

'Saladin' A high-yielding and reasonably flavoured mid-season variety.

'Troubador' Probably the best flavoured and most versatile late-fruiting variety.

'Baron Solemacher' A small, late-fruiting alpine strawberry. Most gardens can accomodate a dozen or so plants of this variety, for they can be grown at the front of an herbaceous border, even in partial shade, and are often left alone by the birds.

? What is the best way of training raspberry canes?

There are conventional and unconventional ways of training raspberries, the latter being particularly valuable if space is limited. The conventional way is to train them against horizontal wires, tightly secured to firm, upright posts. The most convenient heights for the wires are 0.5m, 1m and 1.5m (20in, 3¼ft and 5ft) above ground level. Especially when the raspberries are young, you may need to place bamboo canes vertically against the wires to help with tying-in the plants against damage by wind. Raspberries should be planted about 45cm (18in) apart, and excess growth cut out each spring to leave not more than eight suitably spaced young canes per plant.

In a limited space or in a windy garden, the row may with advantage be placed against a garden fence. Although normally the canes should run north–south to obtain maximum sunshine, in a windy situation, they are better run east–west. In an even more confined space, two plants may be placed either side of a single stake and up to nine canes in total be allowed to grow up for tying-in.

Where space is strictly limited, one raspberry plant can be set on either side of a sturdy post about 2.25m (7½ft) in height, and up to nine strong canes tied to it.

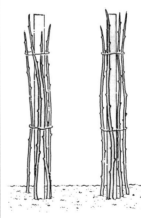

Economical use of space can also be made by growing raspberries in a single row against a garden fence. Space the plants about 45cm (18in) apart, and tie the canes in to the fence as they grow.

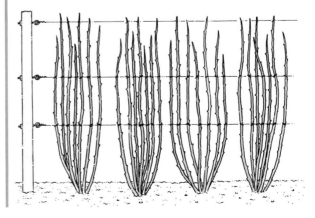

GREENHOUSES

How to garden

under glass

Which is better for greenhouses, wood or metal?

I spend a great deal of time explaining the scientific basis of what is done in gardens and justifying certain courses of action from the underlying principles. But on the subject of greenhouse construction, scientific inclinations usually take second place to aesthetic judgement.

Not many years ago, the notion of a greenhouse constructed from anything other than wood (if it was a small one) or of cast iron (if it was large) would not have entered gardeners' heads. Accordingly, almost all garden greenhouses had a framework of white-painted timber, and many were erected on a base of low brick walls. Over the past 20 years, however, the wooden greenhouse has largely been superseded by the mass-produced aluminium-framed house; so much so that when I set about purchasing a new greenhouse recently, I found only a handful of manufacturers still marketing wooden structures. Why should this be, and is it a desirable trend?

The main reason is financial. The aluminium greenhouse is cheaper to make and, therefore, cheaper to buy than a wooden house of comparable size. Technically, there are some differences in the way they function: a wooden greenhouse usually has thicker glazing bars than an aluminium building with the result that it receives less light. Against this must be balanced the fact that the wooden framework retains heat better. If a wooden greenhouse is constructed of painted or preservative-treated timber, its maintenance is greater than that of an aluminium one. But the maintenance of a high-quality framework of durable red cedar is minimal.

Although wooden greenhouses are thought to be harder to clean and disinfect, this is only marginally true. There need be no more nooks and crannies in a wooden house than in a metal one, and both need scrubbing down and disinfecting at least once a year. Indeed, sulphur, which is a useful greenhouse disinfectant, can actually harm the exposed metal of an aluminium house, and it is the thoroughness with which the greenhouse is cleaned that matters, not the nature of the framework.

Aluminium greenhouses used to be difficult to keep warm in winter because of the difficulty of attaching insulating materials to the framework, but fairly efficient clipping systems are now available. An aluminium greenhouse remains difficult to extend and alter, and structurally is less stable and more likely to be damaged by winter winds than a wooden one.

Ultimately, you can be persuaded by arguments either way and the final choice between metal and wood may rest on nothing more than the attractiveness of the relative manufacturers' brochures. I hope, however, that one further factor may influence you. Little Crystal Palaces tend to appear in the most inappropriate surroundings. For the tranquil garden of an English cottage to be embellished with an aluminium greenhouse is, I believe, an affront to environmental conservation; and this, I trust, is something potential greenhouse purchasers will have close to their hearts.

See also:
Mulching p 14
Garden design pp 22–3
Lifting and storing dahlias pp 19, 77
Lettuce year-round p 122

The aesthetic aspects as well as the practical must be considered when choosing a greenhouse. The older, wooden-framed type looks more at home in a cottage-type garden. Where there is plenty of wall space, a lean-to, either half boarded or aluminium, takes up less garden room.

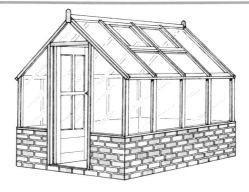

Wooden frame with a base of low brick walls

Half-boarded, wooden-framed lean-to

Least attractive, but cheaper than glass houses and good except where it is very windy, are the tunnels made from plastic sheet supported on a metal framework. Aluminium-framed houses are easy to install and transmit most light, but they add little to the appearance of a garden.

Metal framework covered with plastic sheeting

Aluminium-framed house

Would it be beneficial to install a greenhouse heating system?

The decision depends on why you have a greenhouse and where your gardening interests lie. It is important, also, to clarify what is meant by greenhouse heating, for there are greenhouses heated to the extent of permitting tender plants to be grown or cropped all year round, and there are greenhouses heated only sufficiently to maintain the temperature above freezing in winter. The table indicates the approximate heat output that will be needed to maintain a standard greenhouse at different levels of warmth during the average minimum temperatures in a relatively mild and a relatively cold part of the country (say, Cornwall and mid-Wales).

Obviously, the figures in the table indicate that you need more heat in a cold area than in a mild one to maintain the night-time temperature at just above freezing. But what more do they mean in practice? The lowest temperature permits you to store all your tender plants — dahlias, fuchsias and so on — in complete confidence that they will not be frosted, although you can take other precautions with them. You should also be able to grow winter lettuce, but the temperature will still be too low to prevent most pot plants from becoming chilled.

The middle temperature of 7°C (45°F) enables you to raise early bedding plants satisfactorily (this is made easier still with a small heated propagator) and also many ornamental pot plants. But to raise tomatoes year-round, even the highest level of 13°C (55°F) minimum is inadequate. On balance, I believe that you will be wasting money if you aim for the 'just above freezing' temperature and that unless you can afford the additional heat input to maintain 7°C (45°F), you would be better with an unheated structure.

Check with the heater manufacturers' literature before making a purchase and ensure that your choice has the necessary heat output for your size of greenhouse and locality. The type of heater you choose will, no doubt, again depend on cost. The cheapest to run (gas) is the most expensive to install, and the choice usually lies between the relatively cheap paraffin burner, requiring frequent attention, and the more costly to run, but self-sufficient, electric heater. Radiant electric heaters give much more uniform heating than fans.

Finally, do consider fitting internal partitions in order to heat only part of the greenhouse and don't forget the value of modern plastic insulating sheet (especially of the bubble type) in cutting down heat loss.

UNITS OF HEAT REQUIRED

Temperature	Climate type	Btu/h(Cal/h) needed	
2°C (36°F)	mild	3,000	(756)
2°C (36°F)	cold	5,300	(1,336)
7°C (45°F)	mild	6,000	(1,512)
7°C (45°F)	cold	7,300	(1,840)
13°C (55°F)	mild	8,700	(2,192)
13°C (55°F)	cold	11,000	(2,772)

The figures show the approximate number of units of heat required to maintain a standard greenhouse 2.5 × 1.8m (8 × 6ft) at specific temperatures in different climates.

What type of propagator is best for raising seeds and cuttings?

In return for cost and effort, a propagator probably offers more to a gardener than any other appliance. It is, as its name suggests, a device to aid the propagation of plants, especially by seeds and cuttings. At its simplest, therefore, a propagator need be no more than a seedbox; although a seedbox filled with compost will not propagate plants efficiently without some sort of cover.

When choosing a propagator you should take into account the requirements of the plants you plan to propagate. The priorities are a suitable compost or other growing medium and appropriate levels of moisture, warmth and light. The need for moisture necessitates a cover, which should be easy to remove and, preferably, capable of being ventilated. Although seeds will not germinate well in a growing medium that is allowed to dry out constantly, seedlings rapidly succumb to damping-off if they remain for long after germination in a saturated atmosphere. Cuttings, on the other hand, need a moist environment for much longer.

A simple seedbox can be covered temporarily with a plastic bag, but a rigid, clear plastic cover is more convenient. The better versions have a small ventilator with which to regulate the moisture content of the atmosphere inside the cover. Larger propagators comprise a covered container in which several small seedboxes can be placed.

The second requirement of seeds and cuttings is warmth. The simplest way to provide this is to place a single, small seedbox indoors on a south-facing window-ledge. But most houses cool down quite significantly at night and, to make a really early start with seeds, some form of additional heat is necessary. Once more, there are varying degrees of sophistication.

The most basic aids are flat pads, containing heating elements, which are either placed inside the seedbox (and are, therefore, inefficient in that they cannot be re-used until the seedbox is finished with) or are placed beneath several separate seedboxes. The better types have thermostatic control and operate on low voltage through a transformer. More complex and costly are the propagators with individual, thermostatically controlled heaters in the base.

It is perfectly possible for handy gardeners to build their own heated propagating systems, with varying degrees of complexity. I recommend a wooden framework, built to house one or more of the larger, thermostatically controlled, low-voltage heating pads, with a wooden-framed cover of translucent plastic sheet. The advantage of the low-voltage system is that there is no likelihood of anyone being harmed through faulty electrical connections. But any electrical system should be checked by a electrician, and certainly this is so with the most sophisticated of all propagating systems, the sand bench, with or without a misting facility.

A sand bench is a boxlike construction on a greenhouse bench in which thermostatically controlled electric heating cables are buried in sand. Thus it is possible to obtain regulated and uniform heating over a large area on which seedboxes can be stood. This is undoubtedly the system for the serious gardener who plans to propagate large numbers of plants. The ultimate facility incorporates a misting system: an arrangement of water-pipes, connected to mains pressure and with nozzles automatically spraying an extremely fine mist over the plants at regular intervals. Such a system is used for rooting large numbers of cuttings and is almost essential for success with certain types of plant.

If you raise most of your own seedlings, it is worth acquiring a heated propagator. The best type consists of a plastic tray, with a low-voltage heating element, in which several seedboxes can be placed and which has a hard plastic cover with an inbuilt means of ventilation.

A sheet of glass laid over a box containing a lighting tube makes a simple propagator, *above*. Some thermostatically controlled heating elements can be placed in the bottom of a large tray and then covered with soil, *left*.

See also:
Disinfecting seedboxes p 42
Germination of seeds p 44
Propagating cuttings from trees
    p 110
Lettuces year-round p 122

What are cloches and what are they used for in the garden?

Cloche is a French word that means a cover, a bell or a bell-shaped object. Such covers are used far less than they should be, for many gardeners do not appreciate the benefits that cloching can confer. Although no longer bell-shaped, a cloche, in gardening, is a translucent cover placed over plants, usually with the object of lengthening the growing season — especially of certain types of vegetables and of strawberries. This does not, however, make full use of their potential, for cloches can equally beneficially be placed over bare soil, and they can be used just as well with ornamental plants as with edible crops.

Cloches lengthen the growing season simply by providing protection from frost and enhancing warmth. Using them, vegetables such as lettuces can be sown or planted outdoors several weeks before it is safe to put them out unprotected. And, in the autumn, by placing cloches over growing plants, it is possible to extend the cropping season well beyond the time when frosts and lower temperatures normally take their toll.

Where most gardeners miss out is in not using cloches to pre-warm the soil outdoors before spring sowing. Quite frequently you read directions on seed packets to the effect that the seeds should be sown outdoors in late March or early April. But in many years the soil has barely begun to warm up by early April; so seeds sown then will lie without germinating for a considerable time, at the mercy of insect pests and fungal diseases. Placing cloches over the seed bed ten days or so in advance of sowing will make a great deal of difference to the emergence of the seedlings.

Do not, however, be tempted to use plastic-covered cloches very early or very late in the year; because of the heat-transmitting properties of plastic, the cloches may become even colder inside than out.

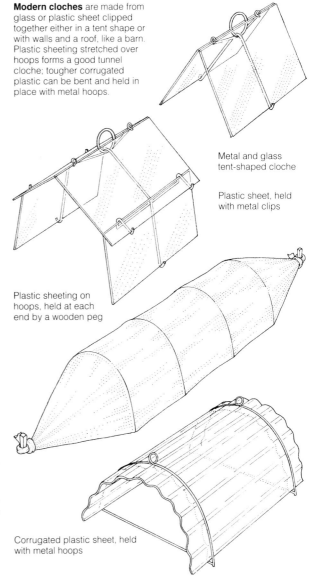

Modern cloches are made from glass or plastic sheet clipped together either in a tent shape or with walls and a roof, like a barn. Plastic sheeting stretched over hoops forms a good tunnel cloche; tougher corrugated plastic can be bent and held in place with metal hoops.

Metal and glass tent-shaped cloche

Plastic sheet, held with metal clips

Plastic sheeting on hoops, held at each end by a wooden peg

Corrugated plastic sheet, held with metal hoops

How frequently should a greenhouse be disinfected?

Greenhouse cleaning is a chore; but whereas some of the less appealing garden tasks can be put off, or short-cuts devised, there can be no half-measures with disinfecting the greenhouse. It must be completely stripped of plants if the cleaning is to be done properly. This is partly to make it easy to reach all the corners and recesses, and partly because most of the disinfectants you are likely to use are potentially damaging to green plants. Mid-winter seems the obvious time for the job, when there is little else to do in the garden, but there are sound reasons for doing it earlier or later, in early autumn or spring.

If you have some heating in the greenhouse to maintain plants over winter, you face the difficulty of finding somewhere to put them for a couple of days. And even if

Cleaning and disinfecting a greenhouse is an annual chore, best carried out in autumn or spring. Remove all plants, then scrub benches, framework, pots and seedboxes, using a mild disinfectant. Clean the glass and, if necessary, fumigate or spray against pests and diseases.

the greenhouse is unheated, the chances of doing the job properly are diminished in cold weather, when the chemical disinfectant will be less volatile and the fungi and insects you seek to control will be in a dormant state. So do the cleansing after the summer crops have been removed but before the weather is so cold as to affect the permanent inhabitants of the greenhouse. Or do it in spring, before growth has started afresh.

Can I grow tomatoes and cucumbers alongside alpines and pot plants in the greenhouse?

If you heed most gardening books, the answer to the question is emphatically no; if you take a look inside my greenhouse, however, the answer is certainly yes. This is one of those areas of gardening where theory does not always match up with practice, and where the standards followed in commercial horticulture are not necessarily applicable to gardening.

Theoretically, tomatoes, cucumbers, pot plants and alpines all need widely differing growing conditions.

Cucurbits (cucumbers, melons and squashes) thrive in hot, steamy conditions. I can never see these plants growing without recalling the mid-summer climate of the countries of Southeast Asia, where they ramble in luxuriant profusion among tropical vegetation. Tomatoes conjure up pictures of the sun-baked gardens of the Mediterranean, in which they crop in abundance; and alpines can only suggest high mountain habitats.

Commercial growers and nurserymen, wanting the maximum possible return from their plants, will not mix the various types. In a garden greenhouse, however, even with such widely contrasting origins, it is possible to achieve a compromise. I adopt two complementary approaches. The first is to choose plants within each group that do not demand extremes; the second is to subdivide the greenhouse. Few tomato varieties suitable

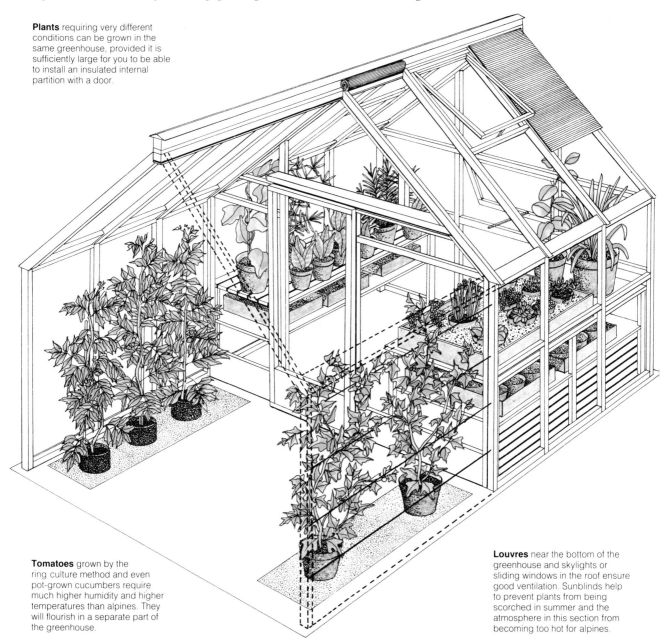

Plants requiring very different conditions can be grown in the same greenhouse, provided it is sufficiently large for you to be able to install an insulated internal partition with a door.

Tomatoes grown by the ring culture method and even pot-grown cucumbers require much higher humidity and higher temperatures than alpines. They will flourish in a separate part of the greenhouse.

Louvres near the bottom of the greenhouse and skylights or sliding windows in the roof ensure good ventilation. Sunblinds help to prevent plants from being scorched in summer and the atmosphere in this section from becoming too hot for alpines.

See also:
Watering hanging baskets p 50
Outdoor tomatoes pp 124–5
Ring culture tomatoes pp 146–7

for a British greenhouse will tolerate high humidity. Although varieties suitable for tropical conditions do exist, they are not worth wasting time on simply to enable cucumbers to thrive. Much better is to choose cucumber varieties more tolerant of lower humidity. In my experience, 'Conqueror' is the best of these, and it will grow well in an unheated greenhouse.

Among alpines and pot plants, avoid any requiring constantly either extreme heat or extreme cold. Even in an unheated greenhouse, you will find it impossible to grow alpines satisfactorily alongside tomatoes and cucumbers because of the humidity resulting from the water given off through their leaves. But it is when you introduce early season heating that the trouble really starts. Your alpines will rot away almost overnight, and an insulated partition becomes essential.

In theory, no greenhouse is too small to subdivide, but a partition across a house smaller than about 2.5 × 1.8m (8 × 6ft) will create one almost unworkably small compartment if the other is to accomodate more than two tomato plants. In addition, the partition itself must be properly insulated and yet permit easy access to the inner compartment.

These limitations underline the importance of thinking carefully before buying a greenhouse. Look at the cost; work out exactly how big a structure you need to satisfy your requirements — and choose one 25 per cent larger. Then check if the manufacturer offers the option of a built-in partition with a glazed door. For relatively little extra cost, this is by far the easiest solution to the subdivision problem, since an effective partition is much more difficult to install later.

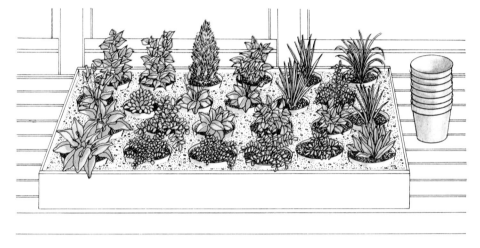

In a temperate climate, where there is relatively little snow and plenty of rain, alpines will do better out of the garden and in a greenhouse. Here they can enjoy the very well-drained, cool conditions they need if their roots are not to rot away. Good ventilation and blinds or white paint on the glass will help to keep them cool, and their roots will remain cool in summer and frost-free in winter if the pots are buried in a trough of coarse grit 10–15cm (4–6in) deep.

How can I keep the plants in my greenhouse healthy when I go away on holiday?

Good neighbours! There is no substitute for them if you expect your plants to receive the amount of heat, ventilation, feed and water they require. There are, however, some ways around the problem if neighbours are unwilling, or simply unavailable. And no matter how 'good' your neighbours are, it is unreasonable to cram your greenhouse to capacity if you know that you will be away for the two hottest weeks of the summer and, even worse, if you are a perfectionist gardener when you neighbour is not.

Assuming that you leave your plants during a fairly hot time of year, the overriding considerations are to provide adequate water and to minimize the danger of the greenhouse over-heating. Leave all vents open; in the middle of summer little serious harm is likely to result from the drop in temperature at night. Ensure also that the greenhouse has adequate shading; various types of blind (some automatic) are now available, but the best solution is still to use the white paint-on method. Do use a 'paint' specially formulated for the purpose; not only are emulsion paints liable to be washed off by rain but they may also filter out some of the beneficial wavelengths of the sun's radiation.

While there are no real shortcuts to minimizing the amount of watering needed by tomatoes and cucumbers, there are ways that even this can be taken care of in your absence without involving the neighbours. Micro-chip technology has reached the garden, and a relatively inexpensive device is now available that incorporates a small, battery-operated, electronically timed valve. This is connected to a mains water supply and can be pre-set to switch on the water at certain times each day, or even automatically, when a soil sensor indicates that the compost is becoming too dry. A system of trickle lines connected through a conventional hose-pipe delivers water precisely to many individual plants.

Less sophisticated, but no less valuable for pot plants standing on the greenhouse bench, is capillary watering: a plastic, absorbent cloth is laid over the bench and the pots are placed on it. A wick is used to deliver water from a small reservoir tank, ensuring that the matting remains uniformly moist.

Should the leaves be stripped from the stems of tomato plants?

Complete stripping of the leaves up to the lowest fruit truss is still sometimes suggested, usually without any indication of the reason for doing it. The logic is probably that the lower leaves may become traps for pests and diseases and that they contribute little to the growth of the plant. Neither of these things need be true.

Certainly, when the leaves are in fairly deep shade, as they often are in a greenhouse, they may be attacked by *Botrytis* and other disease organisms, and they may also become yellow and impaired in function. In such circumstances they should be pulled off. But until they reach this condition they will function satisfactorily, and a tomato plant growing vigorously at the height of summer needs all the nutrient possible.

Tomatoes with blossom end rot

Tomatoes grown in soil in my greenhouse do not crop well; would they do better in pots?

When any type of plant is grown repeatedly on the same site and in the same soil, there is always a risk of problems. These difficulties are partly nutritional and partly pathological, and it is in the hope of avoiding them that rotation is advocated in the vegetable garden. But in the warmth of the greenhouse rather different factors apply, since the conditions used to cosset tomato plants will cosset pests and diseases in the soil also.

After growing tomatoes in the same soil in the greenhouse bed for a few seasons, you will be fortunate if the plants do not show signs of poor and stunted growth, commonly with a sad-looking droop of the leaves as well. If you uproot one of the plants and slice lengthwise through the stem, there will almost certainly be a dark stain within the tissues. This is the tell-tale sign of a disease called wilt.

Although gardeners will be familiar with the word wilt to describe any effects of water shortage on plants, it has, in this instance, a more specific meaning. The cause of tomato wilt disease is a soil-inhabiting fungus that invades the root and stem and causes a blockage of the plant's water-conducting tissues. The disease is incurable and, once established in the soil, it is almost impossible to eradicate.

There are two possible courses of action. The first is to grow a wilt-resistant tomato variety, but these are not of great value for fruit production. They can, however, be used as resistant rootstocks on which a wilt-susceptible, but better fruiting, variety is grafted. It is occasionally

Tomatoes grown in the same soil in the greenhouse for many years are likely to develop wilt. The cause is contamination of the soil by a fungus, which stunts the growth of the plants and makes the leaves droop. If the stem is cut through lengthwise, brown streaks will probably be seen in the tissues. The remedy is to grow plants in containers, growing bags or by the ring culture method.

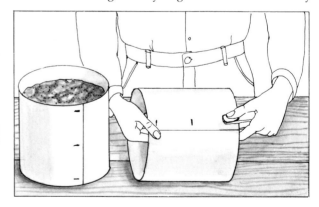

The ring culture method of cultivation is the most popular way of growing tomatoes in greenhouses. The rings are bottomless containers, about 23cm (9in) in diameter and depth, made from fibre or plastic. They are filled with a sterilized compost, such as John Innes No 2 or 3.

See also:
Disinfecting soil p 14
Pansy sickness p 52
Grafting trees and shrubs p 86
Rose replant disease p 91
Budding roses p 92

Disease resistance and 'Super Star'
  roses p 97
Rotation of crops pp 118–19
Outdoor tomatoes pp 124–5
Blossom end rot in cucumbers p 148

What causes the black blotches on my tomatoes?

A clue to the cause of the problem is its great prevalence in hot, dry summers, for tomatoes that have been short of water for even a brief period will almost always develop some symptons of blossom end rot. Water shortage is not the direct cause, but indirectly it gives rise to a deficiency of calcium in the fruit. Most composts used for tomatoes contain sufficient calcium for plant growth, but if the roots are allowed to dry out, the plant is unable to make use of it.

If the symptoms begin to appear, it is sometimes possible to arrest their spread, provided action is taken swiftly, by spraying the fruit (not the leaves) with a calcium-containing compound. The most satisfactory is a solution containing 2g/litre (⅓oz/gallon) of calcium nitrate; this should be sprayed on fortnightly as soon as the first blackening is seen.

Calcium nitrate may not be easy to obtain since garden shops are unlikely to sell it, and only some chemists stock it. The science teacher at your local secondary school might be able to help by giving you the addresses of companies supplying chemicals for laboratory use. As the treament must be applied quickly to have any effect, anyone growing greenhouse tomatoes should have a small stock of calcium nitrate crystals handy.

Another problem sometimes gives rise to blotches on tomato fruit, although more commonly on outdoor than greenhouse crops. The blotches in this instance tend to be brown and leathery, rather than black, and can occur on any part of the fruit; they are caused by potato blight. Although this is not often thought of as a disease of tomatoes, the two types of plant are quite closely related and have several diseases in common.

As with blight on potatoes, it is only worth applying preventative treatments in exceptionally wet seasons. But if the weather at the beginning of July is particularly damp, three sprays at fortnightly intervals with the fungicide mancozeb or with a copper-containing fungicide, such as Bordeaux mixture, are a wise precaution. Once the symptoms of blight have appeared on the tomatoes, however, they cannot be cured and the fruits should be disposed of.

---

possible to buy tomato plants already grafted; and some seed companies sell seed of the rootstock variety with instructions for grafting, so you can try it yourself.

The use of grafted varieties may not appeal to the non-specialist; if so, the answer is to switch to container-raising of the crop. There are three main methods: growing bags, pots and ring culture. Growing bags are perhaps the simplest, each full-size growing bag being used for three plants. Full instructions are supplied with the bags and the main drawback (once you have man-handled them into and out of the car) is that it is easy to over-water or under-water the compost.

The second option is less popular than it once was but remains satisfactory provided you use large enough pots. Choose pots 25cm (10in) in diameter and fill them with John Innes No 3 potting compost. The third method, ring culture, is probably the most popular and most efficient way of growing greenhouse tomatoes.

The principle of the technique is to induce the plants to build up two different root systems, one within the compost of a bottomless pot that serves for feeding, and a second system, lower down in a gravel bed on which the pots stand, for the purpose of taking up water.

Whatever method of tomato-growing is adopted, two important factors should be borne in mind. First, that the compost in the pots or growing bags must have a chance to warm up in the greenhouse before the young plants are transplanted, for tomatoes will always suffer a severe check to growth, often with consequent disease problems, if placed in cold soil. Second, that it does not pay to economise with tomato fertilizer. Tomatoes are greedy and fastidious feeders and should be given a specially formulated proprietary tomato fertilizer in accordance with the manufacturer's directions.

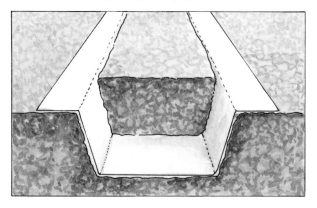

Dig a trench in the greenhouse about 45cm (18in) wide and at least 15cm (6in) deep and line it with heavy plastic sheeting. (Or use a plastic trough of the same dimensions.) Fill it with a mixture of three parts coarse washed gravel to one part of vermiculite and stand the compost-filled rings on this.

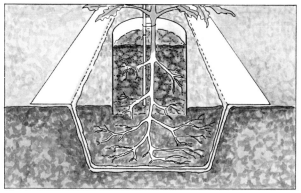

Allow the compost to warm up before planting tomato seedlings and handle them carefully. Their roots will soon fill the rings and penetrate into the gravel. Soak the gravel around each plant with about 2 litres (½ gal) water a day in hot, dry weather and feed the ring pots with a liquid tomato fertilizer once a week.

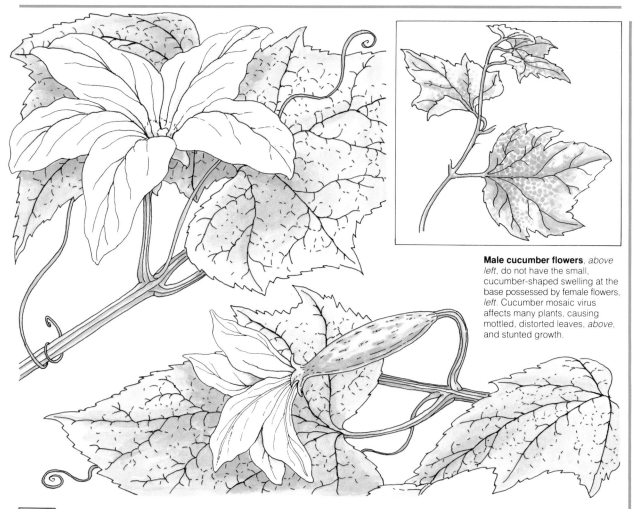

Male cucumber flowers, *above left*, do not have the small, cucumber-shaped swelling at the base possessed by female flowers, *left*. Cucumber mosaic virus affects many plants, causing mottled, distorted leaves, *above*, and stunted growth.

My cucumbers are bitter and inedible; what has gone wrong?

There are three common causes for this complaint that affects both greenhouse and garden crops. Sometimes blossom end rot on tomatoes occurs at the same time as bitterness in cucumber fruits, and one of the causes is similar: a shortage of water as the fruits are ripening. This can often make them taste bitter, and they are usually undersized, too. The remedy is to ensure that the plants have an uninterrupted water supply although, unlike blossom end rot, bitterness in cucumbers is not associated with calcium deficiency and cannot be cured. A sudden drop in temperature can also result in bitter fruit, but this is probably the least common of the various causes.

If the fruits have tendency to be mis-shapen and if the leaves of the cucumber plant show conspicuous crumpling, curling and/or irregular yellowish mottling, the indication is that they have become infected with virus. Once this happens, plants should be destroyed, for the viral contamination can rapidly spread to other cucumbers and related species growing nearby. The possibility of virus infection appearing can be minimized by careful control of aphids throughout the life of the crop, for the disease is most likely to be carried from one plant to another by these insects.

Probably the commonest cause of bitterness in greenhouse cucumbers is that the female flowers have been allowed to become pollinated by the males. The vagaries of the plant kingdom are a source of puzzlement to gardeners and never more so than in the cucurbit, or cucumber, family. For while the flowers of marrows, pumpkins and outdoor cucumbers must be fertilized to obtain a crop, the reverse is true to obtain edible cucumbers in a greenhouse.

On all the older indoor cucumber varieties, such as 'Telegraph', 'Conqueror' and those of the 'Butcher's Disease Resisting' strain, carefully remove all the male flowers as soon as they appear. They are easily distinguishable from the female flowers, for they lack the small, cucumber-shaped swelling at the base. An alternative and simpler solution is to grow one of the modern, all-female varieties that produces no male flowers. The drawback to these plants is that they tend to require higher temperatures than the older varieties, although the small-fruited 'Petita' is probably the least demanding in this respect.

See also:
Turnip mosaic virus in wallflowers
    p 48
Aphid control pp 94, 95, 96

Pollination p 132
Disinfecting greenhouses p 143
Blossom end rot in tomatoes p 148

What is the best way to control whiteflies?

In common with greenflies, blackflies, sawflies and butterflies, whiteflies are not flies at all in the entomological sense. They are sap-sucking insects, closely related to aphids, and they cause somewhat similar damage by weakening plants and by depositing sticky honeydew on which sooty mould fungi grow. Fortunately, unlike aphids, whiteflies are not of major importance in a temperate climate as carriers of viruses.

They occur in extremely large numbers on greenhouse plants of many kinds, and are often not apparent until the foliage is disturbed, when the tiny, white insects, more reminiscent of moths than flies, erupt in a cloud. The secret of successful whitefly control is persistence, for although it is possible to control the adults fairly well with a range of modern insecticides, such as permethrin or resmethrin, the immature stages are relatively unaffected. Spray or 'smoke' treatments must be repeated at weekly intervals in order to catch each fresh generation of adults as they hatch out.

As with the red spider mite, it is possible to try

Whiteflies and their larvae both suck sap from plants, and the honeydew excreted by the adults encourages the growth of mould.

biological control of whiteflies by using, in this instance, a small, parasitic wasp-like insect, *Encarsia formosa*. This lays its eggs on the pupal, or scale, stage of the whiteflies' life cycle, resulting in their death. As with the red spider mite predator, however, insecticides cannot be used in greenhouses containing the parasite.

How can I recognize and control red spider mite in the greenhouse?

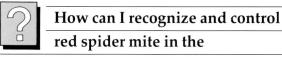

You will need extremely keen eyesight to be able to spot red spider mites with the naked eye, for they are among the smallest of all garden pests, barely exceeding 0.5mm (^{2}/$_{100}$in) in length. Despite their name, they are red in colour only at certain times of the year, and other species of larger, consistently bright red and often beneficial mites are commonly mistaken for them. Mites have eight legs, betraying their relationship to scorpions and

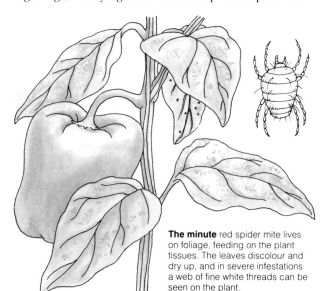

The minute red spider mite lives on foliage, feeding on the plant tissues. The leaves discolour and dry up, and in severe infestations a web of fine white threads can be seen on the plant.

spiders rather than to insects, which have six legs. They betray the fact that they are not insects more significantly, however, in being practically impossible to control by treatment with insecticides.

While you can scarcely see an individual red spider mite, you will soon become all too aware of the presence of a colony in a greenhouse by the effect they have on the plants. A browning or bronzing of the foliage, followed by general withering of the leaves draws attention to affected plants, and, when dead plants are examined closely, a fine cobweb-like growth will become apparent. Infestation is likely to occur on almost any greenhouse plants and is always most severe in hot, dry conditions.

This knowledge suggests one way of minimizing the possibility of attack by red spider mites — regular misting of the greenhouse and the plants during the summer. This helps to maintain the moist environment that deters the mites; but unless it is combined with adequate ventilation there is the risk of encouraging the development of mould and other diseases. Once plants become badly affected, there is no alternative to removing and destroying them and thoroughly disinfecting the entire fabric of the greenhouse.

An alternative method of control can be attempted, but it is rarely as successful on a small scale as it is in commercial practice. The technique involves the use of a form of biological control; not quite setting a thief to catch a thief, but using another species of South American mite, *Phytoseiulus persimilis*, to prey on the pests. It is possible to buy small 'starter' colonies of the mites together with instructions for introducing them into the greenhouse. The *Phytoseiulus* is likely to suffer if chemicals are used in the greenhouse for controlling other types of pest such as aphids, and will, of course, itself die out if it succeeds in eliminating all the red spider mites upon which it feeds.

Topical tips

JANUARY

This is the month to prepare the garden for the forthcoming season, to ensure, above all, that everything is clean and free from potential pest and disease problems. If the greenhouse has not been cleaned and disinfected, therefore, now is the time to do it (provided there are no tender plants within that will suffer at being put outside). Wash and disinfect pots, canes and seedboxes and, as the first seed sowings are not far away, begin to lay in stocks of fresh seed compost.

There are cleaning tasks to be performed outdoors, too, whenever the weather permits. Winter washes should be applied to dormant fruit trees to eradicate overwintering aphids and other pests. A sharp lookout should be kept for signs of the coral spot fungus on dead twigs and branches, and any piles of garden debris or plants left in the ground at the end of the season should be cleared.

FEBRUARY

Frosts are widespread at this time of year, and they can sometimes penetrate into even the most carefully insulated garden stores. During a spell of slightly milder weather, therefore, take the opportunity to check fruit and vegetables, corms and tubers and remove any that have either been frosted or show signs of decay for other reasons. If any rot is discovered among dahlia tubers or other ornamental plants, it would be pertinent to add an additional dusting of fungicide to those still unaffected.

Inspect stored potatoes, too, and, from now on, keep a careful check for signs of sprouting. Rub out any sprouts that you find, for they will act as wicks and withdraw moisture from the tubers; several additional weeks of storage life can be added to potatoes by this simple expedient.

MARCH

Toward the end of this month, lawns will take their turn for gardeners' attention. Specially formulated spring lawn feeds can be applied either in liquid form (which is remarkably laborious) or as powder with a specially designed, calibrated spreader. It is always worth using those lawn feeds that include weedkiller, although you must be prepared, especially at this time of year, for them to give only partial control; almost inevitably, an additional treatment will be needed later. For the first mowing of the season, set the mower a little higher than it will be later on.

APRIL

Sowing of seeds outdoors begins in earnest this month, but the soil will still be relatively cold in most years. Make good use of cloches, therefore, for pre-warming the seedbed, either for vegetables or for early sowing of flower seeds. And, before the foliage of spring-flowering bulbs shrivels and disappears, insert small marker canes to indicate their positions; there is little more frustrating than to slice through a clump of bulbs with a trowel when planting later in the season.

MAY

There is so much to do in the garden this month that some tasks are bound to be neglected. Weeds are probably coming up thicker and faster now than at any other time of the year and anything that helps keep them in check is valuable. Make full use of your hoe whenever the soil is dry, but never hoe wet soil for the weeds will merely be transplanted. Ensure, too, that the hoe blade is sharp; its cutting efficiency will be increased enormously in return for ten minutes worth of effort with a small file.

After digging the beds and borders, make use of the granular weedkiller propachlor, which may be sprinkled over clean soil and will prevent weed seeds from germinating for up to six weeks. But don't, of course, use it where you will be sowing seeds deliberately.

JUNE

After the excitement of the first flush of summer garden flowers, gardeners too often leave plants to their own devices and expect them to bloom repeatedly throughout the season. Many of them will; but with a little care and attention they do so much more efficiently, so don't neglect dead-heading. Remember that spraying once only will not control aphids, mildew or other problems all summer through; regular treatments will be needed as often as the manufacturers direct. Don't forget quick-acting liquid feeds either.

JULY

My advice this month is to look ahead to September and to be prepared. September is the most important month for planting bulbs, and although you will then be able to buy most of the common varieties in garden centres and shops, few of the more unusual ones will be available. Now is the time, therefore, to seek out the catalogues of specialist bulb nurseries and to place your orders well in advance, for stocks will certainly be limited.

AUGUST

One of the most useful garden tasks for this month is also, perhaps, the most pleasant of the year. It is simply to pause occasionally from the feeding and the weeding and to take a long look, both at your garden and at other people's. Now, at the height of the growing season, you can best see what changes would benefit your garden next year. And by visiting some of the innumerable gardens now open to the public, you can observe, and learn from, the way others have approached particular problems and challenges.

SEPTEMBER

Growing bags represent an increasingly important form of gardening, whether used outdoors, on patios and path edges, or in the greenhouse. At the end of the season, when tomatoes and other crops have been removed, the peat-based compost can still be used; but not for growing more crops, since its nutrients will have been exhausted. Its value now is as a protective mulch around the crowns of slightly tender perennials, such as fuchsias, that will remain in the ground during the winter.

OCTOBER

The American term 'fall' is a more telling description of this time of year than autumn, for a great many things are certainly dropping to the ground; fruit very probably, but leaves especially, which need some attention. Rake them up regularly from lawns and paths, being particularly careful to remove any that drop into the garden pool, and put them all to good use by constructing a leaf-mould cage. On the subject of falling fruit, remember that windfalls should be used at once; it is a waste of time storing them since they will quickly start to rot.

NOVEMBER

November is a good month to begin to cultivate an interest in alpines. Many of these delightful flowers can be raised from seed far less expensively than they can be bought. But many need a spell of winter cold to stimulate them into germinating. So sow the seed of alpines this month in shallow seedboxes. Cover them with a sheet of perforated zinc as protection from mice and put them outside, where the worst of the winter weather can get to work.

DECEMBER

Mid-winter frosts can paint a picture in a really quite plain garden. Nowhere more so than on the lawn, which looks both attractive and inviting with a crisp white covering in the morning. But resist the temptation to walk on it. The frozen grass blades will be broken, and the result will be unattractive brown footprints that remain until the spring.

Index of questions

Index

Addresses

It is impossible to detail all those nurseries and plant growers who offer even the general run of garden plants, let alone those who specialize in one or two, but the list gives the names of some leading suppliers of most types of plant.

Allwood Brothers (Hassocks) ltd
Clayton Nursery, Hassocks
West Sussex BN6 9LX
Carnations, pinks and other dianthus

David Austin, Roses
Bowling Green Lane
Albrighton, Wolverhampton
Shropshire WV7 3HB
Roses and herbaceous plant

Avon Bulbs
Bathford, Bath
Avon BA1 8ED
Bulbous plants

Aylett Nurseries Ltd
North Orbital Road
London Colney
St Albans, Herts AL2 1DH
Dahlias

Peter Beales, Roses
London Road
Attleborough
Norfolk NR17 1AY
Old-fashioned Shrub and Climbing Roses

Burnett's Water Lily & Fish Farm
Putton Lane, Chicherell
Weymouth, Dorset DT3 4JL
Aquatic plants

Blackmore and Langdon
Stanton Nursery
Pensford, Bristol
Avon BS18 4JL
Delphiniums and other herbaceous perennials

Walter Blom & Son Ltd
Coombelands Nurseries
Leavesden, Watford
Herts WD2 7BH
Bulbs

Blooms Nurseries plc/ Bressingham Gardens
Bressingham. Diss
Norfolk IP22 2AB
Hardy perennials, alpines and shrubs; conifers and heathers

Broadleigh Gardens
Barr House, Bishop's Hull
Taunton, Somerset TA4 1AE
Hardy small bulbs

John Chambers
15 Westleigh Road
Barton Seagrave, Kettering
Northants NN15 5NJ
Wild flowers and herbs

Beth Chatto
White Barn House
Elmstead Market, Colchester
Essex CO7 7BD
Unusual herbaceous plants

Jack Drake
Inshriach Alpine Plant Nursery
Aviemore
Inverness-shire PH22 1QS
Alpines

Fisk's Clematis Nursery
Westleton, Saxmundham
Suffolk IP17 3AJ
Clematis

Fryer's Nurseries Ltd
Manchester Road, Knutsford
Cheshire WA16 0SX
Roses

C. Gregory & Son Ltd
The Rose Gardens
Toton Lane, Stapleton
Notts NG9 7JA
Roses

R. Harkness & Co Ltd
Cambridge Road, Hitchin
Herts SG4 0JT
Roses

Highfield Nurseries
Whitminster, Gloucester GL2 7PL
Fruit trees and herbs

Hillier Nurseries (Winchester) Ltd
Ampfield House, Ampfield
Near Romsey, Hants SO5 9PA
Trees and shrubs

W.E.Th. Ingwersen Ltd
Birch Farm Nursery
Gravetye, East Grinstead
West Sussex RH19 4LE
Alpine plants and dwarf shrubs; plants for shady conditions

Reginald Kaye Ltd
Waithman Nurseries
Lindeth Road, Silverdale
Lancs LA5 0TY
Alpines and hardy ferns

Knaphill & Slocock Nurseries
Barr's Lane, Knaphill
Woking, Surrey GU21 2JW
Hardy plants

Millais Nurseries
Crosswater Farm
Churt, Farnham
Surrey GU10 2JN
Rhododendrons and azaleas

Ken Muir
Honeypot Farm, Wheeley Heath
Clacton on Sea, Essex CO16 9BJ
Soft Fruits

Treasures of Tenbury Ltd
Burford House, Tenbury Wells
Worcs WR15 8HQ
Clematis

Van Tubergen
Oldfield Lane, Wisbech
Cambs PE13 2RJ
Bulbous plants

Details of individual specialist societies can be obtained from:

The Royal Horticultural Society
Vincent Square
London SW1P 2PE

SEED SUPPLIERS

Dobie's Seeds
Upper Dee Mills
Llangollen
Clwyd, Wales LL20 8SD
A wide range of selected and unusual varieties. Mail order

Suttons Seeds Ltd
Hele Road
Torquay, Devon TQ2 7QJ
Large selection of all vegetable and flower seeds; sweet peas, pansies; unusual seeds

W.J. Unwin Ltd
Impington Lane, Histon
Cambs CB4 4LE
Large selection, especially sweet peas; trees and shrubs

Information regarding chemicals for use in the garden can be obtained from:

British Agrochemicals Association Ltd
Allembic House
93 Albert Embankment
London SE1 7TU

Bibliography/Acknowledgements

Beckett, K.A. *The Concise Encyclopedia of Gardening Plants* Orbis, London, 1983

Biggs, T. *Vegetables* Mitchell Beazley, London, 1980

Boyd, L. *Which? Kind of Garden* Consumer's Association, London, 1983

Brickell, C. *Pruning* 1979; *Fruit* 1980; *Growing Under Glass*, 1981; (Editor in Chief) *The Royal Horticultural Society's Concise Encyclopaedia of Gardening Techniques* 1981; Mitchell Beazley, London

Brookes, J. *The Small Garden* Marshall Cavendish Editions, London, 1977; *A Place in the Country* Thames & Hudson, London, 1984; *The Garden Book* Dorling Kindersley, London, 1984

Brooks, A. and **Halstead, A.** *Garden Pests and Diseases* Mitchell Beazley, London, 1980

Brown G.E. *Shade Plants for Garden and Woodland* Faber & Faber, London, 1980

Browse, P.M. *Plant Propagation* Mitchell Beazley, London, 1979

Buczacki, S.T. and **Harris, K.M.** *Collins Shorter Guide to the Pests, Diseases and Disorders of Garden Plants* Collins, London, 1983

Carr, D. (Ed) *All About Shrubs and Hedges* Ortho Books, USA, 1982; W. Foulsham & Co, UK, 1984

Crockett, J.U. *Crockett's Victory Garden*, 1977; *Crockett's Tool Shed*, 1979; *Crocket's Flower Garden*, 1981; Little Brown, Boston/Toronto

Edlin, H.L. *Collins Guide to Tree Planting and Cultivation* Collins, London, 1970

Evison, J.R.B. *Shrubs* Sundial, London, 1979

Gault, S.M. *The Dictionary of Shrubs in Colour* Royal Horticultural Society, Ebury Press and Michael Joseph, London, 1976

Genders, R. *Bulbs: A Complete Handbook of Bulbs, Corms and Tubers* Robert Hale, London, 1973

Gibson, M. *Shrub Roses for Every Garden* Collins, London, 1973

Grey-Wilson, C. *Bulbs: The Bulbous Plants of Europe and Their Allies* Collins, London, 1981

Grey-Wilson, C. and **Matthews, V.** *Gardening on Walls* Collins, London, 1983

Grounds, R. *Ornamental Grasses* Pelham Books, London, 1979

Halliday, G. and **Malloch, A.** *Wild Flowers: Their Habitats in Britain and Northern Europe* Collins, Glasgow, 1981

Harkness, J. *The Rose* Macmillan, London, 1979; *The World's Favorite Roses* McGraw-Hill, New Jersey, USA, 1983

Harris, R.W. *Arboriculture* Prentice-Hall, New Jersey, USA, 1983

Harrison, C.R. *Conifers* David & Charles, Newton Abbot, 1975

Hay, R. *Gardener's Calendar* Granada, London, 1983

Hessayon, D.G. *The Rose Expert*, 1981; *The Lawn Expert*, 1982; *The Tree and Shrub Expert*, 1983; *The Flower Expert*, 1984; *The Vegetable Expert*, 1985; pbi Publications, Waltham Cross, Herts

Hillier's *Manual of Trees and Shrubs* David & Charles, Newton Abbot, 1981

Huxley, A. (Ed) *Deciduous Garden Trees and Shrubs* Blandford, London, 1973

Ingwersen, W. *Classic Garden Plants* Collingridge, London, 1985

Jekyll, G.A. *A Gardener's Testament* Antique Collector's Club, UK, 1982

Kaye, R. *Modern Water Gardening* Faber & Faber, London, 1973

Lloyd, C. *The Well-Tempered Garden* Collins, London, 1970

Mathew, B. *Dwarf Bulbs*, 1973; *The Larger Bulbs*, 1978; Batsford/The Royal Horticultural Society, London

Menninger, E.A. *Flowering Vines of the World: An Encyclopedia of Climbing Plants* Hearthside Press, New York, 1970

Mitchell, A. *A Field Guide to the Trees of Britain and Northern Europe* Collins, London, 1982

Phillips, R. *Trees in Britain, Europe and North America* Pan Books, London, 1978

Pycraft, D. *Lawns, Ground Cover and Weed Control* Mitchell Beazley, 1980

Reader's Digest (Hay, R. Consultant Ed) *The Gardening Year*, 1968; *Illustrated Guide to Gardening*, 1975; *Encyclopaedia of Garden Plants and Flowers* (2nd ed), 1978; Reader's Digest Association, London

Rix, M. and **Phillips, R.** *The Bulb Book* Pan Books, London, 1978

Rose, G. *The Low Maintenance Garden* Frances Lincoln, London, 1983

Royal Horticultural Society (various authors) *Encyclopaedia of Practical Gardening: Plant Propagation, Pruning*, 1978; *Fruit, Lawns, Ground Cover & Weed Control, Garden Pests and Diseases, Vegetables*, 1980; *Growing Under Glass, Gardening Techniques*, 1981; Mitchell Beazley, London; *Wisley Handbooks* (many subjects; various dates)

Seabrook, P. *Shrubs for Your Garden* Floraprint, Nottingham, 1973

Seddon, F. and **Radecka, H.** *Your Kitchen Garden* Mitchell Beazley/Edenlite, London, 1975

Smith, G. *Shrubs and Small Trees*, 1973; *Easy Plants for Difficult Places*, 1984; Hamlyn, London

Squire, D. *Window Boxes, Pots and Tubs* David & Charles, Newton Abbot, 1983

Stephenson, A. (Consultant Ed) *The Garden Planner* Fontana/Collins, London, 1981

Swindells, P. *Ferns for Garden and Greenhouse* J.M. Dent & Sons, London, 1971; *Making the Most of Water Gardening* Floraprint, Nottingham, 1981; *Waterlilies* Croom Helm, London; Timber Press, Portland, Oregon, 1981

Thomas, G.S. *Plants for Ground Cover* J.M. Dent & Sons, London, 1970

Thrower, P. *Everyday Gardening in Colour* (13th impression) Hamlyn, London, 1982; *First-time Gardening* Hamlyn, London, 1979

Wright, M. (Ed) *The Complete Book of Gardening* Ebury/Michael Joseph, London, 1978

Verey, R. *The Scented Garden* Michael Joseph, London, 1981

Author's acknowledgements
It gives me great pleasure to express appreciation to my friend and colleague Geoffrey Smith for so carefully reading the script and making a number of very valuable suggestions. I must dissociate him, nonetheless, from any errors of fact that may remain, and I certainly did not ask him to agree with all my opinions; especially those regarding *Rhus typhina*.

Publishers acknowledgements
The publishers of *Gardeners' Questions Answered* are especially grateful to Dr Brent Elliott and Barbara Collecott of the Royal Horticultural Society Lindley Library for their invaluable assistance.

Artists
l = left, r = right, t = top, c = centre, b = bottom

Norman Bancroft Hunt: 1, 2bl, 18b, 20bl, 22–3, 28t, 44–5, 66r, 67, 76–9, 88–97, 128–9, 132–3, 144–5

Jim Channell/Linden Artists: 42–3, 46–51

Jeanne Corville: 2r, 38, 52–4, 58–61, 66l, 70–5, 98l, 102–5, 108, 110–13, 116–17, 126–7, 134–5, 140, 146–9

Karen Daws/John Craddock: 6, 33, 62–3, 98r, 99–101, 118–25, 136–7, 141–3

Carole Johnson: 2lc, 20–1, 31, 34–5, 55–7, 64–5, 68–9, 80–7, 106–7, 109, 114–15, 130–1, 138–9

Dee McLean: 18t, 19, 28b, 29, 30

Jane Pickering: 2tl, 8r, 9–13, 14t, 14c, 16–17, 24–5, 32, 39, 40–1

Gabrielle Smith: 26–7

Clive Spong: 8l, 14b

Index Valerie Lewis Chandler